The
Practical PC
4th Edition

Includes a multimedia BookOnCD with the entire contents of the printed book, interactive step-by-step animations, pop-up definitions, skills tests, and more!

June Jamrich Parsons

Dan Oja

THOMSON

™

COURSE TECHNOLOGY

25 Thomson Place, Boston, MA 02210

Australia • Canada • Mexico • Singapore • Spain • United Kingdom • United States

The Practical PC, 4th Edition is published by Course Technology.

Managing Editor	Rachel Goldberg
Senior Product Manager	Amanda Shelton
Product Manager	Brianna Hawes
Associate Product Manager	Emilie Perreault
Editorial Assistant	Shana Rosenthal
Marketing Manager	Joy Stark
Media Specialists	Fatima Lockhart and Donna Mulder
BookOnCD Production	Keefe Crowley
BookOnCD Development	MediaTechnics Corp.
Desktop Publishing	Tensi Parsons
Prepress Production	GEX Publishing Services
Text and Design Composition	MediaTechnics Corp.
Production Editor	Catherine DiMassa
Cover Art Designer	MaryAnn Southard

Disclaimer
Course Technology reserves the right to revise this publication and make changes from time to time in its content without notice.

Some of the product names and company names used in this book have been used for identification purposes only and may be trademarks or registered trademarks of their respective manufacturers and sellers.

Microsoft and the Office logo are either registered trademarks or trademarks of Microsoft Corporation in the United States and/or other countries. Course Technology and MediaTechnics Corporation are independent entities from the Microsoft Corporation, and are not affiliated with Microsoft in any manner.

ISBN 0-619-26799-2

Printed in the United States of America

1 2 3 4 5 6 7 8 9 10 BM 09 08 07 06 05

Preface

About this book

At last, here is a book about the computers that people really use, with practical tips about how to use them. *The Practical PC* provides a state-of-the-art introduction to Windows-based PCs, written in an easy-to-read style. Every book includes an action-packed multimedia BookOnCD. Each page of the BookOnCD looks exactly like its corresponding page in the printed book and contains interactive elements such as pop-up definitions, figures that become videos, and end-of-chapter quizzes. The BookOnCD requires no installation, so it's easy to use at home, at school, or at work.

Each 12-page chapter of *The Practical PC* focuses on a specific topic. The first page introduces the chapter topic, lists the chapter contents, and highlights BookOnCD media. Each chapter includes the following:

- Five **FAQs**, or "frequently asked questions," address key questions, provide background information, and give specific tips for becoming a more proficient computer user.
- A three-page **Hardware** section in each chapter explains the devices that are typically associated with the chapter topic.
- An **Issues** page highlights an ethical or cultural issue that's relevant to the chapter topic.
- A **Tutorial** section provides step-by-step instructions on developing important computer skills.
- A **QuickCheck** page contains self-test activities.

About the BookOnCD

Every book includes the innovative BookOnCD, which is loaded with features to enhance and reinforce learning.

 On the CD, the PlayIt! button makes figures come to life as videos and screen animations. You'll see PC hardware in action and tour some of today's most popular software packages.

 GrabIt! buttons connect to Internet sites with free or demo versions of software featured in the book.

 The Get It? button starts an interactive auto-graded chapter quiz. Take a quiz more than once. Each quiz contains ten randomly selected questions from an extensive test bank. Results can be saved and delivered to an instructor.

What do you think? Interactive "thought" questions focus on current ethical, social, and cultural computing issues. For the classroom, responses can be consolidated by instructors and displayed as pie charts.

QuickChecks Interactive end-of-chapter QuickCheck questions provide instant feedback on what you've learned.

Pop-up Definitions & Glossary Clickable boldface terms display pop-up definitions. A Glossary button provides easy access to all definitions from any page.

Tutorials

Each chapter includes a Tutorial section with step-by-step instructions about an essential computer task.

How to set up your computer

How to use Windows controls

How to download and install software from the Internet

How to create and save files

How to find files

How to use Windows Backup

How to set up a dial-up Internet connection

How to create your own Web pages

How to use your e-mail address book like a pro

How to install and select printers

How to make slides for an effective presentation

How to make your own CDs

How to edit a digital photo

How to work with digitized sound

How to change display settings

How to find the technical specifications for your PC

How to get technical support

How to buy a computer online

Use this book because...

▪ **You want to learn about computers**. *The Practical PC* will help you understand enough "tech talk" so you can decipher computer ads and hold your own when the conversation turns to computers.

▪ **You want to learn Windows**. *The Practical PC* will show you how to use Windows controls and manage files so that you can use your computer to do neat stuff without frustration.

▪ **You want to learn how to use the Internet**. *The Practical PC* will show you how to get connected, use a browser, send e-mail, and launch a search engine.

▪ **You want to find out what a computer can do for you**. *The Practical PC* will demonstrate all kinds of software—in action—including software for word processing, art, video editing, music composition, and 3-D graphics.

▪ **You're a beginner or an intermediate computer user**. *The Practical PC* is great for beginners, but there's enough new and useful information to keep you interested even if you have some experience with PCs.

Teaching Tools

ExamView: Our Powerful Testing Software Package. With ExamView, instructors can generate printed tests, create LAN-based tests, or test over the Internet.

An **Instructor's Manual** outlines each chapter and provides valuable teaching tips.

WebTrack is an exciting new feature that provides automated delivery of tracking data from any student directly to the instructor with minimal setup or administrative overhead.

Check with your Course Technology sales representative or go to *www.course.com* to learn more about other valuable Teaching Tools.

Acknowledgments

The successful launch of this book was possible only because of our extraordinary "ground crews." We would like to extend our profound thanks:

To the students at Northern Michigan University, the University of the Virgin Islands, and countless other universities who have participated in classes and corresponded with us over the 25 (or so) years since we began teaching.

To our development team: Fatima Lockhart, Donna Mulder, Tensi Parsons, and Keefe Crowley for content and media development; to Kevin Lappi, Deanna Martinson, Karen Kangas, and Jackie Kangas for testing; to Chris Robbert for narrations; and to Marilou Potter for her detailed copyedit.

To our team members' patient and supportive parents, spouses, and significant others.

To the New Perspectives team at Course Technology, who once again provided professional and enthusiastic support, guidance, and advice. Their insights and team spirit were invaluable.

To Rachel Goldberg for her editorial support and to our Product Manager, Brianna Hawes.

To Emilie Perreault for her excellent work on the supplements, and the Software Quality Assurance Team for their valuable QA test comments.

To Gary and the crew at GEX, Dean Fossella and Patty Stephan for their valuable input on the book design, and Cathie DiMassa for her careful and cheerful production proofing.

To the professors and reviewers who expressed their ideas and shared their teaching strategies with us for the Practical series: Dennis Anderson, St. Francis College; Mary Dobranski, College of Saint Mary; Mike Feiler, Merritt College; Shmuel Fink, Touro College; Dennette Foy, Edison Community College; Nancy LaChance, DeVry Institute of Technology; Janet Sheppard, Collin County Community College; Pauline Pike, Community College of Morris; and Linda Reis, Garland County Community College.

Media credits

■Brief Contents

Contents

Contents

Contents

■Before You Begin

You're going to enjoy using *The Practical PC* and the accompanying BookOnCD. It's a snap to start the BookOnCD and use it on your computer. So don't delay—get started right away! The answers to the FAQs (frequently asked questions) in this section will help you begin.

■FAQ Will the BookOnCD work on my computer?

The easiest way to find out if the BookOnCD works on your computer is to try it! Just follow the steps below to start the CD. If it works, you're all set. Otherwise, check with your local technical support person. If you are technically inclined, the system requirements are listed inside the front cover of this book.

■FAQ How do I start the BookOnCD?

The Practical PC BookOnCD is easy to use and requires no installation. Follow these simple steps to get started:

1. Make sure your computer is turned on.

2. Press the button on your computer's CD-ROM drive to open the drawer-like "tray" as shown in the photo below.

3. Place the BookOnCD into the tray with the label facing up.

4. Press the button on the CD-ROM drive to close the tray, then proceed with Step 5.

To use the BookOnCD, your computer must have a CD-ROM drive. If you have any questions about its operation, check the manual that was supplied with your computer or check with your local technical support person.

Label side up

Open/close tray button

5. Wait about 15 seconds. During this time, the light on your CD-ROM drive should flicker. Soon you should see the Practical PC Welcome screen.

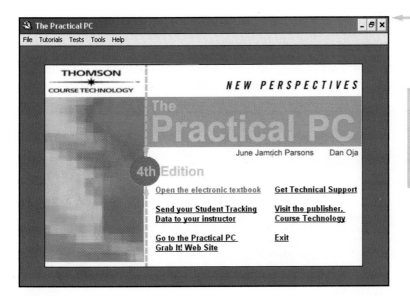

If the Welcome screen does not appear, try the instructions in the Manual Start figure below.

■   ■   ■

Manual Start: *Follow the instructions in this figure only if the Welcome screen did **not** appear automatically in Step 5.*

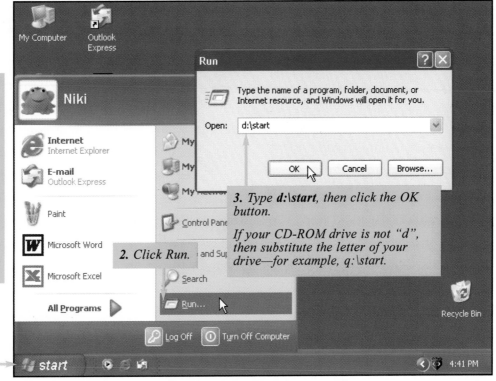

1. Use the mouse to position the arrow-shaped pointer on Start.

Click the left button on your mouse to display the Start menu.

2. Click Run.

*3. Type **d:\start**, then click the OK button.*

If your CD-ROM drive is not "d", then substitute the letter of your drive—for example, q:\start.

▪FAQ What do I do when the Welcome screen appears?

The Welcome screen is the home page for the BookOnCD. Typically, you'll click **Open the electronic textbook** to start using the interactive BookOnCD.

Other options on the Welcome screen allow you to jump directly to pages containing animations, to display your Tracking Disk data, and to turn the sound on or off.

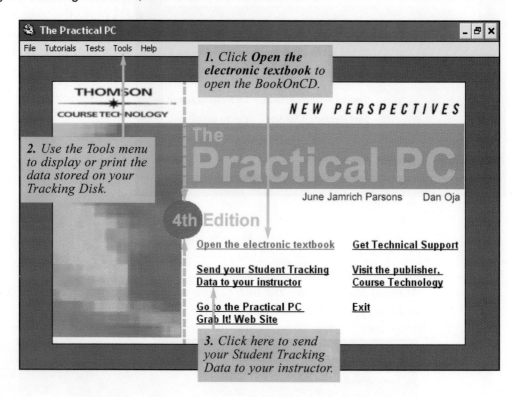

■FAQ How do I navigate through the BookOnCD?

You can use either the mouse or the keyboard to navigate through the BookOnCD.

To scroll up or down the page, press the Page Up or Page Down key or use the vertical scroll bar on the right side of the page. You'll know you've reached the bottom of a page when you see three red boxes.

If you scroll down past the end of a page, you'll move to the next page. If you scroll up past the top of a page, you'll move to the previous page. You can also use the Prev and Next buttons or press the left or right arrow keys to move to the previous or next page.

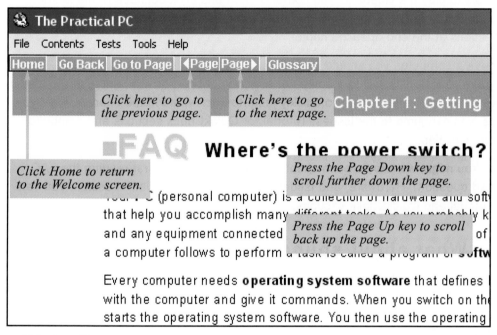

■FAQ What's a Tracking Disk?

A Tracking Disk records your progress by saving your scores on the Skill Sets. You can view or print a summary report of all your scores by using the Tracking Disk menu on the Welcome screen. In an academic setting, your instructor might request your Tracking Disk data to monitor your progress. Your instructor will tell you if you should submit your Tracking Data using the WebTrack system, if you should hand in your entire Tracking Disk, or if you should send the tracking file as an e-mail attachment.

When you start a Skill Set, the program will check in drive A: for a Tracking Disk. If you want to create a Tracking Disk, insert a formatted floppy disk, then click **Create Tracking File A:\TRACKING.TRK**. You'll be prompted to enter your name, student ID, and section number, all of which will be stored on the Tracking Disk. If you don't want to save your results, just click **Continue without a Tracking Disk**. This option allows you try a Skill Set review without saving your results.

You only need to create a Tracking Disk one time. Once you've created the Tracking Disk, just insert it into the floppy disk drive of your computer when you insert the BookOnCD or when you are prompted to do so.

Before You Begin

■FAQ How do I end a session?

You'll need to leave the BookOnCD disk in the CD-ROM drive while you're using it, or you will encounter an error message. Before you remove the CD from the drive, you must exit the program by clicking the File menu at the top of the Welcome screen, then clicking Exit. You can also exit by clicking the Close button in the top-right corner of the window.

■FAQ How do I get the most out of the book and the BookOnCD?

If you have your own computer, you might want to start the CD and do your reading online. You'll then be able to play the videos as you come to them and click boldface terms to see pop-up definitions. Also, you'll be able to immediately interact with the Issues, Tutorial, and QuickCheck sections at the end of each chapter.

If you do not have a computer, you should read through the chapter in the book. Later, when it is convenient, take your BookOnCD to a computer at school, home, or work and use the Media menu at the top of the Welcome screen to quickly jump to each video in the chapter. After you view the videos, you can jump to the Issues, Tutorial, or QuickCheck sections and complete those interactive activities.

Take your time. You might want to do each chapter in two sessions by first reading the FAQ (frequently asked question), Hardware, and Issues sections. Then, in a later session, you can complete the Tutorial and QuickCheck sections.

■FAQ What about sound?

If your computer is equipped for sound, you should hear the audio during the screen tours and interactive simulations. If you don't hear anything, check the volume control on your computer by clicking the speaker icon in the lower-right corner of your screen. If you're working in a lab or office where sound would be disruptive, consider using headphones. You can also use the Options menu on the Welcome screen to turn off the sound; captions will still explain what you are seeing on the screen.

■FAQ Can I make the type appear larger on my screen?

If the type in the BookOnCD appears small, your monitor is probably set at a high resolution. The type will appear larger if you reduce the resolution by following the instructions in the figure below. This setting is optional. You can view the BookOnCD at most standard resolutions; however, your computer should be set to use Windows standard fonts, not large fonts.

If you would like to see larger type on the screen, you can change the Display setting for your monitor by following the numbered steps below. However, you don't have to change this setting to use the BookOnCD.

1. Click the Start button.

2. Click the Control Panel option.

3. Click the Appearance and Themes option, then Display.

4. Click the Settings tab.

5. Move the slider bar to the left for the lowest resolution.

6. Click OK, then follow the instructions on the screen to complete the setting change.

Note: You can skip Steps 1 through 3 if you right-click any empty space on the Windows desktop. On the shortcut menu that pops up, select Properties to open the Display Properties dialog box, then continue with Step 4 above.

Before You Begin

■FAQ Which version of Windows do I need?

Your PC's operating system sets the standard for the way all your software looks and works. Most of today's PCs use a version of the Microsoft Windows operating system—"Windows" for short. The most recent versions of Windows are called Windows 95, Windows 98, Windows Me, Windows NT, Windows 2000, and Windows XP. These versions of Windows look very similar and have a common set of features that you can readily learn to use.

The Practical PC BookOnCD is optimized for use with Windows 95, Windows 98, Windows Me, Windows NT, Windows 2000, and Windows XP. It will not run acceptably on most older computers using the Windows 3.1 operating system.

If you see a screen similar to this one when you start your PC, your operating system is Windows 95, Windows 98, Windows Me, Windows NT, Windows 2000, or Windows XP.

Look for this Start button.

The

Practical PC

4th Edition

Chapter 1

Getting Started

What's Inside?

Chapter 1 provides an overview of your computer system, including the terminology and equipment you need to get started. Some of the material might be a review, but don't ignore the explanations that tell you *why* these things work the way they do.

What's on the CD?

Your BookOnCD contains the entire text of the printed book. But that's not all! On the CD the figures "come to life" through videos and animations. To use the CD, simply insert it into your CD-ROM drive. After a few seconds, you should see the Welcome screen. If the screen doesn't appear, click the Windows Start button, then click Run. In the box type d:\start.exe. If your CD-ROM drive is assigned to a different letter, substitute that letter instead of "d". For more information about using the CD, refer to the Before You Begin section in the front of the book.

■FAQ Where's the power switch?

Your **PC** (personal computer) is a collection of hardware and software components that help you accomplish many different tasks. As you probably know, a computer and any equipment connected to it are called **hardware**. A set of instructions that a computer follows to perform a task is called a program or **software**.

Every computer needs **operating system software** that defines how you interact with the computer and give it commands. When you switch on the computer, it starts the operating system software. You then use the operating system software to start **application software** that helps you produce documents, make calculations, draw pictures, or maintain your to-do list. Most of today's computers use the **Microsoft Windows** operating system ("Windows" for short). For that reason, computers that use Windows are the main focus of this book.

A PC is an electronic device containing a microprocessor. The **microprocessor** is essentially the brain of the computer, carrying out the commands that you issue when you create documents, draw pictures, or manipulate numbers. It works with data representing words, numbers, and pictures held *temporarily* in memory chips called **RAM** (random access memory). Data has a more permanent home on **storage media** such as a hard disk, floppy disk, tape, or CD. Devices that are designed to store data *permanently* on storage media are referred to as **storage devices**. The microprocessor, memory, and storage devices for a PC are typically housed in a **system unit**. Other components—the monitor, keyboard, mouse, and printer—are connected to the system unit.

The PC's power switch is located on the system unit. A small green light indicates when the power is on. The monitor typically has its own power switch. Because the monitor might take a few seconds to warm up, turn it on before you turn on your PC.

Figure 1-1: *A typical desktop computer system consists of a series of components connected to the system unit.*

The microprocessor, RAM, and hard disk drive are inside the system unit

DVD-ROM drive

Monitor

Monitor power switch

Speaker

Floppy disk drive

The power "switch" is usually a round or square push button

Keyboard

Mouse

■FAQ Do I need a disk to start my computer?

You should make it a habit to check that the floppy disk drive is empty before you switch on a computer. The only time you would start the computer with a disk in the floppy disk drive is when the hard disk drive has failed. The reason relates to what happens between the time you flick the power switch and the time your computer is ready to begin the business of computing.

As soon as you switch on the power, your PC starts to "boot up." During the **boot process**, the PC performs diagnostic tests to make sure that the keyboard, storage devices, RAM, and microprocessor are functioning correctly. After testing the hardware, it looks for the operating system programs. Usually, these programs are stored on the computer's **hard disk drive**, a large-capacity storage device located inside the system unit. However, most computers look for them first on the floppy disk drive, just in case the hard disk drive has malfunctioned. You can boot your computer without your hard disk drive by using a special floppy disk called a **system disk**, which contains operating system programs. Most computer manufacturers supply you with such a system disk, or explain how to create one.

What if the hard disk drive is functioning normally and you've inadvertently left a plain data disk in the floppy disk drive? When your computer spots this disk in the drive, it displays a "non-system disk" message. This is your cue to take the disk out of the drive. You can put the disk in later when the boot process ends.

Figure 1-2: When the boot process is complete, you'll see the Windows desktop on your screen. But what happens when your PC doesn't boot correctly? Play this video to find out what to do.

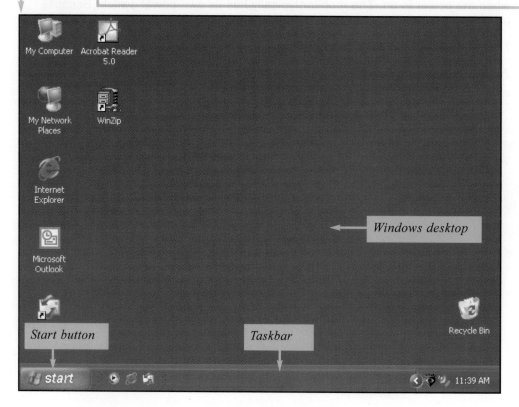

■FAQ What if my computer asks me for a password?

As the boot process proceeds, your computer might display a message asking for your user ID and password. This message often indicates that your computer is part of a network. A **network** is an interconnected collection of computers, printers, and other devices. You've probably heard of a worldwide network called the Internet, but many small local networks are also maintained by businesses, organizations, and schools. By supplying a valid user ID and password, you can access information stored on other network computers or print on a network printer. Your **user ID** or user name is your network identification and is usually a variation of your name. Your **password** is a series of letters and numbers that provide your security clearance for the network. You can tell anyone your user ID, but you should not disclose your password.

> *Figure 1-3: When you type your password, it usually appears as a series of asterisks. This security measure hides your password from anyone who might be looking over your shoulder.*

Some networks provide you with a password that you cannot change. Other networks allow you to create your own password and change it as frequently as you like. A secure password is one that is difficult for someone else to guess. When you create a password, don't use your name, the name of a relative, or your birth date. It is also a good idea not to use any word that you might find in the dictionary because a common way of "breaking" or discovering a password is to run through an electronic dictionary, trying all the words it contains. To create a secure password, combine more than one word or combine words and numbers. For example, "U4got" would probably be a secure password.

In today's connected world, you'll typically spend some time "surfing" the Internet to find information, make travel arrangements, purchase gifts, look for career opportunities, and communicate with other computer users. Before you participate in these online activities, you usually have to register. Should you create a different password for every activity? Probably not, because you'll have a difficult time remembering all of them. However, if you use the same password for everything, a person who discovers your password will have access to all of your information. Some experienced computer users have two passwords: one password for financial transactions and an alternative password for less critical transactions. Whatever passwords you use, you should change them often to maximize security.

■FAQ Which works better, the mouse or the keyboard?

Today's computers generally require you to use both a mouse and a keyboard. These **input devices** help you put information into the computer—the documents you write, the artwork you create, the numbers you want to "crunch," and the commands you want the computer to follow.

Beginning computer users generally use the keyboard to enter text, and use the mouse to select the tasks that they want the computer to perform. Experienced users sometimes use the keyboard rather than the mouse to select tasks when they are working with text. Why? Because moving their hands from the keyboard to the mouse interrupts the flow of their work. There is no right or wrong style for using the mouse and keyboard—over time you'll develop your own style and preferences. In the Hardware section of Chapter 2, you'll learn about some new input technologies that might eventually replace your mouse and keyboard.

Figure 1-4: The mouse helps you move an arrow-shaped pointer on the screen to select the tasks you want to accomplish. Play this video to see how to drag, click, double-click, and right-click the mouse. You'll also find out how to clean your mouse.

Figure 1-5: It is a good idea to understand all the features of your keyboard. Play this video to find out how to use the Ctrl, Alt, and Windows keys; why you should leave the Num Lock engaged; and how to clean your keyboard.

▪FAQ How do I turn off my computer?

Some computers might look like they're off, when they are only asleep! Many of today's PCs have a power-saver feature called **sleep mode** that turns off the screen after a period of inactivity. You can "wake up" your computer by moving the mouse or pressing a key. Even in sleep mode, your computer consumes a small amount of power and remains susceptible to electrical spikes and surges that can damage electronic equipment. It is a good idea to turn off your PC when you've finished with a computing session. But don't just flick off the power switch. If your PC uses the Windows operating system, you should issue the **Shut Down** or **Turn off computer** command before you turn the power off. The shut down process ensures that your work for this computing session is saved and deletes any temporary files that don't need to be saved.

Figure 1-6: *You access the Turn off computer command from the Windows Start menu. This video explains how to turn off your computer safely.*

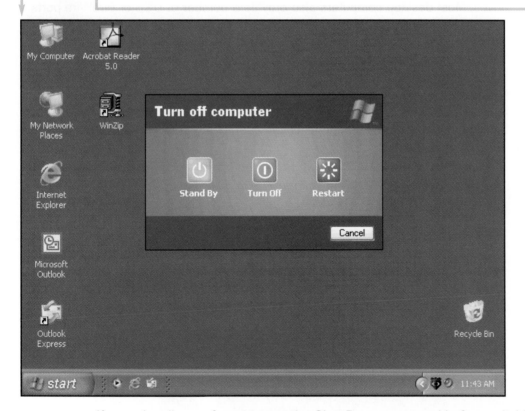

If occasionally you forget to use the Shut Down command before switching off the power, you probably won't damage anything. But you should make it a habit to do things the right way just to avoid potential problems.

Computer software sometimes has "bugs" or errors that cause your computer to "freeze up" or "hang" so it won't respond to your mouse or keyboard commands. If this situation occurs, you won't be able to issue the regular Shut Down command. Before you press the power switch, hold down the Ctrl, Alt, and Del keys at the same time. If only one program has frozen, you'll be able to close that program. You can then try the program again to see if it works correctly.

■Hardware
Desktops, notebooks, and PDAs

Computers come in several configurations that fit on your desk, in your briefcase, or in your pocket. Each has advantages—you might find that you need more than one computer!

A **desktop computer** is designed to be a fairly permanent fixture on your desk. It typically includes hardware components such as a system unit, mouse, keyboard, monitor, speakers, and microphone. You'll tend not to move a desktop computer very frequently because it takes some time to disconnect and then reconnect all the components. In addition, the monitor and the system unit may be fairly heavy, so you don't want to tote it around unnecessarily.

Most current desktop computers are contained in a large, vertical, **tower style** case, which offers room for expansion through addition of internal cards and drives. Most desktop computers also provide a number of USB or FireWire ports that can be used to connect external devices.

Although they are rather large and not very portable, desktop computers provide the most expansion capability and the most computing power for your dollar. You can purchase a very serviceable computer with a basic set of software tools for between U.S.$600 and U.S.$1,200, although a high-performance computer with the latest processor and components can cost as much as U.S.$5,000.

Figure 1-7: *A typical desktop computer with attached devices.*

■Hardware

continued

Notebook computers, sometimes called laptops, are designed for people on the move. All the essential components—keyboard, screen, disk drives, CD-ROM drive, and pointing device—are housed in a single unit. You can plug a notebook computer into a wall outlet or run it from special batteries that last two to five hours on a single charge.

A notebook and its batteries typically weigh between five and seven pounds. However, when you pack a carrying case with a notebook computer and all the paraphernalia needed for computing, you may have 10 to 15 pounds to lug around. Adding substantially to the weight is the "power brick" or **AC adapter**, which allows you to plug the notebook into a wall outlet. Most ads for notebook computers omit this important piece of gear from photos and weight specifications.

A notebook computer includes a flat-panel, light-weight **LCD** (liquid crystal display) screen instead of a monitor. LCDs have lower power requirements than monitors, increasing the time that your notebook can run on a battery charge. A notebook's small size limits the number of devices you can add inside the case. Some notebook computers allow you to insert devices into special drive bays in the notebook case. Most notebook computers also include one or more small PCMCIA slots into which you can insert **PCMCIA cards**, sometimes called PC cards. Most notebook computers include USB and FireWire ports to which you can attach external devices such as mice, CD-ROM drives, and hard disk drives.

Compared with a desktop computer, a notebook provides less computing power for your dollar because you are paying for portability. Notebook computers typically cost between U.S.$1,000 and U.S.$4,000.

Play It!

Figure 1-8: Play this video to get the scoop on notebook pointing devices, such as touch pads and track points.

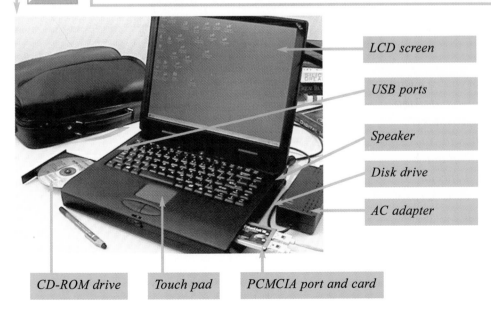

LCD screen

USB ports

Speaker

Disk drive

AC adapter

CD-ROM drive   Touch pad   PCMCIA port and card

■Hardware

continued

A **tablet computer** is similar to a notebook computer, except it typically includes a touch-sensitive screen. Some tablet computers do not include a keyboard; others include a folding or detachable keyboard. Because of the touch-sensitive screen, tablet computers can be used for capturing free-hand drawings and handwritten input, as well as for more traditional computing tasks such as word processing.

A **PDA** (personal digital assistant) is the solution for people who want a basic level of computer power but who don't want to carry a briefcase full of notebook computer paraphernalia. A PDA, sometimes called a palm top, is a hand-held computer in a six ounce, pocket-sized package, typically priced around U.S.$300.

A PDA typically does not include a disk drive. Without a hard disk drive, the operating system and other software programs must be permanently stored in the PDA's circuitry, much like the square root function is hard-wired in a hand-held calculator.

Most Palmtops use an operating system called **Palm OS**, while the Handheld PCs use a scaled-down version of the Windows operating system called **Windows CE**. They also use scaled-down software for scheduling, word processing, spreadsheets, Internet surfing, and e-mail. The documents you create are stored in a special type of **flash memory** that holds data without a constant source of power.

To compensate for a PDA's limited storage capacity, manufacturers provide easy links to connect PDAs to other computers. For example, you can exchange and synchronize your PDA's data with the data on your desktop or notebook computer, so you can keep your schedule up-to-date on both. Also, you can transfer data from your PDA to the storage devices on your desktop computer.

Figure 1-9: When you're away from your full-featured desktop computer, a PDA provides a handy way to maintain your schedule and dash off quick e-mail messages. A special docking bay, or cradle, keeps the data on your desktop computer up-to-date with the data on your PDA.

■Tutorial
How to set up your computer

In addition to its small size, an advantage of a notebook computer is that everything is contained in one unit. The screen, keyboard, pointing device, and disk drives are housed in one easy-to-carry package. Setting up a notebook computer is a breeze. Just swing the screen up into place and plug in the power cable.

Desktop computers present more of a set-up challenge because the system unit, monitor, mouse, keyboard, and speakers are all separate components. When you buy a new computer or move your trusty old computer to a new location, you have to connect each component correctly. As you'll see in the tutorial, the set-up process isn't really difficult. Even if your PC is already set up, the tutorial will help you understand how its components fit together.

When you have completed the tutorial, you should be able to:
■ List the hardware components typically shipped in each of the three cartons that contain a computer system.
■ Safely unpack your computer's hardware components.
■ Connect the keyboard, mouse, monitor, speakers, microphone, and printer to the correct ports on the back of the system unit.
■ Describe two benefits of using a surge strip.

Figure 1-10: Suppose you've just purchased a new computer. Click the PlayIt! button to begin the tutorial and find out how to set up your computer. Estimated time: 10-15 minutes. Tracking Disk points: 10.

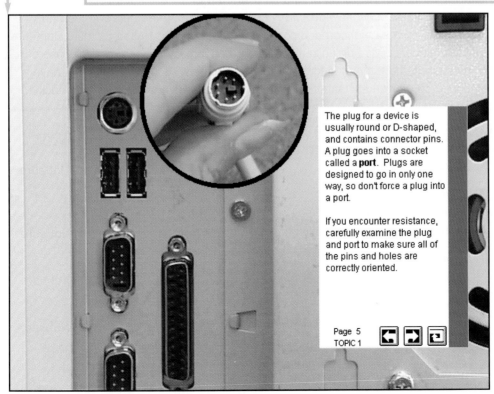

The plug for a device is usually round or D-shaped, and contains connector pins. A plug goes into a socket called a **port**. Plugs are designed to go in only one way, so don't force a plug into a port.

If you encounter resistance, carefully examine the plug and port to make sure all of the pins and holes are correctly oriented.

Page 5
TOPIC 1

■Issue

Computer "haves" and "have-nots"

Microsoft's chairman, Bill Gates, donates millions to supply computers and Internet access to libraries serving low-income communities. By 2003, his foundations had given $250 million to install 47,000 computers in 11,000 libraries in the 50 states and Washington DC. Gates has noted that few low-income families owned computers "and so that's dividing our society and it's moving away from our central belief of equal opportunity."

Is there really a gap between computer "haves" and "have-nots"? Are the economically disadvantaged being denied access to government documents, employment bulletin boards, and other information accessible on the Internet? Are the computer "have-nots" trapped in a low-technology ghetto because they lack the computer skills required to get a well-paying job?

A disturbing report by the U.S. Census Bureau in 2000 indicated that 71% of middle- and high-income families owned a computer, but only 28% of poor families owned one. Also only 32% of low-income children had access to a computer at home while 82% of middle- and high-income kids had access.

Drawing conclusions from this data could be risky. The report is more than two years old. The data doesn't prove whether computer access does, in fact, contribute to economic success. Also, although the data indicates that computers are scarce in low-income homes, it does not indicate if computer access is available through schools or libraries.

Providing information access does not have to involve an expensive government initiative. Computer recycling programs distribute older business computers to schools and libraries worldwide. Many communities have gathered funds and volunteers to create neighborhood computer centers. In the United States, volunteers with the national service organization called Americorps*VISTA promote the use of computers and the Internet in low-income communities. As many volunteers have demonstrated, universal computer and Internet access is a goal that can be tackled one computer at a time.

What do you think?

1. Do you own a computer? ◯ Yes ◯ No ◯ Not sure

2. Do you believe that not having a computer at home is likely to limit a person's chances to improve his or her economic status? ◯ Yes ◯ No ◯ Not sure

3. Do you favor spending tax dollars to make computers available in public libraries? ◯ Yes ◯ No ◯ Not sure

4. Would you favor allowing college students to spend their financial aid money on computers? ◯ Yes ◯ No ◯ Not sure

Save
It!

QuickCheck A

1. A(n) [　　　　　] is the "brain" of your PC, which carries out the commands you issue on data that represents words, numbers, and pictures.

2. Microsoft Windows is [　　　　　] software, which the computer starts during the boot process.

3. True or false? The password "one4all" is more secure than "anarchy". [　　　]

4. The Windows [　　　　　] command makes sure that your work for a computing session is saved before you turn off the computer.

5. A(n) [　　　　　] computer is lighter and more portable than a desktop or laptop computer, but uses scaled-down versions of the operating system and application software.

Check It!

QuickCheck B

Enter the name of the computer components in the numbered boxes below.

5.

1.

2.

4.

3.

1. [　　　　　]

2. [　　　　　]

3. [　　　　　]

4. [　　　　　]

5. [　　　　　]

Check It!

Get It?

While using the BookOnCD, click the Get It? button to see if you can answer ten randomly selected questions from Chapter 1.

Get It?

Chapter 2
Looking at Windows

What's Inside?

In Chapter 2, you'll discover why the operating system is the core piece of software on your PC. Plus, you'll find out how to start your software and how to print. Beyond these basics, you'll find up-to-date information on alternative input devices and software, such as touch-sensitive LCDs, force-feedback technology, and voice recognition.

What's on the CD?

Chapter 2 contains several tours that show you how to use the Windows operating system and some action-packed videos about alternative input devices.

▪FAQ   What's the Windows desktop?

The **Windows desktop** is the gateway to all of the tasks you perform with your PC. It is the screen you see when the boot process is complete, and it remains in the background as you use other software programs.

The Windows desktop is displayed by your PC's operating system. Keep in mind that the main purpose of the operating system is to let you control your computer environment. Graphical objects on the desktop allow you to examine and modify many aspects of this environment, such as the type of printer you'll use, the color scheme for your screen display, or the sensitivity of your mouse.

The desktop contains small graphics called **icons** that represent programs, hardware, and documents. Clicking an icon gives you access to the computer component that it represents. The **taskbar** at the bottom of the screen displays buttons and icons that help you keep track of the status of your computer system, such as the program that you are currently using, the volume setting of your speakers, and the current time.

The **Start button**, which is located on the taskbar, is the main control on the Windows desktop. When you click this button, Windows displays the **Start menu**. You can use this menu to start programs, change your hardware settings, get help, and install software.

Figure 2-1: *Click the PlayIt! button for a guided tour of the Windows desktop. The Windows desktop can be customized, so it might look slightly different on your computer. In later chapters, you'll learn how to customize your desktop.*

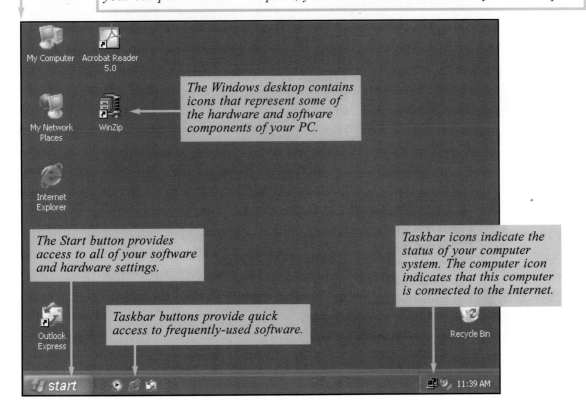

The Windows desktop contains icons that represent some of the hardware and software components of your PC.

The Start button provides access to all of your software and hardware settings.

Taskbar icons indicate the status of your computer system. The computer icon indicates that this computer is connected to the Internet.

Taskbar buttons provide quick access to frequently-used software.

■FAQ   How do I start an application program?

When the boot process is complete and the Windows desktop appears, your PC is ready for your instructions. Ordinarily, when you turn on your PC, you want to use an application program. An **application program** ("application" or "program" for short) helps you accomplish real-world tasks, such as creating personalized greeting cards, balancing your checkbook, or learning to speak Spanish. As you use your PC, keep in mind that an application and the operating system are both programs, but they have distinctly different purposes. The operating system helps you control your "computer world." An application program helps you accomplish tasks for the real world.

The Windows operating system provides several ways to start an application, but typically you'll use the Start button. When you click this button, the Start menu appears. From the Start menu, select the **All Programs option** to display a list of the available application programs. Click any one of the programs and it will start.

In the jargon of computing, starting and using an application is referred to as "running" it. You can run more than one program at the same time. Buttons on the taskbar show you which programs are running. To switch between one program and another, click one of the buttons on the taskbar.

Figure 2-2: Click the PlayIt! button to find out how to start an application program, how to run two programs at the same time, and how to switch between programs.

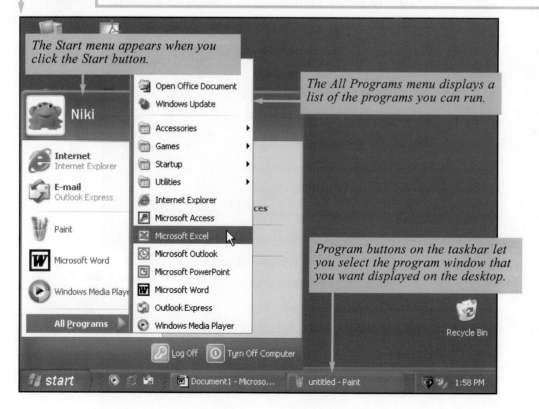

The Start menu appears when you click the Start button.

The All Programs menu displays a list of the programs you can run.

Program buttons on the taskbar let you select the program window that you want displayed on the desktop.

■FAQ What's a window?

The Windows operating system gets its name because everything happens in rectangular viewing areas on the screen called **windows**. Just to clarify, "Windows" with an uppercase "W" refers to the operating system, but "windows" with a lower-case "w" refers to the rectangular areas on the screen. When you start a program, it appears in its own window. The **title bar** of the window indicates the program name and contains three control buttons. The ■ **Minimize button** shrinks the window to a button on the taskbar. The ▣ **Maximize button** enlarges the window to fill the screen. The ☒ **Close button** closes the window and stops the program.

Typically, the windows in which your application programs appear include a **menu bar** that provides access to the commands that control the application. For example, when you have completed a document, you can store it on a disk by clicking the File menu, then selecting Save from the list of command options.

Below the menu bar, you might see one or more **toolbars** containing small pictures, such as a folder, disk, printer, scissors, and clipboard. Each picture is a **toolbar button** that provides you with a shortcut for accomplishing a task. For example, the toolbar button that looks like a disk is a shortcut for saving a document—you can just click this button instead of clicking the File menu and then selecting the Save command. A **scroll bar** on the side of the window helps you move a document or graphic up and down within the window.

Figure 2-3: *Click the PlayIt! button to take a tour of a typical application window and to learn more about using the title bar, control buttons, menu bar, toolbar, and scroll bar.*

■FAQ What's a dialog box?

A **dialog box** is a small window that appears when you click certain menu options. You can think of it as an order form, like one you might use when ordering a gift from a catalog. Just as you would fill in an order form with the color, size, and price of a gift, you fill in a dialog box with the specifications for accomplishing a task.

Most application programs have hundreds of features. These features have so many variations that it would be inconvenient and nearly impossible to list all of them on menus. For example, when you want to print a document, you can select the Print option from the File menu. But do you want to print the entire document or only selected pages? How many copies do you want? If you're printing multiple copies, do you want the printer to collate the pages? If you're in an office with more than one printer, which one do you want to use? Before the computer can print the document, it needs specific instructions that specify the results you want. A dialog box allows you to provide these instructions.

To fill in the "blanks" in a dialog box, you use a variety of **Windows controls**, such as option buttons, list boxes, spin boxes, check boxes, and dialog box buttons. You'll have an opportunity to try these controls in the tutorial for this chapter.

Figure 2-4: When you want to print, click the File menu, then click Print. The Print dialog box contains examples of the numerous controls you can use to specify the results for a task such as printing.

These option buttons let you select how many pages to print.

This list box helps you specify whether to print the document or information about the document.

This spin box lets you specify the number of copies to print.

A check in this check box indicates that you want to collate the pages.

The OK dialog box button starts the print process using the settings you've specified.

■FAQ Which version of Windows do I have?

The operating system is the core piece of software on your PC. You work with it directly to start programs and organize the documents and other information stored on your disks. The operating system sets the standard for the on-screen controls used for all your application software. In addition, the operating system works behind the scenes to detect equipment failure, maintain security, manage storage space, and communicate with the printer, speakers, and monitor. Microsoft has introduced several versions of the Windows operating system, each one slightly different from the others in terms of features and appearance. It is handy to know which version you are using when you purchase new software, when you call for technical support, and when you shop for tutorials.

Microsoft Windows 3.1 was the first commercially successful version of the Windows operating system. **Microsoft Windows 95** offered significant new features and became the operating system of choice between 1995 and 1998. **Microsoft Windows 98** was released in mid-1998 as an upgrade to Windows 95, and was followed by **Windows Me** (Millennium Edition) in mid-2000. Microsoft also offers a line of **Windows NT/2000** operating systems, originally designed for networked environments. In late 2001 Microsoft released **Windows XP**, which unified the 98/Me and NT/2000 lines. Most new computers come equipped with Windows XP, but previous versions of Windows are still widely used on older computers. The various versions of Windows offer similar features and controls, with a slightly different user interface. The images and animations in this book feature Windows XP, but when possible, the information has been generalized so as to apply to most recent versions of Windows.

Figure 2-5: Click the PlayIt! button for a demonstration of two ways to find out which version of Windows you're using.

To find out which version of Windows you're using, use the My Computer icon (or the System icon in Control Panel) to view the System Properties data sheet. It contains the exact version number of Windows.

■Hardware
Alternative input devices

What makes a computer easy to use? The answer is a well-designed user interface. A **user interface** is the combination of hardware and software that manages the way humans and computers interact. In a well-designed user interface, accomplishing any task should be easy and learning a new task should be intuitive.

Windows defines the major elements of the user interface for PCs. Virtually every PC software package follows its **graphical user interface** (GUI, pronounced "gooey") model which includes menus, dialog boxes, and toolbars that you manipulate with the keyboard and mouse. The user interface provides two-way communication between you and your PC. It provides an **input** method that allows you to communicate information to the computer. It also provides an **output** method so that the computer can communicate information to you.

The current Windows user interface is the standard for most PCs, but it is not necessarily perfect, nor is it right for every user or every computing device. For example, the keyboard and mouse are great input devices for a standard desktop PC, but they don't work as well for pocket-sized PDAs or for people who don't know how to type.

A **touch-sensitive LCD** provides an alternative input method for small, portable computing devices and for nontypists. It is similar to the flat-panel LCD screens used on notebook computers, but it includes a matrix of sensors that transmit position and pressure information to the computer. A **stylus** is a pen-like device that you use to "write" on the LCD. The shapes of the characters you produce with the stylus are analyzed instantly by **handwriting-recognition software** that attempts to match your squiggles to the letters of the alphabet. Handwriting recognition is a difficult task given the almost endless variations in handwriting styles. To simplify and speed up the task of analysis, many handwriting-recognition programs require you to print using only a standard set of letters, numbers, symbols, and punctuation marks.

Figure 2-6: The reference card from a pocket-sized PalmPilot PDA shows you how to write the Graffiti alphabet that will be recognized by its handwriting-recognition software. The small squares indicate where to begin each stroke.

■Hardware
continued

As part of the user interface, a touch-sensitive LCD serves a dual purpose—it is both an input and output device. It displays computer output, such as the results of a calculation, but it also collects your written input. A mouse, on the other hand, typically serves only as an input device. This situation is changing, however, as new feedback devices hit the market.

A **feedback device**, as its name implies, supplies you with feedback as you use it. A popular example is the **force-feedback joystick**, an enhanced version of the ordinary joystick you might have used in the past with popular computer games. An ordinary joystick helps you move a screen-based object, such as a pointer, an action figure, or a simulated aircraft. A force-feedback joystick adds another level of interactivity. The computer outputs instructions to this device so that, for example, if your simulated aircraft begins to stall, the joystick starts to vibrate. If you try to take your plane into a steep climb, you feel more and more resistance as your rate of climb increases. Force-feedback steering wheels are popular with racing game enthusiasts.

Force-feedback technology gives the user tactile feedback and is not limited to gaming applications. It can also be utilized in both desktop and Web computing to expand the user experience. For example, with a "touch-enabled" mouse you can feel the contours and shapes of icons on your Windows desktop. You can feel a window's elasticity when you stretch or shrink it. While Web surfing, you can sense a "sunken" feeling to graphic and text links, which are sometimes difficult to identify in a visually cluttered Web page. Obviously, force-feedback mice are very useful for the visually impaired. They typically cost about U.S.$25, while the joysticks are around U.S.$50 and above.

Figure 2-7: A force-feedback joystick works best with software that contains feedback capability. One of the classic feedback games is Sierra Trophy Bass. You use the joystick as a fishing rod to cast out your lure. When a fish grabs the bait, you'll feel a tug. Click PlayIt! to see it.

■Hardware
continued

Fans of the original Star Trek will remember Captain Kirk dictating his captain's log to the on-board computer. That was back in 1966. So after all these years, why aren't we talking to our computers? **Speech recognition**, sometimes referred to as voice recognition, is the ability of a computer to identify and interpret human speech. It has not been an easy technology to successfully implement. Even recognizing a single word such as "pen" can be difficult. A Southerner might pronounce the word more like "pin." Coming from a New Englander, it might sound like "payen." A person with a cold might make it sound like "fenmph!" Background noise can also create interference. And how is the computer supposed to know whether you're talking to it or yelling at your dog?

After many years of laboratory research, speech recognition is finally emerging as a viable technology. Many people would prefer to compose a document by dictating, rather than by typing. Is this option possible today? The answer is a qualified "yes." Speech recognition works, but there's a little more to it than just connecting a microphone to your PC and talking into it.

Before you can dictate to your PC, you must install speech-recognition software and train it to understand your speech patterns. This training consists of reading a fairly lengthy section of text provided by the software manufacturer. Today's speech-recognition software has a limited vocabulary—20,000 to 300,000 words, depending on the software you've chosen. You can add new words through a training process in which you type in a new word and repeat it several times. Even after training, however, the software sometimes makes mistakes. For example, you might dictate, "He knew better, but he ate eight steaks." The software interprets this sentence as "He new better, but he 88 stakes." Obviously, it is important to proofread documents that you dictate before printing them.

Speech-recognition software is typically included as part of the Windows XP operating system. It typically requires that your computer be equipped for sound input and output using a microphone and speakers or a headset.

Figure 2-8: Using today's speech-recognition software is a learning experience both for you and for the software, but you might find the end result worth the effort. Click the PlayIt! button to see speech-recognition technology in action.

■Tutorial
How to use Windows controls

Windows controls are fairly easy to use, but there are certainly many different types: menus, buttons, lists, check boxes, spin boxes, option buttons, and scroll bars. Why such a variety? Different controls allow you to enter different types of specifications. For example, a spin box might be ideal for indicating how many copies of a document you want to print, whereas option buttons might be better for choosing whether to print the whole document or a single page.

Microsoft provides a standard set of Windows controls that you'll find in virtually all application software. Knowing how these controls work makes it easier to learn new software. In this tutorial, you'll have an opportunity to practice using a variety of Windows controls.

When you have completed the tutorial, you should be able to:
- Use the Start button to start a program.
- Identify useful controls on the taskbar.
- Use menus and dialog boxes.
- Use check boxes, option buttons, spin boxes, lists, ScreenTips, and scroll bars.

Figure 2-9: Click the PlayIt! button to begin the tutorial and try out Windows controls such as those described below. Estimated time: 20–25 minutes. Tracking Disk points: 10.

Monopoly is not just a game

In a recent U.S. congressional hearing, a senator asked everyone present to raise their hands if they owned a computer. Almost every hand went up. Next, he asked everyone who had a PC to keep their hands up. A few Macintosh computer owners lowered their hands. Finally, the senator asked those who were using the Microsoft Windows operating system to keep their hands raised. All the hands stayed up. "Now that's a monopoly!" concluded the senator, triumphantly.

A **monopoly** is the exclusive control of a trade, commodity, or service. Does Microsoft have a software monopoly? It is certainly true that more than 80% of the world's computers run Microsoft Windows. However, a monopoly is not necessarily bad—not unless a company uses it to illegally eliminate competition.

Microsoft has been rapidly expanding the features and capabilities of its operating system software. In the past you needed to purchase numerous add-on programs to diagnose hardware problems, add sound capability, display videos, and so on; today this capability is included in Windows. Consumers benefit because they don't have to purchase add-ons. However, an unfavorable result could be that other companies have little hope of publishing and selling similar add-on products.

In the past, some U.S. senators have tried to prevent Microsoft from tying its browser, Internet Explorer, to its distribution of its Windows operating system. Recent antitrust suits are now focusing on Microsoft's distribution of its media player with Windows. One was filed by RealNetworks Inc., makers of a competing digital media player called RealPlayer. Early this year, the European Commission passed a decision requiring Microsoft to unbundle Windows Media Player from its Windows distribution package. Microsoft is appealing the decision. A number of states have also accused the software giant of violating their state's antitrust and unfair competition laws. You may want to explore these cases further on the Internet or at your local library.

What do you think?

1. If you purchase a new computer, would you prefer to use preinstalled Internet software instead of obtaining and installing the Internet software of your choice? ◯ Yes ◯ No ◯ Not sure

2. Do you think Microsoft has used its operating system monopoly to illegally force people to use its Internet Explorer software? ◯ Yes ◯ No ◯ Not sure

3. Did you try to find additional information on this issue? ◯ Yes ◯ No ◯ Not sure

Save It!

QuickCheck A

1. The Windows _____ appears on the screen when the boot process is complete and remains in the background as you use other software programs.

2. If two programs are running at the same time, you can switch between them using the buttons on the _____.

3. A(n) _____ box provides you with controls for entering specifications for a task or command.

4. True or false? Microsoft Windows is classified as application software. _____

5. True or false? Wide variations in pronunciation were one factor that delayed speech-recognition technology from becoming a standard part of the user interface. _____

Check It!

QuickCheck B

Indicate the letter of the desktop element you use to perform each of the following tasks:

1. Close a window ____

2. Display a menu containing the Print option ____

3. Display the Start menu ____

4. Take a shortcut to a menu command ____

5. Shrink a window to a button on the taskbar ____

Check It!

Get It?

While using the BookOnCD, click the Get It? button to see if you can answer ten randomly selected questions from Chapter 2.

Get It?

Chapter 3

Installing and Learning Software

What's Inside?

Chapter 3 provides you with some handy tips for figuring out how to use the software you currently have and for installing new software on your PC.

What's on the CD?

Chapter 3 videos and screen tours show you how to find information about your software using Help, the Office Assistant, and PDFs. Plus, you'll see how to install, uninstall, and download software.

■FAQ   Where's the instruction manual?

When you're installing software or learning how to use it, you might need to refer to **software documentation**. Software publishers typically provide several types of documentation, and each type serves a specific purpose.

A **reference manual**, sometimes called a user manual or user reference, contains detailed descriptions of the software's features. Don't try to read this manual from cover to cover! Like a dictionary or encyclopedia, you should use it to look up information when you run into a problem or when you want to find out how a particular software feature works. Many software publishers have stopped including printed reference manuals with their software, so you may have to purchase this separately from a bookstore.

An **installation guide** provides information about installing the software on your PC. Sometimes it is separate from the reference manual—you typically find this guide in the CD case.

A **Readme file** is an online document that contains installation notes and information about last-minute changes to the software and its features.

A **software tutorial** provides step-by-step lessons on how to use the features of a software product.

The documentation that's included with a software package is not always sufficient for everyone, so you might want to purchase supplemental reference manuals and tutorials from a bookstore or computer store. When selecting a manual or tutorial, make sure that it is written for the same version of the software that you're using.

Figure 3-1: A Readme file is sometimes installed along with the software and then can be accessed from the All Programs menu. If the Readme file is not installed, you can locate it manually. You'll read about locating files in Chapter 4 and Chapter 5.

Typically, a Readme file contains technical information about specialized problems. If you can't find a solution in the reference manual, the Readme file is the next place to look.

■FAQ What's a PDF?

In the past, software reference manuals were typically distributed in printed format. As publishers added more features to their software, however, printed manuals became huge and costly. For example, one popular software tool for computer programmers included printed documentation weighing 26 pounds! The trend today is to convert reference manuals into electronic documents that can be viewed on a computer screen, stored on a CD, or distributed on the Internet.

A **PDF** (portable document format file) is a special type of electronic document that can be displayed on virtually any PC. Many software publishers use PDFs for software documentation because the text and diagrams they contain appear on the screen just about the same way they would look in a printed book. PDFs are also used for many other types of documents. Examples include back issues of magazines, NCAA sports statistics, and U.S. Census Bureau tables and graphs. Many software publishers have stopped including printed reference manuals with their software, so you may have to purchase this separately from a bookstore.

To display a PDF on your PC's screen, you need a software program called **Adobe Acrobat Reader**. Luckily, this program is available for free—it comes preinstalled on many computer systems, it is supplied on most CDs that contain PDFs, or you can transfer it to your computer from the Internet.

Figure 3-2: *Click the PlayIt! button to discover how to use Adobe Acrobat Reader to look through a PDF file that contains documentation for a software product.*

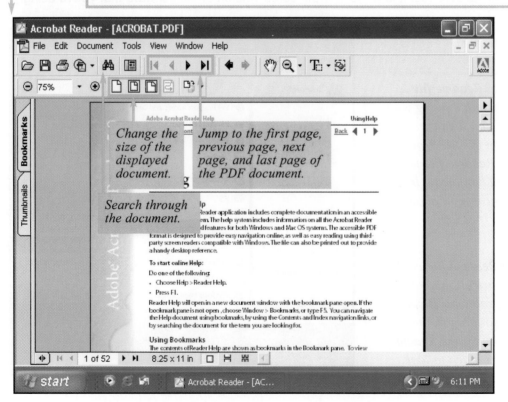

∎FAQ   How do I use online Help?

The documentation that you're likely to use most frequently is an on-screen reference guide called **online Help** or just "Help." Virtually every software application comes with online Help that you can access by clicking Help on the menu bar. The Windows operating system has its own Help that you access from the Start menu. Online Help typically provides you with several ways to look for information: a table of contents, an index, and a search facility. Like the table of contents in a book, **Help Contents** lists the major sections and topics of the online Help. The **Help Index** resembles the index of a book in that it lists the key terms and features of the software. A **Search** or **Find** option allows you to search through the entire text of the online Help to find every occurrence of a specific word.

The question mark "?" is a widely used symbol for Help in the computer world. If you need assistance, look for the nearest ❓ button on the screen and click it. In many Windows applications, a wizard or assistant will appear so you can type in a question or search for specific information.

Most Windows software also provides a "What's this?" feature or menu option. When you click the "What's this feature?" menu option, the on-screen mouse pointer changes to the **Help pointer** ⬚?. Using this pointer, you can point to any label or object on the screen to find out what it does.

Figure 3-3: *Online Help has no page numbers. Instead of turning to a page, you just click any item listed in the Contents or Index to display the information you seek. Click the PlayIt! button for a tour through Windows online Help.*

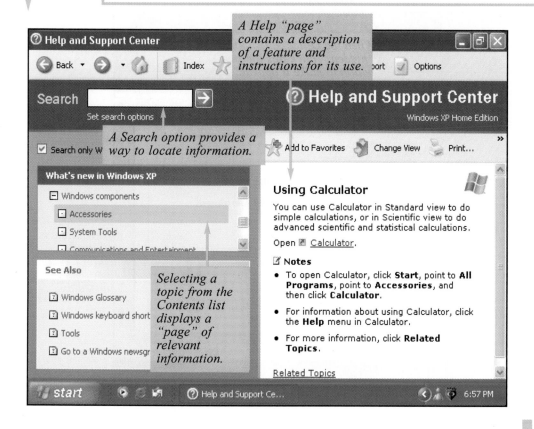

■FAQ What's the purpose of the paperclip cartoon?

Some Microsoft applications provide a friendly, animated **Office Assistant** to help you figure out how to use their features. The Office Assistant typically appears as a paperclip cartoon, and you can use it in several different ways.

First, you can use the Office Assistant to access online Help by entering questions about a task you want to complete. You might ask, "How do I make columns?" In response, the Office Assistant displays relevant information from the online Help.

The Office Assistant also provides suggestions about the specific task that you are performing. These suggestions appear even before you ask for Help. For example, if you click the Office Assistant while you're creating a newsletter that places text in two columns, it automatically provides a list of Help topics about how to work with columns.

How about some tips that point out how to use the features of your software more effectively? At regular intervals, the Office Assistant displays a light bulb to indicate that it has a new tip for you. Click the light bulb to see the tip.

If the Office Assistant gets in your way, you can right-click it, then click Hide to temporarily remove it from the desktop. To display it again, click the ⬚ Office Assistant button in the upper-right corner of the screen.

Figure 3-4: When you need help with a software task, ask the Office Assistant. Click the PlayIt! button to see how you can ask questions in your own words and get tips on how to use the software more effectively.

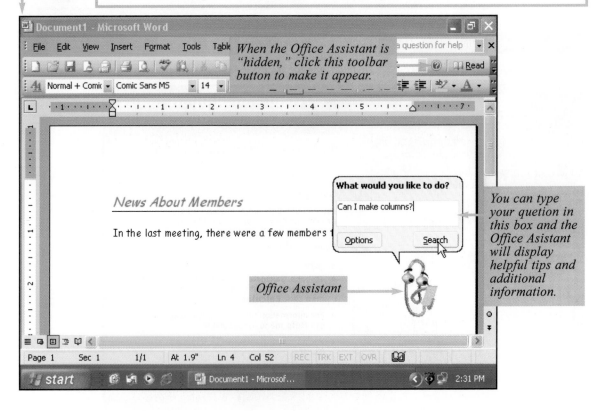

▪FAQ Can I contact the software company for help?

Documentation and online Help are supposed to supply the information that you need to figure out how to install new software and use all its features. However, you might run into problems that don't seem to be addressed in the documentation. For example, you might have trouble installing the software, or you might see an **error message** that signals a problem or software "bug."

Many software publishers provide **toll-free support lines**. By dialing a toll-free number, you can talk to a technical support professional who will try to answer your questions. The personalized help you receive is generally useful, but be prepared to wait—sometimes for more than an hour. The volume of calls is enormous, especially for newly released software.

Before you call for technical support:

▪ Check the documentation and online Help to make sure that your question is not answered there.

▪ Have your distribution CD and software serial number (if applicable) handy.

▪ Compose a brief, but clear explanation of the problem.

▪ Write down any error messages that appeared at the time of the problem.

▪ Make sure your phone is near your computer.

▪ Read the company's support policy. Even though it is a toll-free call, some software publishers charge by the minute or by the call for technical support.

Figure 3-5: *If you have access to the Internet, you might be able to avoid the telephone wait by checking the software company's Web site.*

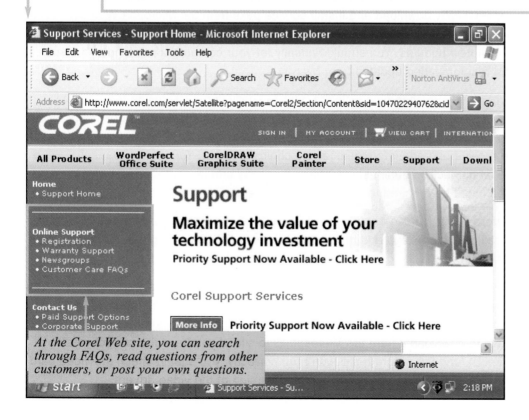

At the Corel Web site, you can search through FAQs, read questions from other customers, or post your own questions.

■Hardware

Install and uninstall software on your PC

Installing and uninstalling software might seem like an odd topic for a *hardware* section, but somehow you've got to get the software "out of the box" and onto your PC hardware. **Installing software** refers to the process of adding software to your PC so that it is available for use. **Uninstalling software** means removing it.

When you first learn how to use computers, you'll likely be using a PC at home, school, or work that contains most of the software you need. Even if you have just purchased your own PC, it is likely to include enough preinstalled software for you to create documents, make calculations, and draw simple graphics. Therefore, you usually don't have to worry about installing software when you're first learning about PCs.

Eventually, you'll want to install more software so that you can do new things with your PC, such as learning to speak Spanish or playing the new game that has drawn rave reviews from your friends. You might also install software upgrades. A **software upgrade** is a new version of a software product, usually with enhanced or more sophisticated features than are available with older versions. A software upgrade provides new features, so you must typically pay for the upgrade.

A **patch** or a **service pak** is a software update that corrects errors or security problems with the original version of the software. Service paks typically do not provide a lot of new features, so they are usually distributed as Internet downloads at no extra cost. Computers running Microsoft Windows are typically configured to automatically download and install service paks from the Microsoft Web site. Your computer may sometimes display a prompt asking if you want to download or install new updates. You should typically let your computer download and install the recommended updates from Microsoft.

When you purchase new software, you'll usually find a CD inside the box. This CD, called the **distribution CD**, contains your new software. The box might also contain a registration card that you can fill out and return to the software publisher to receive upgrade information and technical support. Your software might have a serial number that uniquely identifies that copy and discourages unauthorized use. You might be required to enter this number as part of the installation process.

Before you purchase and install new software, check the **system requirements** listed on the package and make sure that your PC has enough memory, adequate disk space, and the correct version of Windows to run the software.

If you are installing a game or other program that uses sophisticated graphics, you might need to install the latest version of Windows **DirectX**. Sometimes the required version of DirectX is included on the program CD, but if it's not, you might have to download it from the Microsoft Web site. If you have the correct version of DirectX, and the program still won't run correctly, you should check the video card manufacturer's Web site for an updated version of the video drivers.

■Hardware
continued

You might be surprised to learn that a software application is not a single huge computer program, but rather a collection of **program modules** that work together to accomplish a task. When you install software, some or all of these program modules are copied from the distribution CD to your PC's hard disk.

The installation process also adds the name of the software to the Programs menu and provides Windows with the technical information it needs to run the new software most efficiently on your PC. This information is stored on the hard drive in a special document called the **Registry** that keeps track of all installed hardware and software. You can envision the Registry as a sort of hotel register that keeps track of the guests who check in and check out.

The software installation process is automated by a **Setup program** that's included on the distribution CD. The installation process is a one-time procedure. Once a software package has been installed, you don't have to install it again unless it inadvertently gets deleted or unless your PC's hard disk develops problems.

After you've completed the installation, hang on to that CD! Some applications, such as multimedia encyclopedias, would require too much space if all the program modules were copied to the hard disk. Instead, the installation process copies only essential modules and leaves others on the CD. To access all the modules, you'll need to put the CD in the CD-ROM drive every time you use the application.

Figure 3-6: *On most computers, the Setup program starts automatically when you insert the distribution CD in the CD-ROM drive. You can also start the Setup program manually. Click PlayIt! to find out how to install software.*

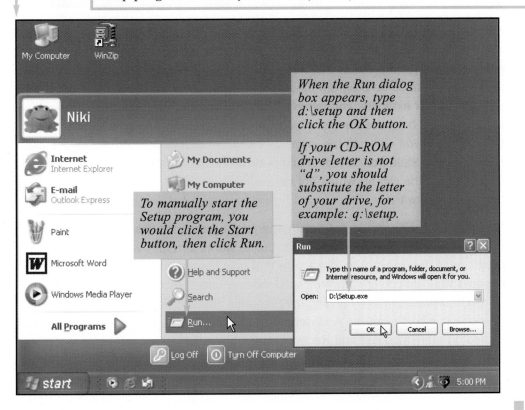

■Hardware
continued

At some point, you might want to remove software from your PC. You might want to make room on the hard disk drive for other programs, documents, or graphics. You might no longer need one of your programs. You might want to replace a program with one that has a better collection of features.

The uninstall process removes programs from the hard disk, removes the program name from the All Programs menu, and updates the Registry. You'll find it quite easy to uninstall software using the Windows **Add/Remove Programs icon**. Although its name implies that you can use it to install and uninstall software, you should use the Add/Remove Programs icon only to uninstall software. To install software, use the Setup program that's included on the distribution CD because it is easier and more efficient.

Figure 3-7: You'll find the Add/Remove Programs icon in the Windows Control Panel, which you access from the Settings option on the Start menu. Click the PlayIt! button to learn how to use the Add/Remove Programs icon to uninstall software.

Although the uninstall process seems straightforward, behind the scenes your PC is very busy. Its major concern is to correctly update the Registry by removing the entries for the software you're uninstalling. This process is not as simple as it sounds because some program modules are used by more than one software application. For example, your word processing software and your graphics software might both use the same program module containing a collection of clip art pictures. If you uninstall the graphics software, should your PC delete the clip art program module from the disk and remove its entry from the Registry? No, because then the clip art would not be available when you use your word processing software.

Generally, your PC should not delete shared program modules when you uninstall software. The Add/Remove Programs routine works carefully with the list of programs in the Registry to make sure that only nonshared files are removed. In the days when computer software contained only one or two modules, you could uninstall software simply by finding the programs and deleting them. On today's PCs, however, it is best to let the Add/Remove Programs icon handle the complexities of shared program modules and Registry updates.

▪Tutorial

How to download and install software from the Internet

Grab It!

Adobe Acrobat Reader

Many companies and organizations maintain Internet computer "sites," containing software, documentation, and other information that is available to the public. The Internet is a great source for free software and trial versions of commercial software. For example, if you need the Adobe Acrobat Reader software, you can find it on the Internet. The GrabIt! buttons featured in the margins of this book will help you locate software on the Internet.

Before you can install and use software from the Internet, you have to transfer it to your PC. This process is called **downloading**. If you're using a PC at work or at school, check with a supervisor to make sure that it's OK to download software. Some software is very large and takes a long time to download, so be prepared to wait. After you download software, you should follow the rules given for its use.

When you have completed the tutorial, you should be able to:
▪ Use a GrabIt! button to download software from the Internet.
▪ Print the installation instructions.
▪ Understand how installing software from the Internet differs from installing software from a CD.

Play It!

Figure 3-8: Click the PlayIt! button to learn how to download and install software from the Internet. You can use this tutorial even if you don't currently have Internet access. Estimated time: 15–20 minutes. Tracking Disk points: 10.

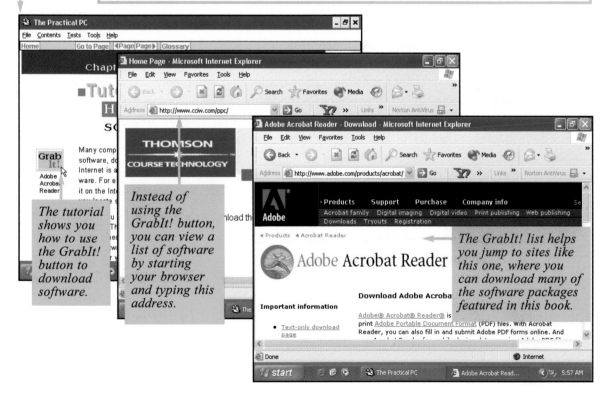

The tutorial shows you how to use the GrabIt! button to download software.

Instead of using the GrabIt! button, you can view a list of software by starting your browser and typing this address.

The GrabIt! list helps you jump to sites like this one, where you can download many of the software packages featured in this book.

Is it legal to install this software?

To answer the question "Is it legal to install this software?" you'll have to read the package or documentation to find out whether it is commercial, freeware, shareware, or demo software. Like books, movies, and music, software is protected by copyright law in most countries. Under copyright law, it is illegal to copy software except to install it and to make a backup copy in case the original version stops working correctly.

Commercial software is marketed for a profit by a software publisher that requires strict adherence to copyright rules. This software often comes with a **license agreement** that further restricts the way you can use it. Look for the terms of the license on the box, CD case, or disk packaging.

Although copyright law protects all software, a software developer can ease the restrictions on copying by creating freeware, shareware, or demo software. **Freeware** is usually provided free of charge. The software developer retains the copyright, but gives blanket permission to download the software from the Internet, install it, copy it multiple times, and give copies to friends. **Shareware** is also copyrighted, but the developer lets you install the software and share it with friends on a trial basis for a short period of time. You and your friends are on your honor to register and pay for the software if you use it beyond the trial period. A **demo** is a special version of commercial software that is often scaled down for demonstration purposes. You can install the demo software to see how it works before you purchase the full commercial version.

If you don't follow regulations for the use of commercial, shareware, freeware, and demo software, you might not be using it legally. Software that is illegally copied, installed, sold, and used is called **pirated software**. According to the Software and Information Industry Association (SIIA), a leading anti-piracy watchdog, piracy of business application software costs the industry $12 billion a year. This figure reveals only part of the piracy problem—it does not include losses from rampant game and educational software piracy.

What do you think?

1. Have you ever used pirated software? ○Yes ○ No ○ Not sure

2. Before reading about this issue, did you understand the difference between freeware, shareware, commercial, and demo software? ○ Yes ○ No ○ Not sure

3. If you discovered pirated software in use at your school or office, would you report it? ○ Yes ○ No ○ Not sure

Save It!

QuickCheck A

1. True or false? You must install all of the program modules from the distribution CD every time you want to use the software it contains. ☐

2. True or false? The easiest way to access a PDF is to click Help on the menu bar at the top of the screen. ☐

3. The operating system maintains a(n) ☐ to keep track of the hardware and software installed on your PC.

4. You have to ☐ software from the Internet before you can install it.

5. You can freely copy and install ☐, but if you use it beyond the trial period you are supposed to register it and pay the developer a fee for its use.

Check It!

QuickCheck B

Type the letter of the object that helps you accomplish each of the tasks listed below.

1. The Help Pointer ☐

2. The Office Assistant ☐

3. Display the Office Assistant in Office ☐

4. Look for a specific word or term in the online Help Index ☐

5. Display an index listing Help and Support topics ☐

Check It!

Get It?   While using the BookOnCD, click the Get It? button to see if you can answer ten randomly selected questions from Chapter 3.   **Get It?**

Chapter 4

Naming and Saving Files

What's Inside?

All of the documents, pictures, and music that you create with your PC are stored as files. Chapter 4 helps you understand how to best name your files, where to store them, and how to use them. It emphasizes how to open and save files from within your application software.

FAQs:

What's on the CD?

Don't miss the Chapter 4 videos and screen tours that provide all the basics about files and floppy disk storage. You'll pick up information on hard disk storage in Chapter 5.

■FAQ What's a file?

A **file** is a collection of data that has a name and is stored on a computer disk, tape, or CD. Virtually all of the information that you can access from your PC is stored as files. For example, each document, graph, or picture that you create with application software is stored as a file. The Web pages that you view from the Internet are also stored as files, as are the program modules shipped on the distribution CD of a software package. Files can be divided into two categories: executable files and data files. Understanding the difference between these two categories is important because you use executable files in a different way than you use data files.

An **executable file** is a program module containing instructions that tell your PC how to perform specific tasks. Your PC "executes" these instructions to complete tasks such as sorting lists, searching for information, printing, or making calculations. For example, the word processing program that tells your PC how to display and print text is an executable file. The main executable files on your computer are listed on the Windows All Programs menu, and you typically use this menu to select the one that you want your PC to execute.

A **data file** contains words, numbers, and pictures that you can manipulate. For example, a document that you create using word processing software is a data file. You have several ways to access a data file, including the Open option on your application software's File menu, and in some versions of Windows, the Start menu's Documents option.

Figure 4-1: You can open recently used files from your application software's File menu. Click the PlayIt! button to learn another handy method for opening files.

The Open option on your application software's File menu lists the data files in the folder. You can click any one of these files to open and display it.

The Documents option on the Start menu lists the data files you've accessed most recently. You can click any one of these files to open and display it.

■FAQ Can I use any name for a file?

You'll create many files as you use application software. You'll create documents with word processing software, graphs with spreadsheet software, and pictures with graphics software. As you're creating documents, graphs, and pictures, your PC holds your data in memory. When you're ready for your PC to **save a file** by transferring it to more permanent disk storage, you must give it a unique name.

PC operating systems, such as MS DOS and Windows 3.1, originally limited the length of a file name to eight characters or less. Also, a file name could not contain any spaces. These limitations made it difficult to create descriptive file names. A file name such as "Letmjord" might indicate a letter written to Michael Jordan. "Orgch504" might be the name of a file containing an organizational chart updated in May 2004. Even when using more recent versions of Windows, you might encounter older software that has not been updated to allow longer file names. If you're not sure about file name limitations for an application, check Help or refer to the reference manual.

Beginning with Windows 95, file names containing as many as 255 characters became permissible. With Windows 95, 98, Me, NT, 2000, and XP you can use file names such as "Letter to Michael Jordan" and "Organizational Chart-Updated May 2004". This capability, which came to be known as **long file names**, makes it much easier to find a specific file based on its name.

Long file names also allow you to control capitalization. Most people tend to use the same capitalization for file names as they would use for a title, using uppercase for the first letter of every word except articles and prepositions. Windows is not **case sensitive**, however. Even though you can use uppercase and lowercase, the file name "Report" is the same as "report" or "REPORT".

Figure 4-2: You can give virtually any name you want to a file as long as it conforms to the rules summarized in this table.

	Operating System	
	Windows 95, 98, Me, NT, 2000, XP	**Windows 3.1**
Maximum length	255 characters	8 characters
Spaces allowed?	Yes	No
Numbers allowed?	Yes	Yes
Characters not allowed	/ < > " \ : | * ?	/ [ ] ; " \ : , | * ?
File names not allowed	Aux, Com1, Com2, Com3, Com4, Con, Lpt1, Lpt2, Prn, Nul	Aux, Com1, Com2, Com3, Com4, Con, Lpt1, Lpt2, Prn, Nul

■FAQ What's a file extension?

A **file extension** is a set of characters added to a file name that indicates the file's type or origin. For example, the file extension .doc indicates a file that was created with Microsoft Word. A file extension is separated from the main file name with a period, but no spaces. File extensions have a maximum length of three characters. The full name of your letter to Michael Jordan, including the file extension, would be "Letter to Michael Jordan.doc".

Each software application that you use typically has a default file extension. In "tech speak," a **default** is a standard setting that always goes into effect unless you manually change it. A default file extension is the extension that an application uses unless you specify otherwise. For Microsoft Word the default file extension is .doc, for Microsoft Excel it is .xls, for Adobe Acrobat Reader it is .pdf, and for Microsoft Paint it is .bmp.

There are hundreds of file extensions and the situation would be pretty grim if you had to remember the extension for each program you use. Happily, you generally don't have to memorize file extensions—instead, your software automatically adds the correct one when you save a file.

A file extension indicates the **file format** in which it is stored. File extensions are sometimes abbreviated versions of the file format names. For example, the three-character .htm file extension indicates that the file is stored in HTML file format.

Files are stored in different formats because they contain different types of data. A document, for example, is typically stored in a different format than a video is. Some file formats, however, allow you to include multiple types of data in a single file, such as a document and a picture. Within a category such as documents, different file formats allow different features. Both DOC and TXT file formats store documents. The TXT file format stores only plain text, whereas the DOC file format allows you to store boldface, italic, and underlined text.

Figure 4-3: A file's format indicates what type of data it contains. This table shows you some of the many file formats that exist for each type of file.

File Contents	File Format
Document	DOC TXT WPS WPD WRI RTF ASCII
Database	MDB DBF
Spreadsheet	XLS WK4
Graphic	BMP TIFF GIF JPEG EPSF PCX WMF
Sound	WAV MIDI
Video	AVI MPEG MOV
Web page	HTML
Programs	EXE COM SYS DLL VBX OCX

■FAQ Can I convert a file from one format to another?

A software application typically works with the one file format indicated by the default file extension. Microsoft Word, for example, uses DOC as its document file format. But suppose you receive a disk containing a document in WRI format. Can Microsoft Word display this document? Most software includes **import routines** that can open different file formats and convert them to the default format. The import routine for the Microsoft Word file format can open documents in WRI format so you can use them in Microsoft Word. An **export routine** allows you to save files in a format other than your software's default format.

Sometimes you must be creative to take advantage of your software's import and export routines. Suppose that you have a customer who uses word processing software that produces documents saved in SAM format, which was used by an older word processor. Your software does not have an import routine for this format, and your customer does not have an export routine for your DOC format. Can you exchange files? The answer is yes, if you can find a common format on your lists of import and export routines. You might discover that your customer can export RTF (rich text format) files, which you can import. Your customer can then convert the SAM file into RTF format. When you receive the RTF file, your software can import it and save it as a DOC file. If you need to send the file back to the customer, you can save it in RTF format, which the customer would then import and resave in the SAM format.

Figure 4-4: *Most software displays a list of import formats in the Open dialog box and a list of export formats in the Save dialog box. Click the PlayIt! button to see how to import and export document files with Microsoft Word.*

■FAQ How do I tell my PC where to store a file?

You'll usually store files on your PC's hard disk—of all your storage devices, it has the highest storage capacity and the quickest retrieval time. If you want to transport a file, however, you might choose to store it on a floppy disk or other removable storage device. If you want to share the file with others, you could store it on a network hard disk. Each storage device on your PC is identified by a unique **device letter**. Typically, the device letter for the floppy disk drive is A and for the hard disk drive it is C. Drive letters are typically followed by a colon (:) and a backslash (\) such as A:\ or C:\.

When you save a file, you must tell the software where to store it. You can select a storage device from the list provided or enter the device letter before the file name. For example, if you enter C:\Journey Home.doc, the file will be stored on the hard disk. Notice that a colon and a backslash separate the device letter from the file name.

Folders allow you to group files for easy retrieval. You might create a folder called Genealogy to hold your family history files. The device letter, folder, file name, and extension provide the information necessary to store a file in a particular location. This information is sometimes referred to as a **path**, because like a woodland path it leads you to a destination. The path C:\Genealogy\Journey Home.doc indicates that the Journey Home file is located on drive C:\ in the Genealogy folder. Notice that the backslash character (\) is used between the components of the path.

Figure 4-5: Click the PlayIt! button to see how to select a storage device, create a folder, and follow a path to a file.

■Hardware
Floppy disks and other removable storage devices

A **floppy disk** is a removable storage medium typically housed in a 3.5-inch square case. The storage capacity of a floppy disk isn't large enough to store a lot of music files, high-resolution photos, or video clips. However, floppy disks are cheap, reusable, and can be used on most computer systems; so they continue to be a convenient way to save and transport smaller files such as word processing documents. Once you've stored a file on a floppy disk, you can transport it between a school lab and your home PC, or between PCs at work and at home. You can also send a floppy disk through the mail to share files with friends or clients.

The disk surface that holds data is protected by a rigid plastic case. A spring-loaded **access hatch cover** on the disk case opens to expose the disk surface when the disk is inserted into a disk drive. You should always insert the metal access hatch first, making sure that the disk label faces up. The disk case also contains a small **write-protect window**. If you open this window, your PC cannot change the data on the disk. This feature is handy when your disk contains an important file that should not be erased or modified.

A floppy disk offers durable and dependable storage if cared for properly. Avoid exposing the disk to high temperatures. Be careful not to leave it on the dashboard of your car in the summer sun, because it might warp or melt. A disk that has been left in freezing temperatures should be allowed to warm to room temperature before you use it.

The data on a disk is stored as magnetized particles, so keep disks away from refrigerator magnets and other magnetic fields. For long-term storage, a clean and dry environment is best. Moisture encourages the growth of mold and mildew that can make a disk unusable. In humid climates, store disks in a sealed plastic bag along with some moisture-reducing desiccant packets. Dust and smoke can also interfere with the ability of the disk drive to retrieve data from a disk.

Figure 4-6: Click PlayIt! for an in-depth look at a floppy disk. A floppy disk gets its name from the thin, flexible disk that's sealed inside its square plastic case. Despite the hard plastic case, you should not call it a "hard disk." Chapter 5 explains more about the difference between floppy disks and hard disks.

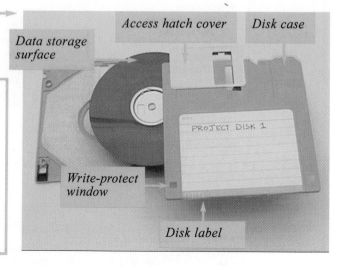

▪Hardware
continued

Unfortunately, many of today's files—especially graphics, sound, and video—are much too large to fit in the 1.44 Megabytes that can be stored on a floppy disk. Over the years, a number of higher capacity floppy disk replacements have been developed, including the Iomega Zip drives which use special Zip disks with capacities up to 750 MB.

For easy transportation of files that are too large to fit on a floppy disk, many users have turned to USB storage devices, often called **USB flash drives**. These devices contain from 32 to 256 Megabytes of solid-state memory which can be used to store and move data between computer systems. When you insert a USB flash drive into the USB port on your computer, it is automatically recognized as a removable storage device and assigned a drive letter. Unfortunately, the USB flash drive may be assigned a different drive letter on each computer, depending on the other storage devices already installed on that system. To minimize the chance of losing data, you should use the Safely Remove Hardware feature before removing a USB flash device from your computer.

Figure 4-7: A typical USB flash drive is small enough to fit on a keychain.

Compared to removable media, USB flash drives are rather expensive, so they are not the best choice if you need to send data to someone or need to store data for long periods of time. If you need to mail a small amount of data to someone, it is better to use an inexpensive floppy disk. If the data will not fit on a floppy disk, the next best option is to write the data to a CD-R disk. CD-R disks are very inexpensive, easy to ship, and can be read on almost any computer system. However, your computer must be equipped with a writable CD drive to save data to a CD-R disk. CD-R disks typically store up to 700 Megabytes of data, the same as 486 floppy disks.

If your data is too large for a CD-R disk, the next best option is to save it on a writable DVD disk using the DVD-R or DVD+R format. These disks can store up to 4.7 Gigabytes of data (4,700 Megabytes), large enough for large video files. Your computer must be equipped with a writable DVD drive to write data to the disks, and the other computer must be equipped with a DVD drive in order to read the disks.

If you need to save and transport large amounts of data that must be modified, you should use a rewritable CD, known as a CD-RW, or a rewritable DVD, using the DVD-RW or DVD+RW formats.

■Hardware
continued

What actually happens when a disk drive stores data on a disk? The answer to this question explains why some disks can store more data than others and why a disk must be formatted before it can be used for data storage.

Internally, a PC represents data using 0s and 1s. For text, a special coding system called **ASCII** (American Standard Code for Information Interchange) uses a series of 1s and 0s to represent letters, numbers, or punctuation marks. In some ways the ASCII code is similar to Morse code, but instead of using dots and dashes, ASCII uses 0s and 1s. For example, the ASCII code 01000001 represents an uppercase "A". To store this character on a disk, the disk drive uses a **read/write head** to magnetize tiny metallic particles on the disk surface. The magnetic polarization of each particle indicates whether it is a 1 or a 0. A group of eight polarized particles represents one character and requires one byte of storage space.

The size and density of the metallic particles determine the amount of data that can be packed into any given area on the disk surface. The smaller the particles and the more densely they are packed, the more data a disk can hold. It is just like packing fruit: you can get lots more lemons than watermelons into a box. This principle explains why a Zip disk can store more information than a standard floppy disk, even though both have approximately the same physical dimensions.

To simplify the process of storing and locating data, a disk is divided into concentric circles called **tracks**. These tracks are then divided into **sectors**. Each sector is numbered. Your PC's operating system records the sector numbers that hold the data for each of your files. The process of dividing a disk into sectors is called **formatting**. A disk must be formatted before you store data on it. Today, when you purchase disks, they're generally preformatted. You just need to read the label to make sure it indicates "IBM PC format," not "Mac format."

Figure 4-8: Click the PlayIt! button to walk through each step in the process of formatting a disk. If you purchase unformatted disks, you'll need to format them before you use them. Formatting erases all data on a disk. Before you reuse old disks, you might want to format them to erase unneeded data.

1. Double-clicking the My Computer icon opens the My Computer window.

2. Clicking the floppy disk icon indicates the location of the disk that you want to format.

3. The File menu contains the Format option that you'll use to format a disk.

■Tutorial
How to create and save files

You can create files using several different techniques, but the process typically begins by opening the application that you'll use to enter your data. Depending on the application, you might have to use the New command before entering the text, graphics, or sounds for the new file. When you are ready to store the file, use the Save option on the File menu. To complete the save process, you will specify the device letter and folder for the file location, then give the file a name.

When you have completed the tutorial, you should be able to:
- Use the New option on the File menu to create a new document.
- Use the Save option on the File menu to save a document on disk.
- Specify the disk and folder in which a file will be located.
- Open a file, modify it, then use the Save As command to save the file under a different name.

Figure 4-9: Click the PlayIt! button to begin the tutorial and learn how to use File menu options to create, save, open, and modify a file. Estimated time: 15–20 minutes. Tracking Disk points: 10.

Should governments regulate encryption?

Encryption
Software

Government agencies, banks, corporations, and individuals sometimes want to keep the contents of their computer files safe from prying eyes. **Encryption software** uses a secret code or "key" to scramble file content. In the course of normal transactions, decoding requires the use of the same type of encryption software and the "key" for unscrambling the file. Although cryptographers can use computer technology to break into encrypted files without the key, this task becomes more difficult as encryption techniques become more complex. Certain encryption techniques, called **strong encryption**, are almost impossible to break.

The increasing use of encrypted files is making some governments uneasy. Information about drug deals, international terrorism, and racketeering might be stored in encrypted format or transmitted on the Internet. What if law enforcement cryptographers can't break the code to access these documents?

Some governments would like to limit civilian use of encryption methods to those for which law enforcement agencies have the master decoding key. Civil rights advocates oppose this scheme because it seems to violate basic privacy rights—analogous to your local police demanding a copy of your house keys.

Some governments regulate strong encryption technology by classifying it as a military weapon, thereby prohibiting a national to send strong encryption software to a colleague in another country in order to exchange encrypted research data. In the year 2000, the United States decided to relax its encryption policy, which now makes it much easier for U.S. companies and individuals to widely export strong encryption in common products despite their strength or the type of technology they utilize.

The new rules do not change restrictions on terrorist-supporting countries like Iran and Iraq. They do not decontrol encryption, so that major concerns about free expression and privacy still remain. The rules also trigger a new debate about appropriate legal protections for decryption keys and other personal data online. Good sources of additional information are the Electronic Frontier Foundation at *www.eff.org* and the Center for Democracy and Technology at *www.cdt.org*.

What do you think?

1. Would you ever want to encrypt the files you have stored on your PC?   ○ Yes   ○ No   ○ Not sure

2. Should your government have a universal key for unlocking all encrypted files?   ○ Yes   ○ No   ○ Not sure

3. If someone devises an unbreakable encryption scheme, do you think that your government should attempt to keep it a secret?   ○ Yes   ○ No   ○ Not sure

Save
It!

QuickCheck A

1. A(n) [＿＿＿＿＿＿＿＿＿] file contains the documents and pictures that you create, whereas a(n) [＿＿＿＿＿＿＿＿＿] file contains instructions that tell your PC how to perform specific tasks.

2. True or false? If your PC has Windows XP, you can name a file ACME Annual Report First Draft. [＿＿＿＿＿]

3. True or false? If your PC has Windows XP, you can have a file named Resume and a file named RESUME in the same folder. [＿＿＿＿＿]

4. The process of [＿＿＿＿＿＿＿＿] a disk divides it into tracks and sectors.

5. C:\JobSearch\Resume.doc would be referred to as the file [＿＿＿＿＿＿＿＿].

Check It!

QuickCheck B

Based on the settings shown in the Save As dialog box, fill in the boxes below to indicate where and how the file will be saved.

1. The file name will be [＿＿＿＿＿＿＿].

2. The device letter is [＿＿].

3. The folder name is [＿＿＿＿＿＿＿].

4. The file extension is [＿＿].

5. The file will be stored on a(n) [＿＿＿＿＿＿] disk drive.

Check It!

Get It?

While using the BookOnCD, click the Get It? button to see if you can answer ten randomly selected questions from Chapter 4.

Get It!

Chapter 5

Organizing Files and Folders

What's Inside?

Chapter 5 provides tips on organizing files and folders so that you can easily locate them. The Hardware section focuses on your PC's hard disk, with information on how it works and how to keep it performing at peak efficiency.

What's on the CD?

In Chapter 5, you'll take an in-depth look at how to use Windows Explorer. You'll also go behind the scenes to explore the mysteries of your hard disk drive.

■FAQ   How do I get a list of my files?

Your application software's Open dialog box and Save dialog box provide a list of files, but their space limitations make it difficult to see the big picture—all of your PC's storage devices, folders, and files. For a complete list of files and a full set of tools for organizing those files, most PC experts turn to Windows Explorer.

Windows Explorer is a part of the Windows operating system that's designed to help you find and organize the files on your PC. It lists files in alphabetical order by title, or in order by size, by type, or by date created so that you can search for a specific file. If locating a file is difficult because you've stored files in the wrong folder or you've jammed hundreds of files into the same folder, you might find it useful to periodically use Windows Explorer to streamline your file system. You can change file or folder names, move files to different folders, move folders to different disks, delete individual files, or delete entire folders and the files they contain.

To start Windows Explorer, select it from the Accessories menu. Windows Explorer provides several methods for accomplishing file management tasks. Experts tend to prefer the right-click method that you'll learn in this book because it works for all the desktops available with all versions of Windows. **Right-clicking** means to press the right, not the left, mouse button. When you right-click a file name or folder, Windows Explorer displays a shortcut menu that lists the options for that file, including Copy, Delete, Open, and Rename.

Figure 5-1: Click PlayIt! for a guided tour of Windows Explorer. Learn how to select a storage device, folder, or file, and how to sort files. You'll even find out how to start programs and display documents without using the Start button.

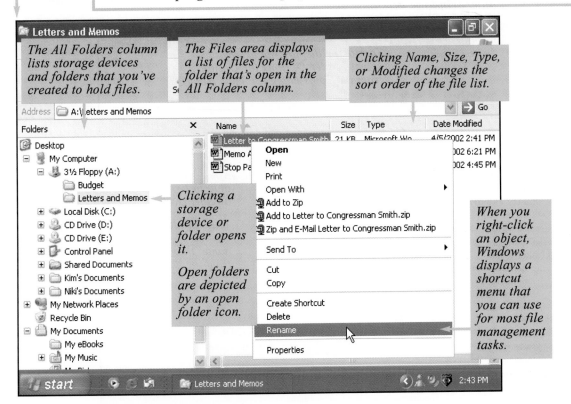

▪FAQ How do I change the name of a file?

Once you have located a file with Windows Explorer, it's easy to change its name. This process is called **renaming**. To rename a file, you select it, then type a new name. You might want to rename a file so its name better describes its contents. You might also want to standardize the names of similar files—Playoff 2003, Playoff 2004, Playoff 2005—so that they appear in sequence.

Renaming files is fairly straightforward, except for a little twist involving file extensions. Windows allows you to hide file extensions. When this option is in effect, file extensions are not displayed, but they still exist. Windows has simply hidden them from your view. If you would like to change this option on your PC, select Folder Options (or Options) from the Windows Explorer Tools menu in Windows XP and Me or the View menu in older Windows versions, then adjust the "Hide file extensions" option on the View tab.

Before you rename a file, look at the file name to see if it includes an extension. If you see .doc or another extension, then Windows is set to display file extensions. In this case, when you rename a file you must type the file extension along with the new name. As a rule, you should use the same file extension as in the original name. If you forget to type the file extension, Windows displays a reminder. If Windows is hiding file extensions, it is not necessary to type the file extension. In this case, when you rename a file your PC automatically retains the old file extension for the new file name.

Figure 5-2: To hide or display file extensions, select Folder Options (or Options) from the Tools menu in Windows Me and XP, or the View menu in older Windows versions.

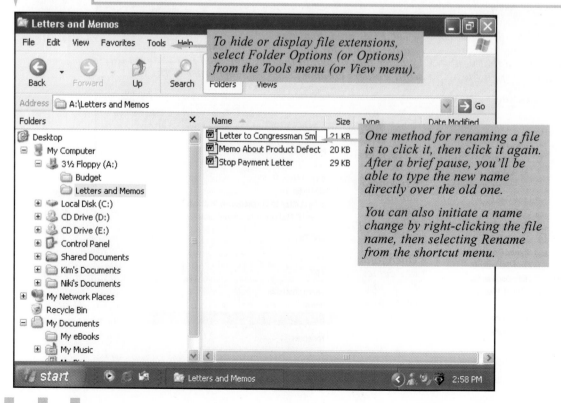

■FAQ What's the best organization for my files?

Folders help you organize files. The key to organizing your files is to create a clearly structured set of folders. If the number of files in a folder exceeds what you find to be a manageable size, don't hesitate to create additional folders and move files into them. To create new folders while in Windows Explorer, click the File menu, then select New. You can also create folders within folders, called **subfolders**, to further compartmentalize or group files.

When you **move** a file, Windows removes or "cuts" the file from its current location and places it on the **Windows Clipboard**—a temporary holding area in your PC's memory. After you select a new location for the file, Windows "pastes" it from the Clipboard to that location. Associating the process of moving files with "cut and paste" will help you remember the sequence of commands needed to move a file.

Here are a few hints to help you improve the organization of your files:

■ Always store your data files in a folder.

■ Create subfolders of the hard disk folder called My Documents to hold your data files. Use descriptive names for all your folders.

■ Group your data files into folders by project or by type.

■ Try not to store your data files in the folders that contain program modules for your application software.

■ The first level under a device should contain only folders, not files.

Figure 5-3: *Click the PlayIt! button to learn how to use Windows Explorer to move single files, groups of files, and folders.*

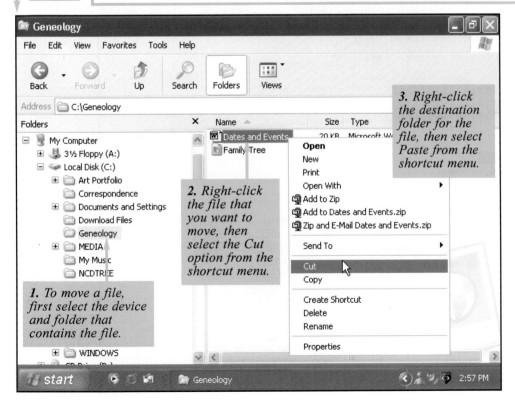

■FAQ How do I copy files to other disks?

Typically, you copy a file when you want to create a duplicate. You could copy a file onto a floppy disk to send to a friend or co-worker. You might copy a group of important files to a Zip disk, which you could store in a secure location. To **copy** a file, Windows places a duplicate of the file on the Clipboard. The original file remains in its present location. After you select a location for the copy, your PC pastes the file from the Clipboard to the new location. Think of copying files as "copy and paste" to help remember this sequence of commands.

Because most PC owners store their files on their PC's hard disks, floppy disks are seldom used except for transporting files from one computer to another. In some circumstances, however, a floppy disk—not the hard disk—becomes your primary storage medium. For example, you might be a student using a university computer lab. You never know which lab computer you'll use, so you must keep your files on a floppy disk.

Windows has a **Copy Disk** feature that quickly and easily makes a copy of your floppy disk, even if you only have one floppy disk drive! Copy Disk copies the entire contents of the floppy disk into the memory of your PC, then asks you to take the disk out of the drive and replace it with a blank disk. The contents of memory are then transferred to the blank disk, and you end up with an exact duplicate of your original floppy disk.

Figure 5-4: Click the PlayIt! button to learn how to copy an entire floppy disk. If you're using a Tracking Disk, apply what you learn to make a copy of it.

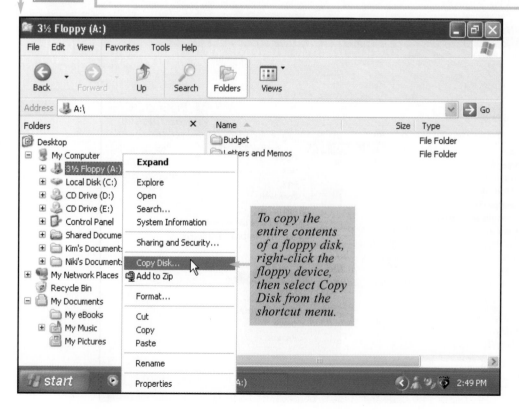

To copy the entire contents of a floppy disk, right-click the floppy device, then select Copy Disk from the shortcut menu.

■FAQ   What if I run out of disk space?

If you run out of disk space, Windows displays a "Disk Full" message. This message usually means that it's time for some PC housecleaning. If your hard disk gets full, start by emptying your PC's Recycle Bin.

The **Recycle Bin** is a holding area for the files you've deleted from your PC's hard disk. When you delete a file from the hard disk, its name is removed from the Windows Explorer file list, but the file itself remains on the disk and continues to occupy disk space. This space is not released until you empty the Recycle Bin. It's nice to know that a deleted file is not gone forever until you empty the Recycle Bin, but you should remember that it holds only hard disk files. The Recycle Bin doesn't keep files that you've deleted from removable media such as floppy disks and Zip disks.

If emptying the Recycle Bin does not free up enough hard disk space for you to continue working, your next step would be to uninstall any software that you no longer use. Deleting a single software application might provide room for hundreds of data files. When you uninstall software, remember to use the Control Panel's Add/Remove Programs icon—don't delete it using Windows Explorer.

You delete data files not so much because you've run out of disk space, but because you no longer need the files. Using Windows Explorer you can easily delete a file by right-clicking it, then selecting the Delete option.

Figure 5-5: Click the PlayIt! button to find out how to delete a file and how to use the Recycle Bin.

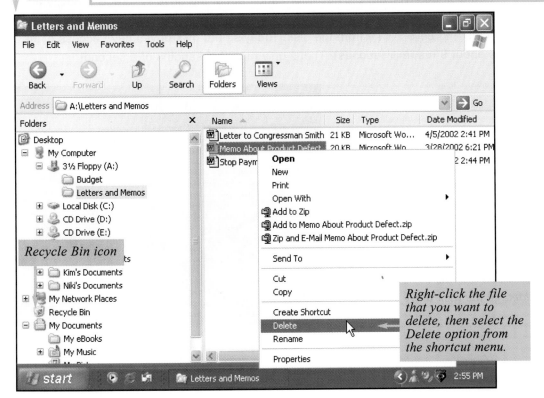

■Hardware
Hard disk drives

In this chapter, you've learned about managing files with Windows Explorer. Where are most of those files stored? The answer—on your PC's hard disk. A **hard disk** is a circular, rigid storage medium that is made of aluminum or glass and coated with metallic particles. One or more of these disks and their corresponding read/write heads are sealed inside a **hard disk drive**, which is then usually mounted inside the system unit of your PC. The hard disks inside the drive are called **platters**. A typical PC hard drive usually contains two to four platters.

Because hard disk platters are sealed inside the drive, they cannot be removed. This constraint would seem to be a disadvantage. In a sense, a floppy disk drive has unlimited storage capacity because you can insert and remove floppy disks. With a hard disk drive, the storage capacity is limited to the hard disk that's sealed inside the case. Sealing the disk inside the case can also be an advantage. It isolates the disk from airborne contaminants such as dust and smoke particles. With these particles safely locked out, the data on a hard disk can be packed in very tightly and recognized without error by the read/write heads.

Snug inside their isolated environment, hard disks operate very efficiently and store huge amounts of data. A typical hard disk could hold as much as 80 to 250 GB of data. By comparison, a standard floppy disk drive stores only 1.44 MB. Remember that a gigabyte (GB) is 1 billion bytes and a megabyte (MB) is only 1 million bytes.

Hard disk ads typically provide information about the drive's storage capacity and access time. **Access time** is the average time it takes the read/write heads to locate and collect data from the disk. Today's hard disk drives have access times of about 9 ms (milliseconds). That's only nine thousandths of a second!

Figure 5-6: A typical PC hard disk drive contains two to four platters and their corresponding read/write heads. The platters spin continuously to provide fast access time. The drive pictured has had its case removed. Don't try this at home or you'll damage the disk drive.

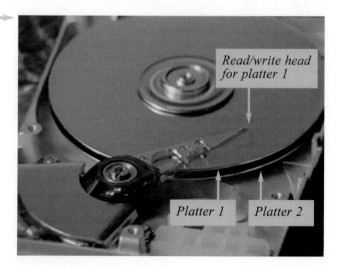

Read/write head for platter 1

Platter 1   Platter 2

∎Hardware
continued

The hard disk that your PC uses in its main storage device is typically a **fixed disk**—a nonremovable disk that's sealed inside the disk drive. If you run out of space on your original hard disk drive, you can typically add a second hard disk drive inside the system unit of most desktop computer systems. An internal 80 Gigabyte hard disk drive typically costs about U.S.$75 and a 250 Gigabyte internal drive costs about U.S.$250.

If you need the storage capacity of a hard disk but the transportability of a floppy disk, a removable hard disk might be the solution. A **removable hard disk**, sometimes called a disk cartridge, is a plastic case that contains a hard disk platter and read/write heads. The hard disk drive stays attached to the computer, while you insert and remove the disk cartridge, using it like an extremely high capacity floppy disk. The Iomega REV drives use removable cartridges that store up to 35 Gigabytes (up to 90 Gigabytes compressed). USB and FireWire versions of the Iomega REV drive cost approximately U.S.$400 and the 35 GB cartridges cost approximately U.S.$50 in packs of four.

Another option is an **external hard disk drive**. These drives typically connect to the USB or FireWire port on your computer. External FireWire or USB drives range from U.S.$150 for a 160 Gigabyte drive, to just over U.S.$300 for a 250 Gigabyte drive. Adding an external hard disk drive is easy—you just plug in the power cord and the USB or FireWire cable. An external hard disk drive can be used to transport large data files from computer to computer. They can also be used as a backup device. You would typically back up or copy your data to the external hard disk drive, then unplug the drive from your computer and from the wall outlet, then store it in a safe location. If your computer is hit by lightning or otherwise destroyed, the backup copy of your data should still be safe on the disconnected external hard disk drive.

Figure 5-7: An external hard disk drive is an easy and inexpensive way to add removable storage to any desktop or notebook computer system.

■Hardware
continued

In the course of adding, modifying, and deleting files, the efficiency of your PC's hard disk begins to decrease so that it takes longer to store, find, and retrieve files. Why does this happen and what can you do about it?

Like a floppy disk, a hard disk is divided into sectors. Each sector is a fixed size and can hold a certain amount of data. Although a file does not have to fill a sector, your PC must use more than one sector for a large file. For most efficient hard disk operation, your PC should place the data for a large file in adjacent sectors so that the read/write head can quickly move from one part of the file to the next. Your files are not always stored so efficiently. In the course of revising your files, the sectors in which they are stored can become scattered all over the disk.

In "tech speak" a file that is stored in nonadjacent sectors is referred to as a **fragmented file**. A disk containing many fragmented files is called a **fragmented disk** and is not operating at peak efficiency. Windows provides a **defragmentation utility** that you can use periodically to put the data for each file in adjacent sectors. Defragmentation does not affect the way your files and folders appear to be arranged in Windows Explorer. Instead, this operation takes place behind the scenes. The only difference you might notice after defragmenting your disk is that it seems to retrieve and store your files more quickly. Most experts recommend that you defragment your hard disk at least two or three times a year.

Figure 5-8: *You can access defragmentation and other handy disk utilities from the Properties dialog box. Click the PlayIt! button to see how to defragment a disk and to find out how much space is available on your PC's hard disk.*

How to find files

You can use Windows Explorer to search for a file by manually checking the list of files in each folder. If you have many folders and don't remember which one holds a particular file, this search process could take quite a long time. Windows provides a way to automate the search process by using the Search program.

The **Search program** accepts information describing the file that you want to find—its title, the date it was created, or its size. If the file contains a document, you can even provide a phrase or two from within its text. In this tutorial, you'll learn how to use the Search program.

When you have completed the tutorial, you should be able to:
■ Start the Search program.
■ Use the Search Criteria options to perform advanced searches.
■ Select and open the file you want from the list of files that the Search program produces as a result of its search.

Figure 5-9: *Click the PlayIt! button to begin the tutorial and discover how to use the Search program. Estimated time: 10–20 minutes. Tracking Disk points: 10.*

Are deleted files legally garbage?

In a highly publicized drug case, police searched through trash bags left on the curb by a suspected cocaine dealer. The evidence they collected led to a conviction, which was appealed because the police had not obtained a search warrant. The conviction was upheld by the U.S. Supreme Court, which ruled that garbage left on the curb is in the public domain and police can search it without a warrant.

What does this case have to do with computers? Files you delete from your PC's hard disk are just marked for deletion and accessed through the Recycle Bin. Even emptying the Recycle Bin does not actually erase your files from the disk. Instead, the file data remains on the disk until the operating system needs those sectors for new data. Deleted data might remain on a disk—a floppy disk, hard disk, or removable hard disk—for years. Anyone who is sophisticated in the use of computers can rummage through this file garbage, but is it legal and ethical to do so? In the Martha Stewart case, key evidence was Stewart's attempt to alter the computer log of a very incriminating phone message from her broker, Peter Bacanovic. Suppose Stewart had thrown out her computer? Would it have been legal for officers to track it down and submit her files as evidence without a search warrant?

Your computer is not on the curb, so it is not in the public domain. The files it contains are probably protected by laws that make it illegal for high-tech thieves to gain unauthorized access and that prevent law enforcement agents from search and seizure without a search warrant. But what about files that you send out on disk? When you send a disk containing files, you expect those files to be accessed in "normal" ways using the Open dialog box or Windows Explorer. If someone uses special software to search for and view the sectors that contain deleted files, is it an illegal activity similar to using special lock picks to enter a locked house? Or is it simply "snooping"—a legal, but not very ethical, activity?

On a closing note, if you want to make sure that you're not sending odd bits of files on your disks, perform a full format on the disk before you copy files to it.

What do you think?

1. If you receive a disk from a friend or client, would it be ethical to use special software to see the contents of deleted sectors? ◯ Yes ◯ No ◯ Not sure

2. Do you agree with the U.S. Supreme Court ruling that curbside garbage is in the public domain? ◯ Yes ◯ No ◯ Not sure

3. Are you familiar with the laws in your country or state that limit access to the data on your computer and on any disks that you send out? ◯ Yes ◯ No ◯ Not sure

Save It!

QuickCheck A

1. "☐ and paste" describes the process of *moving* a file;
   "☐ and paste" describes the process of *copying* a file.

2. Without a set of well-structured ☐, it might be difficult to locate files.

3. True or false? When you see the "Disk Full" message, you should immediately delete some of your data files from the hard disk. ☐

4. True or false? The Recycle Bin allows you to recover files that you mistakenly deleted from a hard disk or a floppy disk. ☐

5. A hard disk becomes ☐ when the sectors that contain a file are scattered in different areas of the disk.

Check It!

QuickCheck B

For each description below, enter the letter of the corresponding Windows Explorer object:

1. The storage device that contains the product defect memo ☐

2. The first file in the Letters and Memos folder ☐

3. The file that's being deleted ☐

4. The control that alphabetizes the files by name ☐

5. The shortcut menu ☐

Folders	✕	Name ← *H*	Size
🖳 Desktop		📄 Letter to Congressman Smith *I*	
⊟ 🖥 My Computer		📄 Memo About Product Defect 20 KB	
⊟ 💾 3½ Floppy (A:) ← *A*		Stop Payment Letter *J*	
📁 Budget		**Open**	
📁 Letters and Memos ← *B*		New	
⊞ 💽 Local Disk (C:) ← *C*		Print	
⊞ 💿 CD Drive (D:) ← *D*		Open With	
⊞ 💿 CD Drive (E:)		🗜 Add to Zip	
⊞ 🗗 Control Panel ← *E*		🗜 Add to Stop Payment L	
⊞ 📁 Shared Documents		🗜 Zip and E-Mail Stop Pay	
⊞ 📁 Kim's Documents		Send To	
⊞ 📁 Niki's Documents	*G*	Cut	
⊞ 🖥 My Network Places		Copy	
🗑 Recycle Bin ← *F*		Create Shortcut	
⊞ 🖨 My Documents		Delete	

Check It!

Get It?

While using the BookOnCD, click the Get It? button to see if you can answer ten randomly selected questions from Chapter 5.

Get It?

Chapter 6

Protecting Your Files

What's Inside?

Chapter 6 has the gruesome details on the disasters that might befall your important data files—fires, floods, hurricanes, tornados, viruses, head crashes, and hard drive failures. It includes tips for avoiding some disasters and recovering from those disasters that you can't prevent.

What's on the CD?

Chapter 6 is a veritable film festival that includes a disaster movie (hard disk crash), a mystery (finding bad sectors), a medical drama (the virus hunt), and a documentary (the tape backup tour). It's fun, but also serious business. Losing files can cost you time and money.

■FAQ Can a computer lose my files?

Yes, files on your PC can become inaccessible or "lost" as a result of an alarming variety of events, including power outages, fires, floods, storms, breakage, and even normal wear and tear. You've probably heard someone complain, "I was almost finished with that project when I lost the whole thing!" The source of the problem might have been a power loss caused by an outage at your community's power plant, a blown house fuse, or simply someone tripping over the PC's power cord and pulling it out from the socket. When you work on files, they are temporarily held in RAM, but this circuitry requires power to hold data. If the power goes out, any open files that have not been saved will disappear.

There are things that you can do to reduce the risk of losing files because of power problems. While you're creating or revising a file, make sure that you save it every five or ten minutes. If your software includes an option to automatically save your files at set intervals, check to make sure that this feature is activated. For basic protection against power variations, you can plug your computer into a **surge strip** which filters out excess power before it reaches your computer. For better protection against both power variations and power outages, you might want to purchase a battery-powered backup device called a **UPS** (uninterruptible power supply), which will feed your computer enough power so that you can close your files and shut down normally when the power goes out. Surge strips typically cost from U.S.$14 to $40, while a UPS can cost from U.S.$40 to $120, depending on the size of the battery and other features.

You can take steps to reduce the risk of power surges, but you can do very little to prevent other things can happen to your data. One such event is a **head crash**. During normal operation, the read/write head of your hard disk hovers just above the disk surface, but does not touch it. But sometimes, perhaps due to jarring the drive or perhaps for no apparent reason, a read/write head might literally crash into the disk surface and damage the particles in the sectors that hold your data.

Even if you take preventative measures, your computer can lose data at any time. To protect your data against events such as head crashes, you should make regular backups of your computer as explained in the Hardware section of this chapter.

Figure 6-1: A head crash can be disastrous. In the worst case, damaged sectors are part of the Registry or other files that keep track of file locations on your hard disk. If your PC is unable to access this information, you might not be able to access any of your data or program files.

▪FAQ Can my PC's hard disk drive fail slowly?

A hard drive often fails without warning, but they do sometimes fail gradually, giving you a chance to do something about it. If you begin to have difficulty accessing some of your files, it might be a signal that the hard disk drive is failing. You should immediately check for bad sectors on your hard disk. A **bad sector** is an area of the disk surface that cannot reliably store data because of manufacturing defects, head-crash damage, or deterioration. If a part of a file is stored in a bad sector, you will not be able to access the file at all.

Many hard disks have some bad sectors, but these are cordoned off when the hard disk is initially formatted. Your PC's operating system keeps track of the bad sectors, ensuring that no data is stored there. Sectors can also go bad in the normal course of operation. Until the operating system adds these sectors to the bad sectors list, your PC might try to store data there. You can use the Windows **Error-checking tool** (or **ScanDisk**) to update the operating system's list of bad sectors. If new sectors seem to go bad every few weeks, you should consider replacing your hard disk drive before it fails entirely and all of your files become inaccessible.

ScanDisk is not always able to identify and repair bad sectors on your hard disk drive. To keep your data safe from bad sectors and failing hard disk drives, you should make regular backups of your computer data as described in the Hardware section of this chapter.

Figure 6-2: *Windows includes a tool that checks for bad sectors on a disk's surface. Click the PlayIt! button to find out how to use the Windows Error-checking tool.*

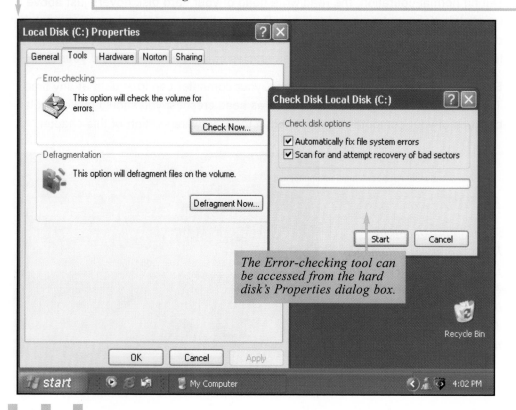

The Error-checking tool can be accessed from the hard disk's Properties dialog box.

■FAQ Can a virus wipe out my files?

A **virus** is a small computer program that's hidden within a legitimate software application or file. It can reproduce and spread from one file to another. For example, when you run a program where a virus lurks, you also run the virus program. Undetected, the virus creates a replica of itself, which attaches to another program. Now, running either of the infected programs will replicate and spread the virus. If you send one of these infected files to another person, the process of replication will begin in his or her PC.

The success of a virus depends on its ability to remain undetected on your PC long enough to spread to other files and to other PCs. By infecting other files, such as those on floppy disks, a virus increases its chances of survival even after being discovered.

In addition to replicating itself, a virus can take action by delivering its payload. A **payload** might simply be an annoying message, or might be something more serious—it might prevent access to the files on your hard disk, erase files, or randomly change data in your files. The events that can trigger the payload include dates (March 6 for the famous Michelangelo virus), a file reaching a specific size, or a certain combination of keystrokes.

Be alert for these symptoms of a virus infection on your PC:

- Your PC displays unusual messages, such as "Your computer is stoned."
- The hard disk suddenly fills up with oddly named files.
- Your PC seems to operate significantly slower than previously.
- You cannot access your hard disk or your PC reboots unexpectedly.
- Some of your files are missing or difficult to access.
- Files that you have not opened recently have become significantly larger.

> *Figure 6-3:* Sources of Virus Infection 1996-2003 according to the ICSA Labs *2003 Virus Prevalence Survey. (Note that e-mail attachments are currently the greatest factor in spreading viruses.)*

Virus Source	1996	1997	1998	1999	2000	2001	2002	2003
E-mail Attachment	9%	26%	32%	56%	87%	83%	86%	88%
Internet Downloads	10%	16%	9%	11%	1%	13%	11%	16%
Web Browsing	0%	5%	2%	3%	0%	7%	4%	4%
Don't Know	15%	7%	5%	9%	2%	1%	1%	3%
Other Vector	0%	5%	1%	1%	1%	2%	3%	11%
Software Distribution	0%	3%	3%	0%	1%	2%	0%	0%
Diskette	71%	84%	64%	27%	7%	1%	0%	0%

▪FAQ How can I protect my files from viruses?

Antivirus
Software

Experts recommend that you practice "safe computing" by using **antivirus software** to scan for and remove viruses from infected files. Antivirus software periodically scans through your PC's memory and the files on any disks that you select, looking for the tell-tale signature of a virus. A **virus signature** is a selection of unique bytes that, like fingerprints, uniquely identify a virus and distinguish it from the legitimate files on your PC. Because new viruses appear every week, you should update your virus software regularly. Companies that publish antivirus software typically provide these updates as free downloads from the Internet.

The following tips will help you protect your files against viruses:

▪ Run antivirus software on your computer.

▪ Configure your antivirus software to automatically download updates so it recognizes new viruses.

▪ Configure your antivirus software to automatically scan incoming mail and any files downloaded from the Internet.

▪ If your application software includes an option to protect against macro viruses that infect document and spreadsheet files, make sure it is activated.

If your computer gets infected with a virus, your virus scanning software might be able to remove it. But, sometimes it cannot remove the virus. As with other computer disasters, your final protection against viruses lies in regular computer backups as described in the Hardware section of this chapter.

Figure 6-4: Click the PlayIt! button to find out how to scan for viruses using antivirus software.

Do I need to make backups if my computer has a recovery disk?

Most computers sold today include a **recovery disk** that makes it possible to restore your computer to the same state that it was in when you first purchased it. The recovery disk might consist of a recovery CD shipped with your computer, or it might consist of a program and special partition on your hard disk drive. You might think this recovery disk means you don't need to worry about backing up your computer. That could be a serious mistake.

Let's assume that your computer was hit by a power surge and you've lost access to your hard disk drive. You weren't worrying about backups, because you planned to use the recovery feature if anything happened to your computer.

The restore option typically sets the computer to *exactly* the same state that it was in when it left the factory. That sounds good, until you think about it for a bit. The restore option will typically reinstall the operating system, drivers, and any software included with the original system.

Anything else that you loaded onto the computer since you received it, including any additional programs and all data that you've created will typically be lost when you restore your computer. After you finish restoring the system, you will have to reload any additional software that you were using. If you can locate the installation CDs for all of your software, this isn't a disaster. It just means that you'll have to spend some hours, or maybe a few days, reinstalling and reconfiguring your software.

Then you're faced with the real problem. All of the documents, digital photos, and music files that you had stored on your computer are gone. If you were using a personal finance program such as QuickBooks, all of the data entered in it is gone. If you were working on a term paper, a business proposal, or a family history, it's gone. If you were using a local e-mail client such as Outlook Express, you'll have to recreate your account with the right user ID, e-mail password, and incoming and outgoing mailboxes. All of the e-mail that you sent and received, and all of the addresses from your Address book are also gone. Your Instant Messenger Buddy List, your list of Favorite Web sites, those digital photos of you and your friends last summer—they're all gone. At that point, you'll wish you had paid careful attention to the backup strategies explained in the following pages.

The recovery feature can help you get your computer up and running, but it is not a substitute for regular backups as explained in the Hardware section of this chapter.

Backup and backup devices

There are two very different approaches to backing up your computer data. One approach is to back up the individual files or folders that you explicitly created, such as your word processing files. If your files aren't very large, you can use almost any storage device for this type of backup. The other approach is to backup your entire computer to ensure that you get copies of everything stored on it. This full backup requires a device large enough to hold a copy of everything on your hard disk drive. In this section, we'll explore the types of devices that you can reasonably use for each type of backup.

If you have only a few documents or other small files that you need to protect, you can easily copy them to a floppy disk. Floppy disks are inexpensive and can be used on most computers, but they only hold 1.44 MB of data, so they can only be used for relatively small files.

Alternatively, you could copy your important files to a USB flash drive and carry that drive with you, perhaps attached to your keychain. With a 128 MB Flash Drive, you might be able to carry a copy of all of your important files with you. If something happens to your computer while you are away, you would presumably have your keys—and your USB flash drive—with you.

If you have a lot of important data files, you could periodically save them on a writable CD or DVD disk. If you save your files to a floppy disk, CD, or DVD, you should store those backup disks in a separate location, such as a friend's house or a safe deposit box. This is known as an **off-site backup**. That way, if your computer is lost to a fire, theft or other major disaster, at least one copy of your data should remain safe in that other location.

The backup options outlined above work well for protecting files that you deliberately create. For example, if you are a writer and store all of your data files in folders underneath the My Documents folder, you can protect your data by periodically copying your My Documents folder to your USB flash drive.

But if you only backup individual folders or files, you're still going to have a lot of work ahead of you if something happens to your hard disk drive. It can be difficult to locate and back up all of the important files stored on your computer system. To further protect yourself against disaster such as hard drive failure, you should periodically make a **full backup** of your entire hard disk drive. That will preserve everything on your computer, including files such as received e-mail, your Address book, your Favorites folder and any other files that you might not otherwise remember to back up.

To back up your entire computer, you would typically use **backup software**. Most backup software, such as the Backup program included with Microsoft Windows XP, allow you to specify if you want to backup all files on the entire hard disk drive, or if you want to backup only specified files. To perform a full backup, you would backup all of the files on your hard disk drive. A full backup can require a lot of space and take a long time, so you'll want to use the largest and fastest backup device available. Removable hard drives, external hard drives, and tapes work well, but DVD disks are acceptable for occasional full backups.

∎Hardware
continued

Figure 6-5: The medium that you select for your backups depends on your budget, the size of your hard disk, the size of the files that you want to back up, and the value of your data.

Backup Medium	Advantages	Disadvantages
Floppy Disks	Inexpensive, a reasonable way to back up smaller individual files such as word processing documents.	Very slow, too small for a full backup.
USB Flash Drive	Portable, relatively fast, a very effective way to back up and transport individual files and folders.	Too small for a full system backup, too expensive for archiving or shipment of data.
Zip Disks	Faster and larger than floppy disks, a reasonable way to back up an entire project.	Relatively slow, requires too many disks for a full backup.
Removable Hard Disks	Fast, large capacity so relatively few disks needed for a full backup, can be used to copy files or a folder or make a full backup.	Relatively expensive, typically proprietary, somewhat less reliable than other devices.
Tapes	Reliable and inexpensive— low-cost tapes make it feasible to keep multiple sets of backup tapes.	Very slow, cannot use backup files directly from tape, multiple tapes are typically required for a full backup.
CD-R or CD-RW	Inexpensive, reliable, good for backup of a large project with many files and folders.	Relatively slow, requires too many disks for a full backup (more than 100 CD-R disks to back up a full 80 GB drive).
DVD-R/DVD+R, or DVD-RW/ DVD+RW	Relatively inexpensive, reliable, large enough to be reasonably used for an occasional full backup.	Relatively slow, still requires multiple disks for a full backup (approximately 17 DVD-R disks for a full 80 GB drive).
External Hard Disk Drive	Reasonably inexpensive, fast, can be used to store a backup file or an exact duplicate of the original files, large enough for a full backup on one drive.	Cost prohibits multiple backup copies, must be removed and stored safely to avoid damage from lightning and other power fluctuations.

continued

Because it takes so long to make a full backup, you won't want to do it very often. You definitely wouldn't want to do it every week, and most individuals probably wouldn't want to do it every month.

In between your full backups, you would perform incremental backups of your entire system. An **incremental backup** stores only those files that have been created or modified since the last backup. Every time you make an incremental backup, only new and revised files are added to your backup tapes. The number of incremental backups that you make between full backups depends on how many files you create and modify each day. Home users might run incremental backups a few times a year, or perhaps every month, but business users typically perform an incremental backup at least once each week.

The amount of data saved with each incremental backup depends on the number and size of the files that you have created or modified since your last incremental backup. In most cases, you will find that an incremental backup will fit on a single DVD disk, perhaps even on a single CD.

Once you've created a full backup and an incremental backup, you can restore everything that was on your computer up to the time of your last incremental backup. You would first restore the original full backup, then each of the succeeding incremental backups.

For example, a business might make a full backup of the entire computer system at the end of every month. In between, they might make an incremental backup every Friday afternoon. Assume that the hard disk drive fails on Wednesday of the third week of the month. To restore the system, they would first restore the last full backup, made at the beginning of the month. They would then restore the incremental backups made at the end of the first and second weeks. Then comes the hard part. Any data entered between the time of the incremental backup on Friday afternoon of the second week and the time the hard disk failed on Wednesday afternoon would need to be re-entered. If they are using an accounting system, they would need to re-enter all invoices and payments. All e-mails sent or received in that time would be lost and any documents created or modified would have to be reconstructed. That's a lot of work, and could easily take several days.

Of course, the business could further reduce the risk by making more frequent backups. For example, they could make an incremental backup at the end of every day. In the worst case, if the computer failed right at the end of the day, they should lose no more than one day worth of work.

Even if you back up your system every day, you will still probably lose some data if your hard disk drive crashes. The idea is to implement a backup plan that balances the time and energy that you put into backups versus the cost of losing any data that is not backed up. If you implement a backup plan that is appropriate for your computer use, then you should always have a reasonable way to recover from hard disk failure or other disasters.

■Tutorial
How to use Windows Backup

The Windows operating system includes a program called **Backup** that you can use to create a full system backup, a backup of selected files, or an incremental backup. Although many backup programs refuse to copy any files that you have open at the time of a backup, the Windows Backup program backs up the Registry file, even though it is open, because it is crucial for restoring your computer system to its original state. If the software supplied with your tape drive does not back up the Registry, you might want to use the Windows Backup program instead.

How can you tell if your backup actually contains files that you can restore to your hard disk? You should test your backup procedure by backing up a few files and then restoring them to your hard disk.

When you have completed the tutorial, you should be able to:
■ Start the Windows Backup program.
■ Perform a complete system backup.
■ Select files for a backup set.
■ Restore files from a backup set.

Figure 6-6: Click the PlayIt! button to learn how to use the Windows Backup program to back up and restore your important files. Estimated time: 20–25 minutes. Tracking Disk points: 10.

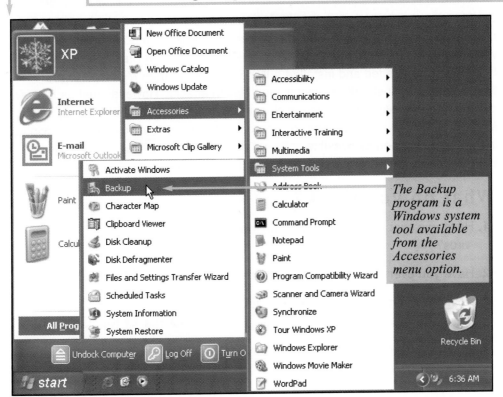

The Backup program is a Windows system tool available from the Accessories menu option.

Issue
What about a "good" virus?

Like "tagging" subway cars with spray-painted graffiti, creating a virus has some element of artistry and risk. The artistry lies in the satisfaction of creating a really brilliant virus that can elude detection from antivirus software and cause just the right amount of mischief on the infected PC. Some twisted person apparently took much delight in creating a virus that bellows in an Arnold Schwarzenegger-like voice, "Your files have just been TERMINATED!", as the file names disappear one-by-one from Windows Explorer.

Creating a virus can be a risky business. Most states have laws that punish deliberate attacks on computer systems. Also, a surprisingly effective ad hoc group of virus watchdogs in the computer community seems to be able to track most viruses to their source. The authors of several viruses have been caught. Some have apologized that their creations somehow "escaped" into the wild of public computing and infected PCs in businesses, schools, and homes. Other virus authors claim that they created viruses as a public service to point out security holes and flaws in antivirus software.

According to recent statistics published by ICSA Labs, which sets standards for information security products, viruses have become more prevalent, increasingly more destructive, and consequently more costly in the past years. The Labs' survey reported the cost for a virus disaster in 2003 to be almost U.S.$100,000 ($99,900) versus U.S.$81,000 in 2002.

Could there be a "good" virus that can be used to eliminate bad viruses? When the vicious Blaster worm wreaked havoc across the globe, a do-gooder released a worm called Nachi as a Blaster antidote. It erased copies of Blaster on infected PCs, then downloaded and installed a Windows update from Microsoft to protect the computer against further Blaster (and Nachi) attacks. However, just as Blaster caused major network traffic, so did Nachi. Still, some believe that the only way to stop major viruses is to out-hack the hackers. Because it is impossible to anticipate interactions between all possible software programs, it is difficult to determine if the benefits of "good" viruses might outweigh their risks

What do you think?

1. Have you ever used a computer that had a virus?   ○ Yes   ○ No   ○ Not sure

2. Have you ever lost a file because of a virus?   ○ Yes   ○ No   ○ Not sure

3. Does the computer you use most regularly have antivirus software?   ○ Yes   ○ No   ○ Not sure

4. Do you think the benefits of "good" viruses outweigh their risks?   ○ Yes   ○ No   ○ Not sure

Save It!

QuickCheck A

1. A power outage is most likely to affect the data (a) in RAM, (b) on the hard disk, or (c) on a floppy disk. The letter of the correct answer is [_____].

2. The Windows [_____] program looks for bad sectors; the Windows [_____] program copies files to a tape or disk for safe-keeping.

3. Antivirus software looks for a unique [_____] that identifies the virus and distinguishes it from the legitimate files on your PC.

4. True or false? A floppy disk is a very reasonable way to make a backup copy of an individual file. [_____]

5. True or false? The recovery feature of your computer system will restore the operating system and drivers, as well as your programs and data files. [_____]

Check It!

QuickCheck B

Select the storage or backup device that would be best suited to each use:

1. [____] Mail a 250 KB word processing document.

2. [____] Carry 14 MB of digital photos with you on your keychain.

3. [____] Mail 320 MB of digital photos.

4. [____] Make a full backup of your entire 80 GB hard disk drive that you can plug into another computer and use directly.

5. [____] Make a full backup of your 80 GB hard disk drive, followed by incremental backups at the end of every month. You couldn't use these backups directly, but you could use them to restore your computer in the event of hard disk failure.

A. Floppy disk

B. External 80 GB hard disk drive

C. CD-R Disk

D. USB Flash Drive

E. DVD-R/DVD+R Disk

Check It!

Get It?

While using the BookOnCD, click the Get It? button to see if you can answer ten randomly selected questions from Chapter 6.

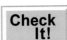
Get It?

Chapter 7
Connecting to the Internet

What's Inside?

The Internet is in the news and on everyone's mind. Chapter 7 provides the information you need to get connected. In Chapter 8 you'll learn about the Web, and in Chapter 9 you'll learn about e-mail.

What's on the CD?

The Internet has so much to offer that the twelve pages in Chapter 7 can merely get you started on an exploration of the fascinating Internet world called "cyberspace." On the CD, you'll get a taste of Internet action by taking a shopping trip to the popular Amazon.com book and music store. Then, you'll find out how to set up and troubleshoot your Internet connection.

■FAQ Why would I want to connect to the Internet?

The Internet has plenty to offer. Just imagine.... After you wake up in the morning, you take a hot cup of java over to your computer, connect to the Internet, and check the latest news. You browse through an online newspaper that's customized to provide your local weather and news topics of interest to you. While you're online, you play a video report of today's financial news. It is not necessary to wait for a scheduled broadcast to find out how your stocks are doing. Then you just have time to check the NBA playoff scores before racing off to work.

At the office, you settle into your cubicle and fire up your computer to check your e-mail. Courtesy of the Internet, you can send and receive mail just about anywhere on the planet—and your message often arrives in less than an hour. An e-mail from your supervisor reminds you to make plans for an upcoming trade show in Cincinnati. You connect to an online travel service, review flight schedules, compare prices, and book a ticket. How about a hotel? You can quickly find lots of information about Cincinnati hotels, restaurants, and entertainment. Before logging off, you check today's Dilbert cartoon. You can relate to it.

During lunch, you munch on a sandwich at your desk and check out your favorite online music store. You listen to a few new tunes and take advantage of a 3-for-$20 CD sale. An afternoon meeting with the sales team from Los Angeles takes place in the videoconference room, with your images and voices transmitted over the Internet. It's almost like being there.

Back home after work, you connect to the Internet to check your bank balance and make sure your latest paycheck was automatically deposited. Then you work on the MBA course that you're taking online. You "hand in" your assignment using the Internet, so that your instructor can grade it tomorrow. You wind up your evening in an online chat group discussing the movie you saw last weekend—two thumbs up. You can do all this and more once you're connected to the Internet.

Figure 7-1: Click the PlayIt! button to take a shopping tour of an Internet bookstore.

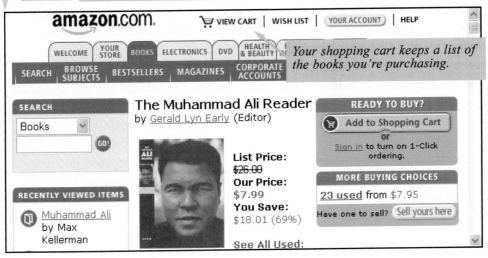

∎FAQ What's an Internet connection?

The **Internet** is a global communications network that carries a variety of computer-generated data, such as documents, e-mail, pictures, videos, and music. It provides numerous services, such as the tremendously popular World Wide Web. Sometimes called a "network of networks," the Internet is composed of computers and other communications devices that are connected by communications lines. An **Internet connection** is simply the way that your computer gains access to this data communications network.

The computer that you use to access the Internet is called a **client computer**. Like a customer who orders food in a restaurant, your client computer orders information and then waits for it to arrive. If you use a computer in a school or corporate network, the network would generally provide an Internet connection. From your home computer, you typically connect to the Internet using a device called a **modem**, which connects to a cable to allow your computer to communicate with the Internet. There are different types of modems for each of the various types of cable connections. Different modems and cable connections provide dramatically different connection speeds. The slowest connection, called a **dial-up connection**, uses a standard telephone line and a **dial-up modem**. For a faster connection through the telephone company, you might be able to connect to a special high-speed telephone line using a **DSL modem**. Another type of fast connection requires a device called a **cable modem** and it uses the same cable that is used to carry cable television signals.

A different type of connection uses a wireless network adapter to connect to a wireless access point, such as those available on many campuses, at airports, and many coffee shops. This type of Internet connection does not use a modem or a cable. Instead, the wireless network adapter uses radio signals to communicate with the wireless access point, which is typically connected to the Internet through a DSL modem or cable modem.

In many areas of the country, cable modem connections, DSL, and wireless Internet connections are simply not available. Users in those areas typically have only two choices—a slow dial-up connection or a satellite Internet connection known as **DSS**. From the marketing literature, DSS sounds like a very good option—high-speed Internet service available anywhere in the country, with communication speeds rivaling those of DSL or cable modems. But DSS connections are slowed by **latency**, or the time required for a signal to travel from your computer, up to the satellite, then back down to the base station where it is transmitted to the Internet. This latency adds a noticeable pause to DSS connections. DSS connections also typically provide limited upstream bandwidth—some users have found that it can take longer to upload a file with a satellite connection than with an ordinary dial-up modem. DSS connections can also be affected by trees, clouds, rain, and snow. Before committing to a DSS connection, you should see if you can try it out for yourself to be sure that it will be adequate for your needs.

■FAQ   What's an Internet connection? (continued)

Whether through a modem and cable or a wireless connection, your client computer connects to an ISP, such as AOL (America Online), AT&T Worldnet, Comcast, Charter, or the telephone company. An **ISP** (Internet service provider) is a company that sells access to the Internet, just as a telephone company sells access to phone lines or a cable company sells access to television broadcasts.

Your ISP connects to an **NSP** (network service provider), such as IBM, MCI, PSINet, or UUnet. The NSP, in turn, connects to other NSPs, to ISPs, and to Internet servers. An **Internet server**, sometimes called a host, is a computer that stores information and "serves" it out to customers, researchers, employees, and other interested parties. Internet servers generally remain connected to the Internet at all times and provide the majority of information that you will access on the Internet.

Other people from around the world connect their client computers to the Internet using their own ISPs. Because you are all connected to the same worldwide network, you can view the same Web sites, play the same games, and send and receive e-mail.

Figure 7-2: To connect to the Internet, your home PC establishes a dial-up connection to one of the ISP's modems. The ISP is connected to an NSP over a high-speed communications link. Interconnections between ISPs, NSPs, and Internet servers provide you with access to information from any of these sources.

■FAQ How do I get connected to the Internet?

The first step in connecting your computer to the Internet is to decide which type of Internet connection you will use: a dial-up connection, DSL, or cable modem connection. For many users, the choice is dictated by the limited options available in your area.

Dial-up Internet access is the default, because it's available in almost every area. If cable TV is available in your area, there's a good chance that your cable TV company provides cable modem connections. DSL service is available in most cities, but availability is limited in small towns and rural areas.

If you want to connect your computer to the Internet using a dial-up connection, you typically need a dial-up modem, an account with an ISP, and either software to configure your computer for dial-up access through that ISP. You connect a standard phone cable between your modem and the telephone jack, then run the software from the ISP to configure your computer for dial-up access. You can use your existing telephone line for your dial-up connection, but you won't be able to use your telephone while your computer is connected to the Internet. If you use your dial-up connection frequently, you might want to pay for a second telephone line for your dial-up connection.

Grab It!

ISP Sign-up Kits

Most ISPs charge about U.S.$20 per month for dial-up Internet access. The ISP supplies you with a phone number that your computer can call to make an Internet connection. When your computer modem dials this phone number, one of your ISP's modems answers and establishes a connection to the Internet. The ISP also supplies you with an e-mail account, a user ID for billing, and a password for security purposes.

To connect your computer to the Internet using a DSL connection, you can contact a company that specializes in DSL Internet connections. This might be the telephone company, or it could be a third-party company that leases telephone lines from the phone company. The company from which you purchase your DSL connection will typically provide you with a DSL modem and configuration software. They can also arrange to have DSL service activated on your telephone line. When the DSL service is activated on your phone line, you typically connect the DSL modem to the Ethernet or USB port on your computer, and run the software from the ISP to configure your computer for the DSL connection.

To connect your computer to the Internet using a cable modem, you can contact the cable television company. They will provide you with a cable modem and software to configure your computer. You, or a cable technician, can then connect the cable modem to the Ethernet or USB port on your computer, and then run the software to configure your computer for the cable modem connection.

DSL and cable modem connections typically cost from U.S.$40 to U.S.$80 per month, depending on the speed of the connection. At first, that can sound much more expensive than a dial-up connection, but many dial-up users are also paying for a second phone line, bringing their total monthly cost into the U.S.$40 range. For most cable modem or DSL users, the extra speed is well worth the extra cost.

■FAQ How do I connect to my ISP?

DSL and cable modem connections are **always-on** connections. Once you've connected the cable and configured your computer, it is remains connected to the Internet as long as your computer is turned on. If you turn you computer off, then turn it back on, it automatically re-establishes the connection to the Internet when it boots up.

A computer with a dial-up connection is not always connected to the Internet. You can manually initiate the connection procedure or a software application can initiate the connection automatically. When a program needs to send or receive data, it typically displays a message asking if you want to go online. Responding "yes" initiates the dialing sequence.

Your computer dials the preprogrammed phone number for your ISP, connects to one of your ISP's modems, and sends your account ID and password for verification. After your ISP has verified your account, you can surf the Internet for information and collect your e-mail.

When data transfers are complete, you should disconnect from the Internet so that your phone line isn't tied up. Use the Disconnect button or menu option in your software to end your connection. Many software applications have a "Hang up when finished" setting that tells the application to automatically disconnect when data transfer is complete.

Figure 7-3: *If you want to manually initiate a dial-up Internet connection, you can use Network Connections (or Windows Dial-Up Networking) by selecting it from the Communications menu.*

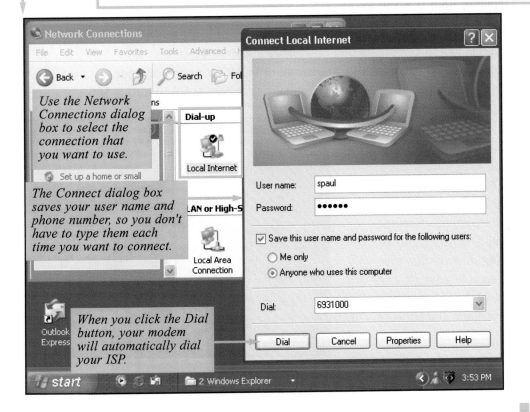

∎Hardware
Modems

The word "modem" is derived from the terms "*mod*ulate" and "*dem*odulate" because a modem has the ability to convert (modulate and demodulate) signals. This ability is especially handy for converting the digital signals from your computer into analog signals that can travel over telephone or cable television lines. Internally, your PC moves and stores data as **digital signals** using a series of 1s and 0s. The Internet, which was designed for computer communication, also works with digital signals. However, the telephone cable television systems were designed to carry sounds and video using wave-shaped **analog signals**. A modem converts your PC's digital data into analog signals for its journey over the cable or phone lines to your ISP. When your ISP receives these analog signals, it converts them back into digital signals that can speed along the Internet's communications links.

Dial-up modems are available in three configurations: internal, external, and PCMCIA. An **internal modem** plugs directly into the main circuit board inside your PC's system unit. An opening in the back of the system unit allows you to connect the phone cable. Internal modems are popular because they do not require desk space. At U.S.$25 to U.S.$50, they are the least expensive type of modem. Most desktop computers are shipped with an internal modem already installed.

An **external modem** is housed in a separate case outside of the PC's system unit. It is connected to the computer using a serial or USB cable, and to the phone jack using a standard phone cable. External modems cost more than internal modems, typically from U.S.$50 to U.S.$75.

A **PCMCIA modem** is housed on a credit-card-sized PCMCIA card and is typically used in laptop computers that don't have standard expansion slots. Many laptop computers are shipped with an internal or PCMCIA modem already installed, but when purchased separately they typically cost from U.S.$40 to U.S.$80.

Figure 7-4: The external modem pictured at the left of the photo requires an external power source. The internal modem (top right) is designed to plug directly into the main circuit board of your PC. The PCMCIA card in the foreground provides both modem and network connections.

continued

Cable and DSL modems are often supplied by the company that provides the cable or DSL connection. You might pay a one-time fee for the use of the modem, or you might pay a monthly rental charge for it.

Cable and DSL modems can also be purchased separately, but you should check with your cable or DSL service provider to determine if they support the use of other modems. Both cable and DSL modems typically cost from U.S.$50 to U.S.$100. Cable and DSL modems are typically external devices consisting of a small box that sits on your desk, a power plug, and cables that connect to your computer and the telephone or cable line.

The speeds of modems and other Internet connections vary dramatically, as shown in Figure 7-5. Notice that Cable and DSL connections are asymmetrical, meaning that the downstream or receiving rate is far faster than the upstream or sending rate.

Figure 7-5: What if your modem stops working or you install a new modem and it doesn't seem to work? Click PlayIt! to learn how to troubleshoot modem problems using the Control Panel.

	Dial-up	DSL	Cable
Typical downstream rate	44 Kbps	384 Kbps	800 Kbps
Typical upstream rate	33 Kbps	128 Kbps to 1.5 Mbps	256 Kbps
Time to download 2MB file	6 minutes	43 seconds	20 seconds
Typical monthly fee	$20	$50 to $200	$40 to $80

A modem is connected to a cable or telephone line that can occasionally carry damaging electrical spikes. To protect your modem you might consider routing the signal through a surge strip or UPS before connecting it to the modem. This can protect the modem—and your computer—from damaging power surges, spikes, and lightning strikes.

■Hardware
continued

Like any other circuit-based component in your PC, a modem can sometimes misbehave. The cause could be as simple as a loose cable, or as serious as a malfunction in the modem circuitry.

If your modem doesn't seem to work, try these troubleshooting tips:
- Make sure that all of the cables are plugged in securely.
- If you're using a cable or DSL modem, verify that the WAN light is on. If it is not on, and if the cables are attached securely, contact your cable or telephone company for assistance.
- If you're using an external modem, make sure it is plugged in and turned on. Verify that the power and connection lights are on.
- If you're using a dial-up modem, make sure the phone line is working. If in doubt, plug a phone into the wall jack, make sure that you have a dial tone, then dial your ISP using a regular phone to ensure that its line is not busy and that your computer is dialing the correct number. You should hear a series of tones when the ISP's modem tries to answer.
- If you're using a dial-up modem, double-check that the phone cable is plugged into the correct jack at the back of your computer. Your computer documentation will indicate which of the two jacks to use for the modem.
- Use the Control Panel to diagnose installation and connection problems.

Figure 7-6: What if your modem stops working or you install a new dial-up modem and it doesn't seem to work? Click PlayIt! to learn how to troubleshoot dial-up modem problems using the Control Panel.

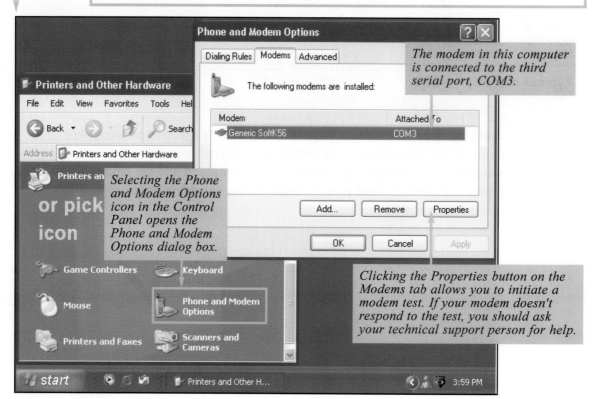

■Tutorial

How to set up a dial-up Internet connection

In this tutorial you'll learn how to use the **Windows Internet Connection Wizard** to establish an account with one of the larger national ISPs. You might wonder why this is important, particularly if you are connected to the Internet using a much faster DSL or cable modem connection.

Cable modem and DSL connections are very fast, but they have one significant disadvantage—you can't use them when you are away from home. Aside from wireless Internet service, which is not available in many locations, a dial-up connection to a national ISP is often the only connection option available while away from home. A **national ISP** operates in a wide geographical area and offers local dial-up connections for many cities and larger towns. If you travel frequently, you might find this coverage handy because you can connect to your ISP from any city that it services.

When you have completed the tutorial, you should be able to:
■ Outline the steps required to set up an Internet connection.
■ Use Windows Internet Connection Wizard to sign up with a national ISP.
■ Cancel Internet service from an ISP.

Figure 7-7: Click the PlayIt! button to begin the tutorial that simulates the process of signing up with a national ISP. Estimated time: 15–20 minutes. Tracking Disk points: 10.

▪Issue

Do we need anonymous digital cash?

The Internet is increasingly used for **e-commerce** activities, such as shopping online, paying utility bills, and subscribing to various online services. E-commerce typically requires e-payment. Today's consumer usually pays for online transactions using a credit card. But many people wonder if it is safe to transmit their credit card information over the Internet. Could their credit card numbers be intercepted, and then used by crooks?

Although it is possible to intercept data flowing over the Internet, it is not so easy to filter out credit card numbers from the rest of the data. Your credit card number is more likely to be stolen by someone who finds a receipt in your trash or by a dishonest restaurant employee who jots down your card number while processing your dinner payment. Online security at most e-commerce sites further protects your credit card transactions by providing a special connection that encrypts your card number as it travels over the Internet. Although it is fairly safe to use your credit card on the Internet, the process has what many people view as a major disadvantage—it leaves a trail of what you buy and who you pay. Many consumers would prefer to use an anonymous form of payment.

Digital cash is an electronic replacement for cash that can be stored by your PC and spent on the Internet—without leaving a trail to its source. Several companies have unveiled prototypes for digital cash, but none has gained widespread use because some critical issues remain unresolved. For example, can private firms issue digital cash, and can they profit from its use? Currently, only governments issue cash because controlling the money supply plays an important role in maintaining a stable economy. Is it possible to create digital cash that cannot be stolen or falsified? Obviously consumers and merchants alike want assurances that the digital cash they receive is authentic. Is it really a good idea to have anonymous transactions? Many honest consumers think so, but so do many criminals. Consumers would enjoy much more privacy with regard to their purchases, but governments would not be able to keep close tabs on taxable income.

What do you think?

1. Have you ever made a purchase from the
Internet using a credit card?   ○ Yes   ○ No   ○ Not sure

2. Do you think that most people believe that
using a credit card in a restaurant is safer
than using a credit card on the Internet?   ○ Yes   ○ No   ○ Not sure

3. Do you think that anonymous digital cash is a
good idea?   ○ Yes   ○ No   ○ Not sure

Save
It!

QuickCheck A

1. A typical Internet connection requires a computer, a modem, and an Internet [_____] provider.

2. A modem converts [_____] signals to digital signals and back again.

3. Cable and DSL modem connections are [_____] connections.

4. Either a cable or a DSL connection would be much faster than a [_____]-up connection.

5. True or false? Cable and DSL Internet connections can often receive data faster than they can send it. [_____]

Check It!

QuickCheck B

Fill in the letter from the diagram that correctly matches each description:

1. An ISP modem [____]

2. An Internet server [____]

3. An NSP [____]

4. A digital connection [____]

5. An analog connection [____]

Check It!

Get It?

While using the BookOnCD, click the Get It? button to see if you can answer ten randomly selected questions from Chapter 7.

Get It?

Chapter 8

Browsing and Searching the Web

What's Inside?

The Web is the real jewel in the crown of the Internet. You've seen references to it in magazines and on TV. Web addresses, such as *www.nationalgeographic.com*, direct you to Web sites where you can find information, order products, interact with other people, and more! Chapter 8 highlights the Web's key features and provides tips for surfing the Web like a pro.

What's on the CD?

In Chapter 8, you'll find out how to use a Web browser and a search engine, the two required software tools in the Web surfer's toolkit. Also, you'll learn how to incorporate the information that you find on the Web in your own documents and Web pages.

▪FAQ What's a Web page?

A **Web page** is a specially coded document that can contain text, graphics, videos, and sound clips. Millions of these pages are interlinked and available on the **Web** (a nickname for the World Wide Web), an Internet service second in popularity only to e-mail. The links between pages, sometimes called **hypertext links**, allow you to follow a thread of information from one Web page to another.

The computers that store Web pages are known as **Web servers**. Each Web server hosts one or more **Web sites** that contain information about a specific topic, company, organization, person, event, or place. The person who creates, updates, and maintains a Web site is called a **Webmaster**.

The main page for a Web site is sometimes referred to as a **home page**. Any page on a Web site can be linked to the home page, to other pages at the same Web site, or to pages at other Web sites anywhere in the world. **Text links** usually appear as blue or green underlined words. Some Web pages also have **graphics links** that appear as pictures, rather than as underlined text. When you point to a text or graphics link, the arrow-shaped pointer changes to a hand-shaped **link pointer**. By clicking a link, you are requesting the Web page indicated by the link. To fulfill your request, a Web server sends a copy of of the linked Web page to your PC's memory. Your PC can then display the Web page on the screen.

Figure 8-1: Click the PlayIt! button to take a guided tour of a typical Web page. You'll learn how to use text and graphics links to "surf" from one page to another, plus you'll see how Web pages play videos and sound clips.

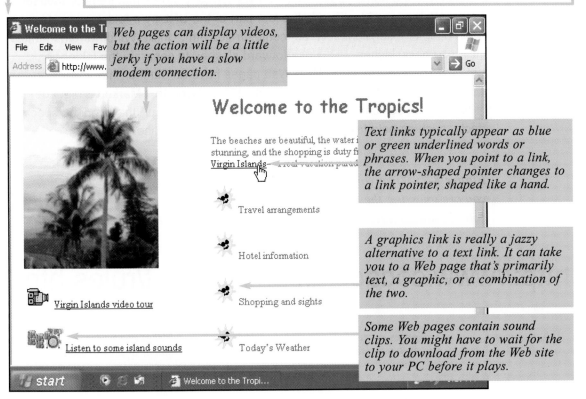

Web pages can display videos, but the action will be a little jerky if you have a slow modem connection.

Text links typically appear as blue or green underlined words or phrases. When you point to a link, the arrow-shaped pointer changes to a link pointer, shaped like a hand.

A graphics link is really a jazzy alternative to a text link. It can take you to a Web page that's primarily text, a graphic, or a combination of the two.

Some Web pages contain sound clips. You might have to wait for the clip to download from the Web site to your PC before it plays.

■FAQ   What's a URL?

A **URL** (uniform resource locator) is essentially a Web page address—it specifies the Web server that stores the page, the folder (or folders) that hold the page, and the name of the page. If you are not using a link to jump to a Web page, you will need to enter its URL manually. As a hypothetical example, suppose that you want to find out about a new promotion sponsored by the Coca-Cola Company. You could look for the URL in one of the many Internet directories on the shelves of a library or bookstore, but you can often guess the URL of a Web site's home page once you understand how URLs are constructed.

Most URLs begin with http://. The acronym **HTTP** stands for Hypertext Transfer Protocol, a standard used by Web servers for transmitting Web pages over the Internet. Some financial Web sites encrypt transmissions by using Secure HTTP or Secure Sockets Layer. The URL for a secure site would begin with https://.

The next part of the URL is the Web server's name, which usually begins with www and includes the name of a company, organization, or person. Periods separate the parts of a server name, as in *http://www.cocacola.com*. The last part of the server name indicates a Web server category or **top-level domain**, such as .com for commercial businesses, .org for professional and nonprofit organizations, .gov for the U.S. government, or .edu for educational institutions. A top-level domain might also indicate a country, such as .ca for Canada or .uk for the United Kingdom. You can generally connect to a Web server by entering the server name. Entering *http://www.cocacola.com* should connect you to Coca-Cola's home page.

In addition to the home page, a Web server typically stores hundreds or thousands of other Web pages identified in the last part of the URL by a folder name, file name, and file extension, such as /contest/rules.htm. Unlike Windows path names which use backslashes, URLs use forward slashes to separate the folder name from other parts of the path. Most Web pages have an .html or .htm extension because they are stored in HTML format. **HTML** (Hypertext Markup Language) is a file format that contains embedded instructions called "tags" that produce specific effects, such as bold text, colored backgrounds, or underlined links.

Figure 8-2: When you enter a URL, make sure you type it exactly as written. If you are guessing the URL of a Web server, use all lowercase letters. URLs don't contain any spaces, so never add a space before or after a period or a slash.

http://www.cocacola.com/contest/rules.htm

Web protocol

Server name, including top-level domain

Web page folder, name, and extension

■FAQ How does a browser work?

Browsers

A **Web browser** (or "browser" for short) is the software that displays Web pages on your computer screen by interpreting **HTML tags** that are embedded in each Web page. Your browser understands, for example, that when it encounters the HTML tag <U> in the text of a file, it should underline text until it reaches a </U> tag. A browser also handles links between Web pages. When you click an underlined link, your browser sends the link's URL to the Web server, which in turn sends the linked page to your PC. Two of today's most popular browsers are Microsoft Internet Explorer and Netscape Navigator.

Special computer programs called **plug-ins** extend the variety of files and media that your browser can display on a Web page. Certain types of video and sound files, for example, might require plug-ins. If a Web page requires a plug-in that your browser doesn't have, you will typically see a message indicating which plug-in is needed and the site from which it can be downloaded.

Sometimes, your browser interacts with a Web server to create a cookie. A **cookie** is a message that contains information to help a Web server identify you and, perhaps, customize the information that it presents. When you access a Web site that uses cookies, you typically fill out a form with information such as your name, e-mail address, and interests. This information is encapsulated as a cookie and sent to your browser, which stores the cookie on your PC. Whenever you access this Web site, your browser sends the cookie back to the Web server for its use.

Figure 8-3: Click PlayIt! to tour a browser and find out how it interprets *HTML tags behind the scenes to display a beautifully formatted Web page.*

▪FAQ How do I use a search engine?

Just as a librarian catalogs books, a **search engine** catalogs Web pages to make it easier to find information. Popular search engines such as Google and Yahoo! help you sift through the millions of Web pages on the Internet. Like any other Web site, a search engine has a URL. To search with Google, for example, you would use your browser to connect to *www.google.com*. Once you've connected to a search engine, you enter words and phrases that describe the kind of information you want to find. Google will search through its database and return a list of links to all of the pages that match your search criteria.

Most search engines can handle both simple and complex searches. For a simple search, you just enter a topic and, perhaps, a few synonyms. To find information about losing weight, for example, you might enter "weight loss diet calories." A search engine will respond by showing you a list of results or "hits" for Web pages that contain information on one or all of these topics. The list will include a short summary of each page and an underlined link that you can use to jump directly to it. With a simple search, a search engine often returns a huge list that might contain more than 10,000 hits. To get a smaller, more targeted list, you must use more sophisticated search techniques. Because each search engine provides a slightly different set of advanced search tools, you should consult your search engine's online Help for details on composing advanced searches.

Figure 8-4: Google lets you enter simple searches, or compose advanced searches. Click the PlayIt! button to find out more about using search engines.

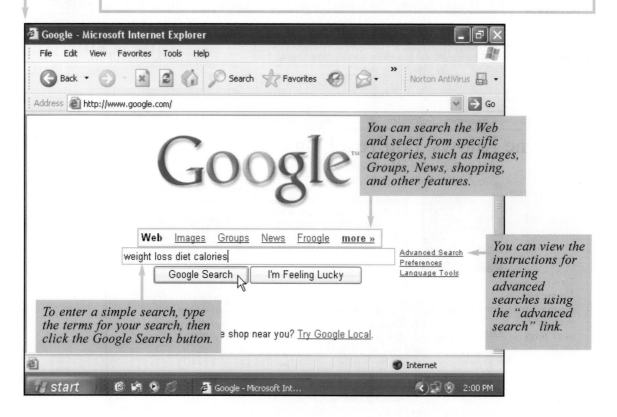

■FAQ Can I save text and graphics that I find on the Web?

If you come across an interesting article or graphic on the Web, you might want to print it or save it on your PC. To print a Web page, use your browser's Print button or the Print option on the File menu. Before printing, you might want to use the Page Setup option on the File menu to ensure that the Web page URL will appear on each sheet of the printout. Instead of printing, you can save a copy of an entire Web page, or just save selected paragraphs. You can also save copies of Web page graphics, including photos and borders.

When using material from the Web, make sure that you respect the author's intellectual property rights. Assume that everything you see on the Web is copyrighted. If you would like to use a graphic that you've downloaded, you should obtain permission first by e-mailing the copyright holder. Look for an e-mail address at the bottom of the Web page that contains the graphic or on the main page for the site. When you incorporate Web page text excerpts into your documents, you must include a citation that follows a standard style such as MLA or APA. The citation must contain the author's name, the title of the Web page, the title of the site, the date of publication, the date when you accessed the page, and the URL for the page. Note the following example of a citation using the MLA style:

Canine, Claire. "No One Knows You're a Dog." <u>Dogs on the Net</u>. 1998. 11 Nov. 1999 <http://www.dogsonthenet.org/intro.htm>.

Figure 8-5: Click the PlayIt! button to find out how to save a copy of the text and graphics that you find on Web pages.

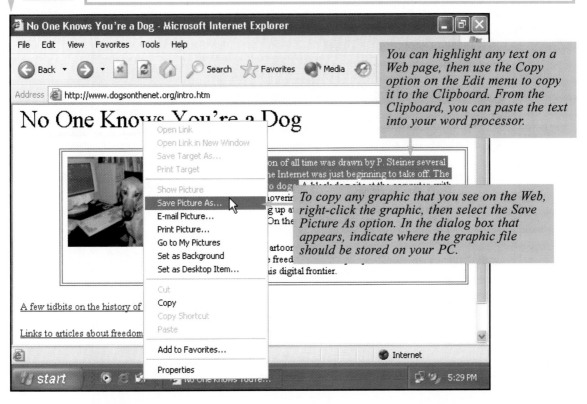

You can highlight any text on a Web page, then use the Copy option on the Edit menu to copy it to the Clipboard. From the Clipboard, you can paste the text into your word processor.

To copy any graphic that you see on the Web, right-click the graphic, then select the Save Picture As option. In the dialog box that appears, indicate where the graphic file should be stored on your PC.

∎Hardware
Protecting and sharing your Internet connection with a router

One of the major advantages of a cable or DSL connection is that it is always on. If your computer is turned on, it is connected to the Internet. This is nice because you don't have to wait for your computer to dial-up and establish a connection every time you want to view a Web page or read your e-mail. However, an always-on connection means that your computer is readily accessible to hackers who might try to break into your computer to copy or damage your files.

Grab It!

Personal Firewall software

If your computer is connected to a cable or DSL modem, you should strongly consider installing a firewall. A **firewall** is a software program or a hardware device that protects one or more computers from outside intruders. If you use only a single computer, you might want to purchase or download personal firewall software such as BlackICE or Norton Personal Firewall. Once you install the firewall software, it will monitor all data sent between your computer and the Internet and will warn you of any suspicious activity that might indicate that a hacker is attempting to break into your computer. Personal firewall software typically includes a number of security settings. Higher security settings can more thoroughly protect your computer, but might interfere with normal use of the Internet. In general, you should select the default security setting unless you have a specific reason to do otherwise.

Play It!

Figure 8-6: Click the PlayIt! button to find out how to configure personal firewall software

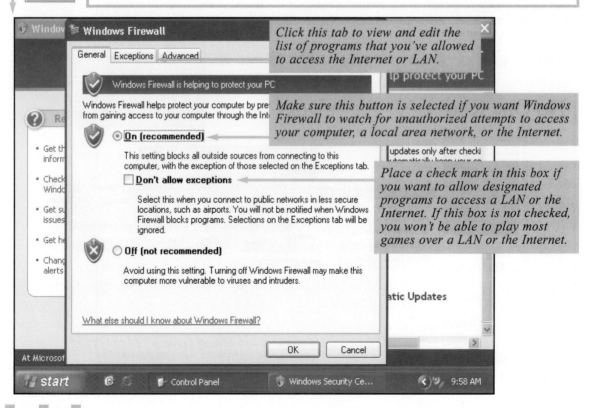

■Hardware
continued

If you use more than one computer, you might want to consider installing a router. A **router** is a hardware device that connects a local area network to a larger network such as the Internet. The router is attached between the cable or DSL modem and your computer. Most routers provide a number of ports so you can connect multiple computers to them. Every computer connected to the router gains access to the cable or DSL modem attached to the other side of the router. Some routers also function as a wireless access point. If your computer includes a wireless Wi-Fi network card, you can use it to connect to the Internet from any location within range of the antenna on the router. Wired and wireless routers have become very inexpensive, typically costing from U.S.$40 to U.S.$100.

Because most routers use **NAT** or Network Address Translation, hackers on the Internet typically can only reach the router. The computers connected to the router are typically not visible, because they are hidden behind the router.

In most cases, installation of a wired or wireless router is relatively easy and painless. Often you can just turn off your computer, plug in the router and connect it to your cable or DSL modem, then connect it to your computer. Then turn on the router and your computer. If your computer has been configured to automatically request a TCP/IP address, it will request an address from the router and everything will work automatically.

If your computer is set to use a specific TCP/IP address, you'll either need to change that setting in your computer or configure the router to use fixed IP addresses. This can get a bit complicated, so if your computer and router do not start working automatically, you might want to call in a computer technician to help you configure your computer. In general, the companies that provide cable and DSL modem service do not support routers and will not provide you with technical support in configuring your router.

There is one important configuration setting that you should always change if you install a router. You should always start by changing the administrator password on the router. Typically, you'll open your browser and enter a specified URL with a TCP/IP address such as *http://192.168.1.100* to open the browser configuration software. The first thing that you should change is the password used to change the configuration of the router. Hackers know the default passwords, so if you leave the default password active, they'll be able to reconfigure your router. Be sure to use a safe password, preferably one that uses a combination of letters and numbers or punctuation marks. Be sure to make a note of the password so you can get back into the router if you need to change the configuration in the future.

∎Hardware
continued

If you have installed a wireless router, there are a few more steps that you should take to secure the router and your computer from intruders. Most wireless routers include a feature that will encrypt all data sent to and from the router. However, this feature is typically turned off by default. You should locate this setting in the router and turn encryption on.

Wireless routers also allow you to configure the router so that it will only talk to computers that are using a specified hardware or **MAC address**. You should read the documentation for your router and configure it so it will only communicate with your computers. This will make it much harder for a drive-by hacker to connect to your wireless router and possibly gain access to your computers.

For extra security, you might also activate the user ID and password feature of your router. This will require you to type in the correct user ID and password each time you connect to your router.

Wireless networks have a very limited range and reception can be affected by other electronic devices such as wireless phones. If you cannot get a good signal on your computer, you might have to try moving the router or computer to different locations to find a place where you get a solid signal.

Figure 8-7: Click the PlayIt! button to find out how to install and configure a wired or wireless router.

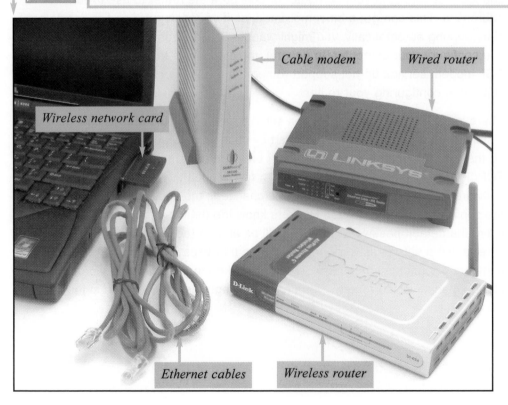

■Tutorial
How to create your own Web pages

Grab It!

Web Page Authoring Software

You can create your own set of Web pages for the world to access. All you need is software that generates HTML documents and an ISP that will host your Web pages. Most word processing software today has the capability to produce HTML documents. For example, Microsoft Word can be quite suitable for creating your personal Web pages. Software specifically designed for creating Web pages includes Netscape Composer and Microsoft FrontPage. You can find this software at a computer store or on the Internet. Your ISP might allow you to post your personal Web pages, and educational institutions sometimes provide this service to students and faculty. In this tutorial, you'll learn how to use Microsoft Word to create and revise Web pages.

When you have completed the tutorial, you should be able to:
- Create a Web page and save it in HTML format.
- Add links and graphics to a Web page.
- View and test the page using a browser.
- Examine the HTML tags embedded in a Web page.

Play It!

Figure 8-8: Click the PlayIt! button to begin the tutorial and learn how to create your own Web page. Estimated time: 20–30 minutes. Tracking Disk points: 10.

Issue
The filtering controversy

Democracies have a rich tradition of free speech and a free press that stands watch against censorship. Developments on the Internet have brought new attention to the tug-of-war between free speech and public decency. Without too much effort, anyone surfing the Internet can find some very unsavory material, including child pornography, hate group rhetoric, terrorist handbooks, graphic violence, and sexually explicit Web pages that go way beyond kinky sex.

Grab It!

Filtering Software

Many parents are concerned about what their children might encounter while surfing the Web. Even an innocent search for "Valentine" might lead to Web sites where sex is on sale. **Filtering software** makes it possible to block access to certain Web sites. Parents can install this software on their home PCs, select the sites that they want to block, and use a password to prevent anyone else from removing the blocks. In many communities, children also have access to the Internet from computers at school and the public library. Although filtering software makes it possible to block access to sites on these PCs, some librarians are reluctant to use it. They fear that it would be impossible to reach a consensus on the sites that should be filtered.

Without agreement on the advisability of using filtering software on computers accessed by children, it would seem improbable that schools and libraries would filter Internet access on PCs that are typically used only by adults. This idea really smacks of censorship. Spam filters are now popular tools for controlling junk e-mail. But popular as they may be, they are not foolproof, and every now and then they can still fail to recognize certain unwanted e-mail or come up with "false positives," i.e., filter out legitimate mail. Consumer advocates have expressed concerns that Internet service providers are imposing e-mail censorship through their use of spam filters. ISPs are now trying to incorporate some kind of feedback from users to identify spam.

What do you think?

1. If you had children, would you use filtering software on your home PC to block access to certain Web sites?   ◯ Yes ◯ No ◯ Not sure

2. Do you think schools and public libraries that provide Internet access to children should use filtering software?   ◯ Yes ◯ No ◯ Not sure

3. Do you believe that in some situations it is appropriate to use filtering software on computers accessed only by adults?   ◯ Yes ◯ No ◯ Not sure

Save It!

QuickCheck A

1. Now that you understand how URLs are constructed, you could guess that the URL for Microsoft's home page is http:// _____ .

2. Your PC is able to display a Web page correctly because your browser can interpret _____ tags.

3. If you enter your name and e-mail address on a Web page form, the Web server will probably create a(n) _____ containing this information and store it on your PC.

4. True or false? When in doubt, enter a URL using all lowercase letters. _____

5. Yahoo! and Google are popular _____ engines.

Check It!

QuickCheck B

Fill in the letter from the diagram that correctly matches each description below:

1. A text link _____

2. A URL _____

3. The link pointer _____

4. Connection icon _____

5. Browser toolbar _____

No One Knows You're a Dog - Microsoft Internet Explorer   A   D

File Edit View Favorites Tools Help

B   Search   Favorites   Media

Address http://www.dogsonthenet.org/intro.htm   C   Go

No One Knows You're a Dog

My favorite cartoon of all time was drawn by P. Steiner several years ago when the Internet was just beginning to take off. The cartoon shows two dogs. A black dog sits at the computer, with *E* artfully hovering over the keyboard. A spotted dog sits on the floor gazing up at the obviously computer-savvy *F* dog, who says, "On the Internet no one knows you're a dog."

To me, Steiner's cartoon captures the character of the Internet and highlights the freedom and anonymity that have attracted so many people to this digital frontier.

G

A few tidbits on the history of the Internet

H

Links to articles about freedom and anonymity on the "Net"

I

http://www.cciw.com/np   Internet

start   No One Knows You're...   5:29 PM

Check It!

Get It?

While using the BookOnCD, click the Get It? button to see if you can answer ten randomly selected questions from Chapter 8.

Get It?

Chapter 9

Sending E-mail and Attachments

What's Inside?

Chapter 9 takes you from e-mail basics to more advanced topics such as attachments and file compression. You'll get some tips on "netiquette" and in the hardware section you'll learn how networks provide an alternative to dial-up connections for accessing the Internet and e-mail.

What's on the CD?

In addition to the basics of creating, reading, replying to, and forwarding e-mail, you'll learn how to send attachments, how to compress those attachments for more efficient transmission, and how to use your e-mail address book.

■FAQ   How does e-mail work?

E-mail is an electronic version of the postal system. An **e-mail message** is an electronic document that can be transmitted from one computer to another, usually over the Internet. E-mail has become enormously popular because it is easy to use, delivers mail in a matter of hours, and lets you broadcast the same message simultaneously to more than one person. The computers and software that provide e-mail services form an **e-mail system**. At the heart of a typical e-mail system is an **e-mail server**—a computer that essentially acts as a central post office serving a group of people. It runs special **e-mail server software** that provides an electronic mailbox for each person, sorts incoming messages into these mail-boxes, and routes outgoing mail over the Internet to other e-mail servers. Many ISPs maintain an e-mail server to handle e-mail for their subscribers.

Grab It!

E-mail
Client
Software

To access an e-mail system, you must have an account on its e-mail server and your PC must have **e-mail client software** that helps you read, compose, and send messages. Most e-mail client software is inexpensive or free. For example, Microsoft Outlook Express is shipped with Windows, Netscape Mail is shipped with Netscape Navigator, and Eudora is available on the Web as shareware. Before using your e-mail client, you must provide it with configuration information. Your ISP will typically supply this information when you subscribe.

E-mail is a **store-and-forward technology**, which means that the e-mail server *stores* incoming messages until your client computer connects and requests them. The server then *forwards* this mail to your computer when you're ready to read it. Using store-and-forward technology, you don't miss any messages that arrive when you're not connected—they're stored on the server. This approach also allows you to minimize your connect time because you can read and compose messages offline, then connect only when you want to download your new mail from the server or upload mail that you've composed.

Mail arrives
from other
e-mail servers.

Your ISP's e-mail server
receives and stores incoming
mail until you request it.

Your PC receives a batch of
new mail when your e-mail
client software connects
and downloads the mail
from the server.

Figure 9-1: Your e-mail server receives your mail and stores it until you request that it be downloaded to your computer.

When you compose new messages, they are typically stored on your PC until you are ready to transmit them to the e-mail server, which then sends them on to the recipients.

■FAQ How do I send and receive e-mail messages?

Basic e-mail skills include composing new messages, reading messages that you receive, replying to those messages, and forwarding messages. To compose a new message, simply fill in the e-mail header and then type the text of your message. When you use a dial-up connection, you'll typically compose your messages offline and queue them in your Outbox. The **Outbox** is a folder on your PC's hard disk that temporarily stores your newly created e-mail messages. When you're ready to send the messages, you connect to the mail server. Your e-mail client software will then transmit the message files from your Outbox to the mail server.

To read your mail, you must first connect to the mail server and download new messages to your **Inbox**, a folder on your PC's hard disk that holds incoming e-mail. Your e-mail software displays a list of messages in your Inbox. Unread messages are indicated by an icon, boldface, or colored type.

To reply to a message, simply click the Reply button. Your software will automatically open a new message, address it, and fill in the subject line. Typically, it will also display the text of the original message, with each line being preceded by a ">" symbol. By incorporating the original text with your reply, both you and the message recipient can have a complete record of the correspondence. It is customary to type your reply above the original message, or intersperse your reply within the lines of the original message. You can also forward the entire text of a message to a third party if you would like to share its contents.

Figure 9-2: Click the PlayIt! button for an overview of sending, reading, replying to, and forwarding e-mail.

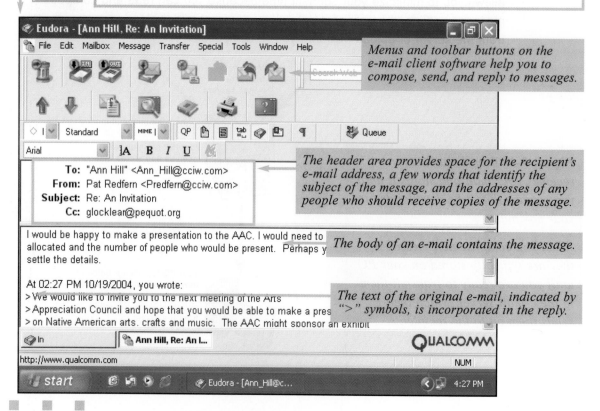

■FAQ   What's an e-mail attachment?

You don't have to know what kind of computer or software the recipient of your e-mail uses because the e-mail system makes any necessary translations. However, the system is set up to handle only plain, unformatted text files. To send formatted text, graphics, video, or sound files, you can use e-mail attachments. An **e-mail attachment** is a file that travels along with an e-mail message. You can attach a file with virtually any format, including DOC, BMP, WAV, and EXE.

Most e-mail software indicates the existence of an attachment with an icon, such as a paper clip. Typically, the person who receives an attachment can double-click the icon to open the attachment. However, it will open only if the recipient's PC has software that can work with files stored in the format of the attachment. For example, if you receive an e-mail message with a DOC attachment, your PC must have Microsoft Word software to open and display the attachment. To help the recipient open your attachment, in the body of the regular e-mail message you should indicate which software you used to create it. You might say, for example, "This e-mail includes a DOC attachment that I created with Microsoft Word XP."

Some attachments harbor viruses, so you should exercise caution when opening them—especially those with an .exe extension. You might want to use antivirus software to scan attachments before you open them. Refer to the Help facility of your antivirus software for recommendations on how to use it for attachments.

Figure 9-3: Click the PlayIt! button to learn how to attach files, open attachments, and scan attachments for viruses.

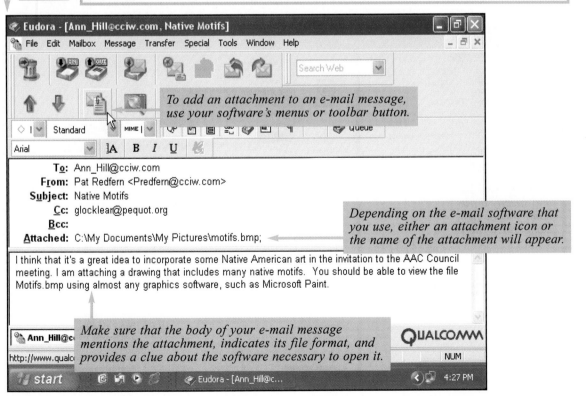

∎FAQ Is there a size limit for e-mail messages and attachments?

Some e-mail systems limit the size of the e-mail messages and attachments that they will accept and forward. Typically, this limit is anywhere between 2 MB to 10 MB, but you should try to keep the size of your attachments below 1 MB. If you need to send a larger file, you may be able to "zip" it to make it smaller before you attach it.

Compression Software

Compression software "zips" or reduces the size of a file using techniques such as scanning for patterns of words in a text file or patterns of colors in a graphics file and recoding those patterns using fewer bytes. The compressed version of the original file is then stored in a new, smaller file that requires less storage space and transmission time. Compressed files typically have a .zip file extension. Before they can be viewed, they must be "unzipped" to their original size.

Some file formats can be shrunk to less than half their original size, whereas other file formats don't seem to compress at all. Many video and sound formats shrink to about half their original size. Most text formats, such as DOC and TXT, shrink quite dramatically, as do some graphics formats, such as BMP and TIFF. Other graphics formats, such as JPEG and GIF, are already compressed, so using compression software does not affect the size of these files. If you're not sure whether compression software will shrink a file, first try to compress the file, then compare the original and compressed file sizes shown by your compression software.

Figure 9-4: If you receive e-mail with a compressed file attachment, you'll typically need to unzip the file before you can use it. Click the PlayIt! button to find out how to use compression software to zip and unzip attachments.

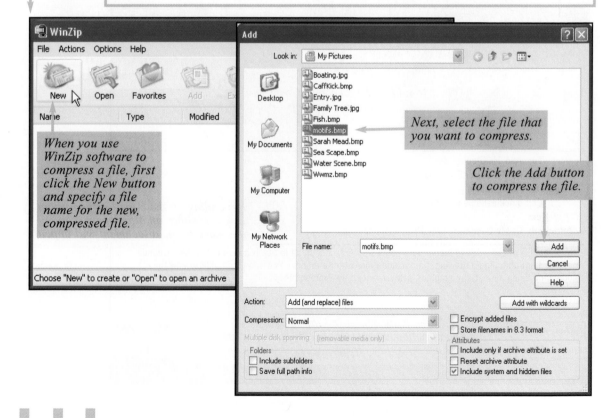

∎FAQ What are smileys, flame wars, and spams?

It doesn't take long to get initiated into the e-mail club. Within days of sending your first e-mail, you're likely to receive replies containing odd little symbols called **smileys** or emoticons. E-mail communication lacks the body language and vocal intonations that give us clues to meaning and intent in face-to-face conversations, but e-mailers have devised a visual way to add some of these clues. The original smiley :-) is formed using a colon, a hyphen, and a right parenthesis. Tip your head to the left to see the smiling face. This smiley usually means that the preceding statement is intended to be friendly, not inflammatory.

To add emphasis or emotion to e-mails, some people resort to TYPING IN ALL CAPS—the Internet equivalent of shouting. Use this technique sparingly, because you probably don't want your message to start a flame war. A **flame war** is an exchange of controversial or insulting messages that become increasingly nasty as one person tries to get the other's goat, so to speak.

The Internet might seem like an "anything goes" sort of place, but there exists an unwritten code of behavior or etiquette, sometimes referred to as **netiquette**. Flame wars are considered bad netiquette because they are rude and use Internet bandwidth unproductively. **Spams**—sending unsolicited junk e-mail to huge numbers of people—are another dubious use of Internet bandwidth.

When you send e-mail, follow these tips to ensure that you use correct netiquette:
- Read your mail regularly. E-mail travels rapidly and your correspondents expect a quick response.
- Maintain a professional image by using standard grammar and capitalization. If your e-mail software includes a spelling checker, use it.
- Think before you send potentially controversial or inflammatory mail. You don't want to start a flame war. Use smileys to help clarify your intentions.
- Don't reply to a group if your reply is meant for only one member of a group.
- Don't waste bandwidth with unnecessary mail. For example, it is rarely necessary to send a message saying "I received your e-mail."
- When possible, zip e-mail attachments to reduce their size and transmission time.

Figure 9-5: Smileys, sometimes called emoticons, can help your e-mail messages convey the correct tone.

;-)   :-(:-O

The winking emoticon means "don't take this seriously."

The frowning emoticon indicates unhappiness or displeasure.

The "o-shaped" mouth on this emoticon indicates surprise.

∎Hardware
Local area networks

A **LAN** (local area network) is a collection of computers and other devices connected within a limited geographical area. Sometimes simply called a "network," a LAN differs from the Internet in that it is smaller, privately owned, and does not necessarily use the same communications technology.

Some LANs are very simple. If you've connected your computer to a router as described in the Hardware section of Chapter 8, you've created your own basic local area network. Many routers, such as those discussed in Chapter 8, combine the traditional functions of router with those of a network hub. A **hub** is a device to which multiple computers or network devices can be attached. Every device attached to the hub can communicate with all other devices attached to the hub.

To create a basic network, you just connect one or more computers, or workstations, to the hub. A **workstation** is a standard PC that's connected to a LAN to take advantage of network resources, such as the cable modem or DSL modem attached to the router.

If desired, the workstations on a network can be configured to share resources. For example, the laser printer attached on one computer can be configured as a shared device so you can print files on it from other computers on the network. You can also configure workstations for shared access to storage devices such as hard disk drives and even CD-ROM and DVD drives. You can use **drive mapping** to assign drive letters to shared devices on other workstations. For example, drive C: on one computer might be configured as drive F: on another computer. Both computers can then read and write files on that hard disk drive. Of course, the computer with the shared device must be turned on before other users can access its devices.

A **NIC** (network interface card) is a small circuit board that connects a PC to a local area network. In a desktop PC, the NIC plugs directly into the main board inside the system unit. An opening in the back of the unit allows you to connect the network cable to the NIC. In a notebook computer, the NIC can be built-in or might be a credit-card-sized PCMCIA card that can easily be removed to disconnect the computer from the network when you travel.

Workstations are typically connected to a network using 10Base-T cables. A **10Base-T cable** has square plastic connectors that look much like those on a standard telephone cable.

■Hardware
continued

Figure 9-6: *If your workstation is a desktop PC, you'll see the network interface card connections at the rear of the system unit. For basic troubleshooting, make sure that the cable is securely connected to the NIC.*

To avoid having to make sure that all workstations are turned on in order to reach their attached devices, you can install devices such as printers and storage devices directly to the network.

A **network printer** includes an Ethernet port. You plug it directly in to the network, then configure the workstations to print to it. A **network server** is a computer that provides some service to the workstations. There are many kinds of servers. For example, a **file server** provides access to data files and software; a **print server** controls the activities of one or more shared printers; and an **e-mail server** provides e-mail service. Smaller home or small business LANs might include a file server and perhaps a network printer. More complex networks in larger businesses and organizations might include include many different network devices including specialized servers and a number of network printers located in different offices and departments.

Figure 9-7: *Large networks often include many types of network devices. The most popular LAN technology today is Ethernet, which uses a hub as the centralized point of connection for all workstations and servers on the network. On larger networks, local hubs may be attached to larger hubs, effectively connecting many small networks into one larger network.*

■Hardware
continued

When you boot your PC, the Windows operating system automatically checks the Registry to find out whether a network interface card has been installed. As the boot process continues, you will be asked to enter a password supplied by your network specialist. Typically, Windows will then execute a special set of instructions called a **login script** that automatically connects your workstation to one or more servers and printers. Your login script is generally created and installed by your network specialist.

From your workstation, you can get an overview of the entire network by using the **My Network Places icon** on the Windows XP or Me Desktop (or **Network Neighborhood icon** on older Windows versions). Clicking this icon displays a window that lists the servers and printers connected to the network. Your workstation's ability to access the network devices displayed in the Network Neighborhood window depends on which access rights you've been assigned by your network specialist. Your login script gives you automatic access to one or more servers. In addition, your network specialist might provide you with login passwords to access other servers or even other workstations on the network.

When using a network, you should do your part to maintain its security. Do not provide your password to unauthorized users. Also, make sure that you follow the recommended logoff procedure to disconnect from the network when you have completed your computing session.

Figure 9-8: *Click the PlayIt! button to find out how the My Network Places window lists the devices connected to a LAN.*

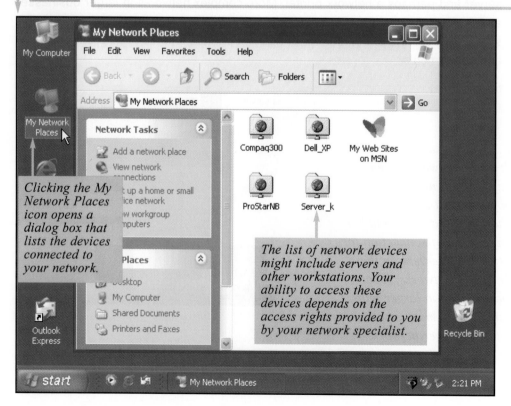

Clicking the My Network Places icon opens a dialog box that lists the devices connected to your network.

The list of network devices might include servers and other workstations. Your ability to access these devices depends on the access rights provided to you by your network specialist.

∎Tutorial

How to use your e-mail address book like a pro

Although you can manually type the address of each e-mail recipient in the message header, you might forget someone's address. It is also easy to make a typing error that will bounce the e-mail back to you, branded "address unknown." Most e-mail software includes an address book that keeps a list of frequently used addresses. Instead of manually typing the address for each message, you can select an address from the address book.

The address book also allows you to create mail groups composed of multiple e-mail addresses. By selecting the group from your address book, you can conveniently send an e-mail message to everyone in the group.

When you have completed the tutorial, you should be able to:

- Open an e-mail address book.
- Enter individual e-mail addresses in the address book.
- Send a message to an individual listed in the address book.
- Create a group in the address book and send mail to everyone in the group.

Figure 9-9: *Click the PlayIt! button to begin the tutorial. You'll learn how to use an e-mail address book and discover how to simplify e-mail addressing tasks. Estimated time: 10–15 minutes. Tracking Disk points: 10.*

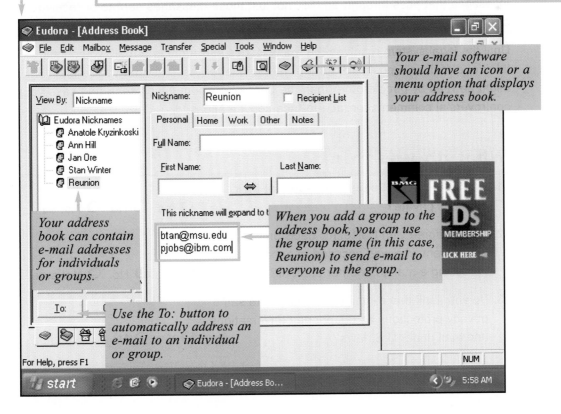

■ **Issue**

Just how private is e-mail?

Most people assume that e-mail has similar privacy protections as telephone conversations and as letters that are carried by the postal service. That is not necessarily the case, however. The electronic technology that makes e-mail so popular also tends to make it less private than a phone call or a letter. It is easy for the recipient of an e-mail message to forward copies of it to other people. The contents of an e-mail message might appear on a technician's screen in the course of system maintenance or repairs. Also, your e-mail messages—including those that you have deleted from your own PC—might be stored on backups and archives of an e-mail server where you cannot control access to them.

When a CalTech student was accused of sexually harassing a female student by sending lewd e-mail to her and to her boyfriend, investigators retrieved all of the student's e-mail from archives of the e-mail server. The student was expelled from the university even though he claimed that the e-mail had been "spoofed" to make it look as though he had sent it, when it had actually been sent by someone else.

To eavesdrop on e-mail from suspected terrorists and other criminals, the FBI developed a technology called Carnivore, which scans through messages entering and leaving an ISP's e-mail system to find e-mail associated with a person who is under investigation. Privacy advocates are concerned because Carnivore scans all messages that pass through an ISP, not just those messages sent to or received by a particular individual.

Until the legal system resolves the many issues surrounding e-mail, you should think of e-mail as a postcard, rather than as a letter. Assume that your e-mail might be read by people other than the person to whom it was sent, and save your controversial comments for face-to-face conversations.

What do you think?

1. Do you think most people believe that their e-mail is private?   ○ Yes   ○ No   ○ Not sure

2. Do you agree with CalTech's decision to expel the student who was accused of sending harassing e-mail to another student?   ○ Yes   ○ No   ○ Not sure

3. Do you think that e-mail should have the same privacy protections as telephone conversations and mail under U.S. laws?   ○ Yes   ○ No   ○ Not sure

Save It!

QuickCheck A

1. True or false? Store-and-forward technology allows you to minimize dial-up connect time because you can read and compose messages offline. _____

2. An e-mail attachment might harbor a virus, and you should be particularly suspicious of attachments with a(n) _____ extension.

3. Because some e-mail systems impose a size limit on the mail they accept, as a rule of thumb attachments should be smaller than _____ megabyte(s).

4. Compressed files typically have a(n) _____ file extension.

5. True or false? You must use the Network Neighborhood as your e-mail client software if your computer is connected to a LAN. _____

Check It!

QuickCheck B

Fill in each blank, based on the e-mail shown at right.

1. The name of the person who wrote this e-mail:
_____

2. The recipient's e-mail address: _____

3. Does this e-mail include an attachment? _____

4. The name of this e-mail software: _____

5. The symbol that indicates the lines of the original message: _____

Eudora - [Ann Hill, Re: An Invitation]

File   Edit   Mailbox   Message   Transfer   Special   Tools   Window   Help

Search Web

Standard   MIME   QP   Queue

Arial   A   B   I   U

To: "Ann Hill" <Ann_Hill@cciw.com>
From: Pat Redfern <Predfern@cciw.com>
Subject: Re: An Invitation
Cc: glocklear@pequot.org

I would be happy to make a presentation to the AAC. I would need to know the time that you have allocated and the number of people who would be present. Perhaps you could phone me and we can settle the details.

At 02:27 PM 10/19/2004, you wrote:
> We would like to invite you to the next meeting of the Arts
> Appreciation Council and hope that you would be able to make a presentation
> on Native American arts, crafts and music. The AAC might sponsor an exhibit

In   Ann Hill, Re: An I...

QUALCOMM

http://www.qualcomm.com

start   Eudora - [Ann_Hill@c...   4:27 PM

Check It!

Get It?

While using the BookOnCD, click the Get It? button to see if you can answer ten randomly selected questions from Chapter 9.

Get It?

Chapter 10

Writing and Printing Documents

What's Inside?

A computer with preinstalled software typically includes a software suite or an integrated software package that provides a set of basic tools for producing documents, making calculations, creating presentations, and getting organized. Chapter 10 focuses on the software you use to produce documents.

What's on the CD?

Chapter 10 screen tours show you how to improve your writing with word processing software and how to create professional publications with desktop publishing software. This chapter's video feature looks at laser printers.

■FAQ Can word processing software improve my writing?

Word processing (WP) software provides a set of tools for entering and revising text, adding graphical elements, then formatting and printing documents. Although many people regard WP software as a tool for improving the appearance of documents, it also provides resources for improving the quality of your writing. Popular WP software includes Microsoft Word, WordPerfect, and Lotus Word Pro.

Good writing requires a coherent progression of ideas expressed in grammatically correct sentences using carefully selected descriptive words. Before you focus on how your document looks, pay attention to how it reads by using your WP software to organize your ideas and clarify your wording. Entering text on screen gives you the flexibility to first sketch in your main points, then move them around to improve the progression of your ideas.

Once you're satisfied with the flow of ideas, use your WP software to improve wording and sentence structure. A built-in **grammar checker** can help you spot awkward sentences and other grammatical faux pas. It reviews your document sentence-by-sentence and offers suggestions for improvement. To make your writing really sparkle, boost your vocabulary by using the built-in **thesaurus**, which displays synonyms for any word that you select. Your WP software can also help you find and fix spelling errors. A **spelling checker** compares each word in your document to an electronic dictionary. If you've used a word that is not in the dictionary, the spelling checker displays a list of possible alternatives.

Figure 10-1: Click the PlayIt! button to see how your writing can improve when you use a thesaurus, grammar checker, and spelling checker.

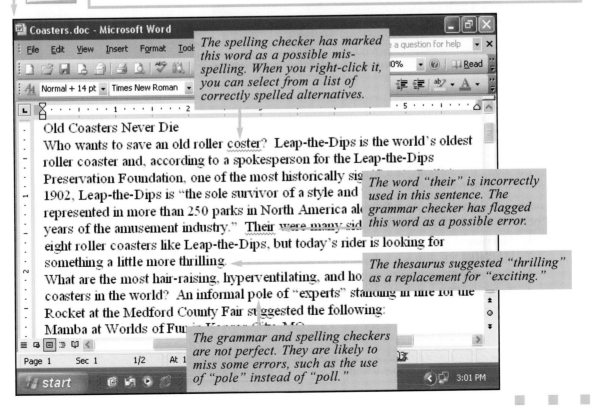

■FAQ How does WP software help me format a document?

You can use your WP software to **format** a document and change its appearance to create a professional, high-impact, or casual look. When you first type the "raw" text for a document, don't press the Enter key at the end of each line—just keep typing. Your WP software will automatically **word wrap** to the next line. You should, however, press the Enter key at the end of a title or paragraph. Think of this "raw" text as strings of characters that form paragraphs that exist on a page. You will later be able to apply formats at the character, paragraph, or page level.

Grab It!

Fonts

You can format one or more characters in a document to change the font, color, and size. The term **font** refers to the design or typeface of each text character. You can also add effects such as bold, italics, and underlining. To apply character formats, you'll typically use the mouse to select the text to be formatted, then use a toolbar button or menu option to indicate the format that you want.

Paragraph format options include margin settings, line spacing, bulleted and numbered lists, columns, centering, left and right alignment, and "justification" that creates even right and left margins. To apply paragraph formats, make sure that you're working within the paragraph, then use a menu option to select a format.

Page format options apply to an entire document and include adding header text at the top of each page, adding footer text at the bottom of each page, changing the page size, and automatically numbering pages.

Play It!

Figure 10-2: Click the PlayIt! button for a quick tour of character, paragraph, and page formatting.

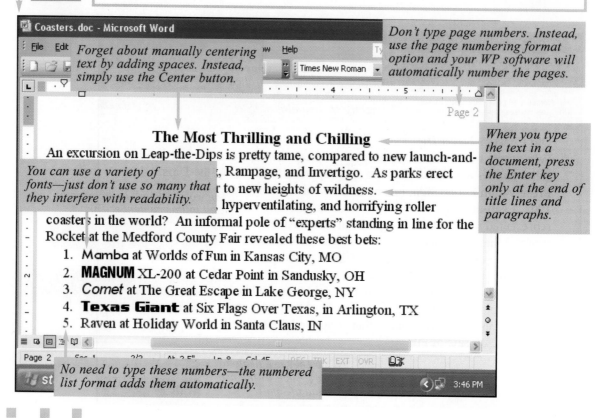

■FAQ   Does WP software provide standard document styles?

A **style** is a set of character and paragraph attributes that you can name and define. For example, you might name a style "body text" and define it as a small-size Arial font, single-spaced, and left-aligned. Your word processor typically keeps track of the styles you define in a **style list**. Once you have defined a style, you can apply all of its attributes in one operation by making a selection from the style list.

Word Templates

The "look" of a document depends on the style settings that you use for each element, such as titles, body text, tables, and footnotes. A collection of such settings is referred to as a **style sheet**. You can save style sheet settings as a **template** so that you can produce documents with a similar "look." If you are unsure about the proper style to use for a document such as a business memo, your WP software might provide a predesigned template with appropriate headings, margin settings, and so on. Using a template is easy. Simply open the template, type the text for your document, and apply styles as needed.

In addition, your WP software might provide **template wizards** that further simplify the process of creating a document. A template wizard asks you a series of questions about the document that you want to create, then essentially creates the document for you based on your answers. Wizards are commonly supplied for letters, memos, resumes, and faxes.

Figure 10-3: Click the PlayIt! button to find out how to create styles, use templates, and activate a template wizard.

■**FAQ** **What's desktop publishing software?**

Grab It!

DTP
Software
Demos

Desktop publishing (DTP) software provides a set of tools to design and print typeset-quality documents using your PC. It is the software of choice for documents that will be widely distributed, such as newsletters, brochures, corporate reports, and books. Popular DTP software includes Adobe PageMaker, Microsoft Publisher, and QuarkXPress.

Typically, DTP software is not the tool that you use to author and edit a document. Instead, you use it to collect and incorporate all the elements for a publication. For example, you would write, edit, and check the spelling of a document using WP software, then import that text into your DTP software. You would also prepare photos and diagrams using graphics software, and then import them as well.

DTP software's major advantage is the flexibility and precision it provides for positioning text and graphical elements on a page. You can designate rectangular areas on the page called **frames** and fill each one with either text or graphics. To achieve a pleasing layout, you can move, resize, and overlap these frames.

The appearance of your printed document is affected by the quality of your printer. If your printer cannot produce high-quality output, you might be able to use it to print only drafts of your document. For the final printout, you can deliver your files to a professional printing press. You'll learn more about printers in the Hardware section.

Play It!

Figure 10-4: DTP software has essentially replaced typesetting, even for glossy magazines, newspapers, and books. Click the PlayIt! button to take a tour of DTP software.

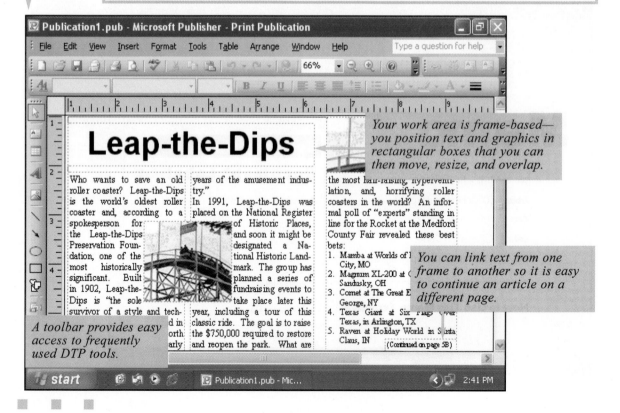

■FAQ Do I need DTP software in addition to WP software?

As a rule of thumb, you can probably create most of your documents using word processing software. You might consider adding desktop publishing software to your PC if you frequently produce graphics-intensive brochures, magazines, newsletters, or professionally printed books.

Today's WP software has evolved far beyond typewriter emulation and now incorporates many DTP features. Therefore, the capabilities of WP and DTP software overlap to some extent. The difference between these two types of software is often one of degree. For example, although WP software can work with color graphics, DTP software provides more flexibility for positioning, modifying, labeling, and color-adjusting those graphics. You can send documents produced with WP software to a professional print shop, but you might find that more print shops can accommodate files created with DTP software.

After you have worked with both WP and DTP software, you will be better able to judge which one is appropriate for a particular project. In the meantime, don't hesitate to start by using WP software for any project. If layout and formatting become too complex for your WP software, you can easily import the document into DTP software, then lay it out and format it.

Figure 10-5: Use this chart to compare the strengths and weaknesses of WP and DTP software to see if you need both.

Document Production Feature	WP	DTP
Create outlines and autonumbered paragraphs	☺	☹
Check grammar	☺	☹
Track revisions made by authors and editors	☺	☹
Generate footnotes	☺	☹
Generate an index or table of contents	☺	☺
Check spelling	☺	☺
Generate tables	☺	☺
Work with columns of text	☺	☺
Control spacing between letters and lines for typeset look	☺	☺
Incorporate and manipulate graphics	☺	☺
Add callouts or text labels to graphics	☹	☺
Incorporate elaborate page headers	☹	☺
Generate full-color "plates" for a professional printer	☹	☺

☺ strong   ☺ adequate   ☹ weak

■Hardware
Printers

A **printer** is a device that converts computer output into images on sheets of paper or other media, such as labels, envelopes, transparencies, or iron-on transfers. Today's printers tend to use one of three technologies: dot matrix, ink jet, or laser. Despite their differences, all three technologies produce characters and graphics as a series of small dots.

The quality or sharpness of an image depends on its **resolution**—the density of the gridwork of dots that create it. Printer resolution is measured by the number of dots it can print per linear inch, abbreviated as **dpi**. At normal reading distance, a resolution of about 900 dots per inch appears solid to the human eye, but a close examination of color sections on a page will reveal the dot pattern. Although 900 dpi might be considered sufficient for magazines, expensive "coffee-table books" are typically produced on printers with 2,400 dpi or higher resolution.

When PCs first began to appear in the late 1970s, dot matrix printers were the technology of choice. Still in use today, **dot matrix printers** produce characters and graphics by using a matrix of fine wires. As the print head noisily clatters across the paper, the wires strike the ribbon and paper in a pattern prescribed by your PC. With a resolution of 360 dpi, a dot matrix printer produces low-quality output with clearly discernible dots forming letters and graphics. Dot matrix speed is typically measured in characters per second (cps). A fast dot matrix device can print at speeds up to 569 cps—about six pages per minute.

Today, dot matrix printers, which are sometimes referred to as "impact printers," are used primarily for "back-office" applications that demand low operating cost and dependability, but not high print quality. A U.S.$4 ribbon can print more than eight million characters before it needs to be replaced. Unlike many newer printer technologies, a dot matrix printer actually strikes the paper and therefore can print multipart carbon forms.

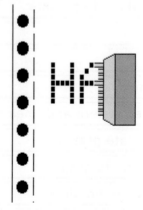

Figure 10-6: *The print head in a dot matrix printer contains a row of fine wires that strike the ribbon and paper to produce a matrix of dots that form characters or graphics. Click the PlayIt! button for a quick demonstration.*

■Hardware
continued

An **ink jet printer** has a nozzle-like print head that sprays ink onto the paper to form characters and graphics. Today's most popular printer technology, ink jets produce low-cost black-and-white or color printouts. The print head in a color ink jet printer consists of a series of nozzles, each with its own ink cartridge. Most ink jet printers use **CMYK color**, which requires only cyan (blue), magenta (pink), yellow, and black inks to create a printout that appears to have thousands of colors. Alternatively, some printers use six ink colors to print additional midtone shades that create slightly more realistic photographic images.

Operating costs for an ink jet printer are reasonable. You'll need to periodically replace the black ink cartridge and a second cartridge that carries the colored inks. Each replacement ink cartridge costs between U.S.$25 and U.S.$35. Under realistic use, your costs for color printing will be between 5 and 15 cents per page. A potential hidden cost of operating an ink jet printer is special paper. Although you can satisfactorily print documents with small graphics and line art on the same type of inexpensive paper that you might use in a photocopier, high-quality photo printouts require special paper that can cost between U.S.$0.08 and U.S.$1.50 per sheet. Typically, this special paper has a super smooth finish that prevents the ink from bleeding and creating dull colors.

Today's ink jet printers have excellent resolution; depending on the model, it can range from 600 dpi to 2,400 dpi. You can expect to pay more for a printer with a higher resolution to get better quality when printing photographic images. Some ink jet printers achieve their ultra-high resolution by making multiple passes over the paper. Although it might seem logical that this technique would slow down the printing process, even multiple-pass ink jet printers produce a respectable twelve pages per minute. You can purchase a good-quality ink jet printer for about U.S.$100. Manufacturers include Hewlett-Packard, Epson, Lexmark, Okidata, Canon, and NEC.

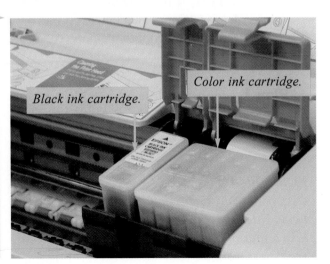

Black ink cartridge.

Color ink cartridge.

Figure 10-7: An ink jet printer sprays colored inks from its nozzle-like print heads. A color ink jet printer typically uses one black ink cartridge and another cartridge that contains the rest of the ink colors.

continued

A **laser printer** uses the same technology as a photocopier to "paint" dots of light on a light-sensitive drum. Electrostatically charged ink is applied to the drum, then transferred to paper. You can purchase laser printers at two price points. Inexpensive "desktop" or "personal" models, priced under U.S.$400, are quite suitable for black-and-white printing of a limited number of copies. More expensive "professional" laser printers with color or extended-run capacity begin at U.S.$700 and quickly exceed the U.S.$3,000 mark.

As with other printer technologies, print speed and resolution will be key factors in your purchase decision. Personal laser printers produce 8 to 15 pages per minute at a resolution of 600 dpi. Professional models pump out 19 to 40 pages per minute at 1,200 dpi. The **duty cycle** of a printer is specified in pages per month (ppm) and indicates how much work you can expect your printer to produce without breaking down. A personal laser printer has a duty cycle of about 3,000 ppm—that means about 100 pages a day. You won't want to use it to produce 5,000 campaign brochures for next Monday, but would find it quite suitable for printing ten copies of a five-page outline for a meeting tomorrow.

Some people are surprised to discover that laser printers are less expensive to operate than ink jet printers. On average, you can expect to pay about 2 cents per page for black-and-white laser printing. This per-page cost includes periodically replacing the toner cartridge and drum. A toner cartridge and a drum unit each cost about U.S.$70, though prices vary by manufacturer and model.

Laser printers accept print commands from a PC, but use their own printer language to construct a page before printing it. **Printer Control Language** (PCL) is the most widely used printer language, but some printers also use the **PostScript** language, which is preferred by many publishing professionals. Printer languages require memory, and most lasers have between 2 and 32 MB. A large memory capacity is required to print color images and graphics-intensive documents. A laser printer comes equipped with enough memory for typical print jobs. If you find that you need more memory, check the printer documentation for information.

Figure 10-8: A laser printer uses electrostatically charged ink called toner. Click the PlayIt! button to take a tour of a laser printer and see how it works.

■Tutorial

How to install and select printers

In the tutorial for Chapter 1, you learned how to set up a printer and connect it to your PC. Windows will spot this new equipment and display the Add Printer wizard to help you install the necessary printer driver. A **printer driver** is a software program that sets up communications between the printer and your PC. Windows includes a set of printer drivers, but if you have just connected a new-model printer, Windows might require a driver from the floppy disk or CD supplied by the printer manufacturer. After installing the printer driver, you can use the printer.

Windows allows you to connect multiple printers to your PC. You must designate one as the **default printer** that Windows will use for all your printouts unless you specify otherwise. In this tutorial, you'll learn how to install printer drivers, choose a default printer, and select a printer when you print a document.

When you have completed the tutorial, you should be able to:

■ Use the Add Printer wizard to install a printer driver.
■ Designate a default printer.
■ Select the printer that you want to use for a printout.
■ Check the status of a print job.

Figure 10-9: *Click the PlayIt! button to learn how to use the Add Printer wizard and select the printer for your printout. Estimated time: 10–15 minutes. Tracking Disk points: 10.*

Issue
What's truth got to do with it?

You live in the Information Age. Ironically, much of the information that you read and hear is just not true. False and misleading information predates the Information Age, but now it propagates more rapidly, fed by new technologies and nurtured by "spin doctors." As one commentator has suggested, "The danger is that we are reaching a moment when nothing can be said to be objectively true, when consensus about reality disappears. The Information Age could leave us with no information at all, only assertions."

In a more innocent era, the source of information provided a clue about its reliability. Television network news was usually dependable. You could generally rely on newspaper reports and information in books. Now, however, the yardstick once used to measure the reliability of information is being challenged by technology and by changes in the relationship between mass media and their audience. Using DTP software, virtually anyone can produce brochures, pamphlets, and books that look professional and official. Using Web authoring software, it is easy to design a professional Web site and stock it with misinformation. In an Internet chat group, anyone can start a rumor that propagates via the Net and eventually achieves the status of an "urban legend." Editorializing has softened "hard" news, and news stories are often selected for their sensationalism, rather than for their importance.

Who should be responsible for ensuring the accuracy of information? Holding writers accountable for their "facts" does not seem to be working. Governments, already overburdened with other problems, have scant resources available to sift through mountains of information and set the record straight. It seems, then, that the burden of verifying facts is ultimately left to the reader—or watcher, as the case may be. But many of these individuals do not have the time, motivation, expertise, or resources to verify facts before they pass them on through the information mill. This information problem might prove particularly difficult to solve.

What do you think?

1. In your opinion, can people typically recognize false information in print, on the Web, or on TV?   ○ Yes ○ No ○ Not sure

2. Have you believed information from a reliable source that you later discovered was false?   ○ Yes ○ No ○ Not sure

3. Do you think that governments should penalize people who knowingly disseminate false information?   ○ Yes ○ No ○ Not sure

Save It!

QuickCheck A

1. True or false? In the phrase "Goldilocks and the tree bears," a spelling or grammar checker will flag the word "tree" because it is missing the letter "h." _____

2. When you initially type the "raw" text for a document, you should press the Enter key only at the end of a title or _____.

3. A(n) _____ includes the style settings necessary to duplicate the look of a previously designed document.

4. True or false? WP software was designed to produce documents that look professionally typeset. _____

5. DTP software uses rectangular _____ to hold text and graphics.

Check It!

QuickCheck B

In the right-hand column of the table, indicate which type of printer would **best** fit the job. Abbreviate your answers using **D** for dot matrix, **J** for ink jet, and **L** for laser.

1. An individual wants to print color photographic images of family and friends	
2. A school secretary wants to print 75 copies of the black-and-white program for tomorrow's school play	
3. A salesperson needs to print out a multipart carbon invoice form	
4. A professional publisher specializes in full-color brochures	
5. A student wants a dependable low-cost color printer	

Check It!

Get It? While using the BookOnCD, click the Get It? button to see if you can answer ten randomly selected questions from Chapter 10.

Chapter 11

Making Spreadsheets and Presentations

What's Inside?

Chapter 11 begins with a whirlwind tour of spreadsheet software. If you want to make a presentation based on the results you produce with spreadsheet or any other software, you'll be interested in the overview of computer projection devices in the Hardware section. The tutorial focuses on a related topic—how to use presentation software.

What's on the CD?

Chapter 11 animates spreadsheet software to show you how to create worksheets and graphs. In addition, a video shows you how to set up presentation equipment.

■FAQ What's a spreadsheet?

A **spreadsheet** is a tool for working with numbers. It is arranged in a grid of columns and rows forming **cells** that hold labels, numbers, and formulas. You can use spreadsheets for simple or complex calculations, such as computing loan payments, figuring out your taxes, or dividing expenses with your roommates.

Spreadsheet software, such as Microsoft Excel, Quattro Pro, and Lotus 1-2-3, allows you to create electronic spreadsheets that you can easily edit, print, save, post on the Web, or transmit via e-mail. An electronic spreadsheet is often referred to as a **worksheet**. A worksheet functions much like a visual calculator. You place each number needed for a calculation in a cell of the grid. You can then enter formulas to add, subtract, or otherwise manipulate these numbers. Your spreadsheet software automatically calculates the formulas and displays the results. As an added bonus, it can create graphs based on the data in a worksheet.

Using spreadsheet software helps ensure the accuracy of your calculations by displaying all of your data and formulas on screen. It can also help you to create numeric models of real-world entities. As an example, you could create a numeric model of a new business, then examine projected income and expenses to determine whether the business will make you rich beyond your wildest dreams. You can even use your model to examine several alternative **"what-if" scenarios**, such as "What if sales are double what I projected?" or "What if sales are only half of what I projected?"

Figure 11-1: Click the PlayIt! button to take a tour of some handy and innovative spreadsheets.

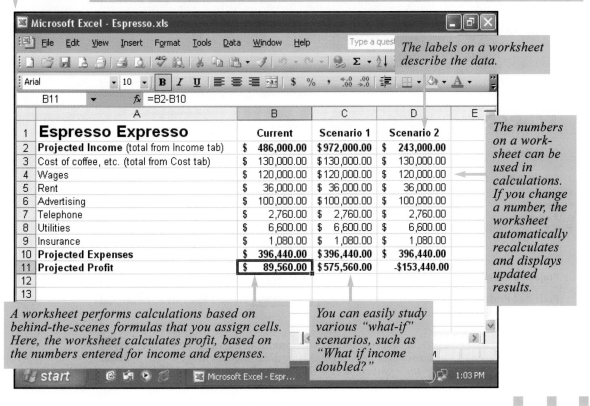

The labels on a worksheet describe the data.

The numbers on a worksheet can be used in calculations. If you change a number, the worksheet automatically recalculates and displays updated results.

A worksheet performs calculations based on behind-the-scenes formulas that you assign cells. Here, the worksheet calculates profit, based on the numbers entered for income and expenses.

You can easily study various "what-if" scenarios, such as "What if income doubled?"

■FAQ How do I create a worksheet?

After you have a clear idea of the purpose of your worksheet, you can begin by entering the title and the labels that will identify your data. Next, you enter the numbers or "values" that will be incorporated in calculations. Finally, you enter formulas in any cells where you want the result of a calculation to appear.

A **formula** specifies how to add, subtract, multiply, or divide the numbers in worksheet cells. Typically, a formula begins with an equal sign (=) and contains cell references instead of the "raw" numbers for a calculation. A **cell reference** is the column and row location of a cell. In Figure 11-2, the projected income of $486,000.00 is in column B and row 2, so its cell reference is B2. To create the formula that calculates profit (=B2-B10), you should use this cell reference instead of the actual number. Then, if the projected income changes, you can simply enter the new number in cell B2, but you won't have to change the formula. The worksheet will recalculate the profit based on the new number you've entered.

After you've entered labels, numbers, and formulas, you can format your worksheet to make it more attractive and easier to understand. Formatting options include font treatments, cell colors, and data alignment within the cells. An additional set of formatting options helps you control the way your numbers are displayed, such as whether to include $ signs, decimal places, and commas.

Figure 11-2: *Seasoned worksheet veterans have developed tips and tricks for making effective worksheets. They'll share some of these with you when you click the PlayIt! button.*

*The formula for the selected cell (B11) is displayed here. Excel formulas begin with an = sign and can contain mathematical operators, such as + (add), - (subtract), * (multiply), and / (divide).*

You can use fonts, graphics, and color to jazz up the appearance of your worksheet.

Enter a formula in the cell where you want the results to appear. The formula in this cell adds up all the expenses.

When referring to a number in a formula, use its cell reference. The formula for this cell, =B2-B10, calculates profit by subtracting the number in cell B10 from the number in cell B2.

∎FAQ What if I don't know the right formula?

Some formulas are easy to figure out. If you follow baseball, you know that a player's batting average is the number of hits divided by the number of times at bat. Easy. But suppose that you're looking at new cars and you want to calculate your monthly payments for a spiffy red Toyota. You'll need to factor in interest rates, the number of payments, and the cost of the car. What's the formula?

Spreadsheet software includes built-in **functions**, which are predefined formulas that perform simple or complex calculations. Handy functions include AVERAGE, SUM, PMT (calculate monthly payments), STDEV (calculate a standard deviation), and ROUND (round off a decimal number). To use a function, simply select it from the function list, then follow the on-screen instructions to select the cells that contain arguments for the calculation. An **argument**, sometimes called a "parameter," is a value or cell reference that a function uses as the basis for a calculation. When you use the PMT function to calculate monthly car payments, the arguments include the interest rate, number of payments, and cost of the car. The arguments for a function are generally separated by commas and enclosed in parentheses.

$$=PMT(B7/12,B8,B6)$$

Function name   *Arguments*

Play It!

Figure 11-3: Click the PlayIt! button to explore worksheet functions and learn how to incorporate them into your worksheets.

How do I know if worksheet results are accurate?

The person who creates a worksheet is responsible for its accuracy. Therefore, before you use or distribute a worksheet, you should test it to verify that it produces the correct results. Most spreadsheet software includes sophisticated tools for testing worksheets. If possible, however, you should first simply check the results using a hand calculator or data that is known to be correct. Worksheet errors typically result from one of the following factors:

■ A value that you entered in a cell is incorrect due to a typographical error.

■ A formula contains a mathematical operator that is not correct, includes an incorrect cell reference, or is simply the wrong formula.

■ A formula produces the wrong results because the order for the calculations is not correct. Spreadsheet software first performs any operations in parentheses, then performs multiplication and division, and finally performs addition and subtraction. For example, the result of the formula =2+10/5 is 4, whereas the result of =(2+10)/5 is 2.4.

■ A specified series of cells does not encompass all the values needed for a calculation. For example, you may have intended to sum the values in cells C5 through H5, but specified cells C5 through G5.

■ The worksheet was created using a built-in function, but the wrong cells were selected as the arguments. For example, in the PMT function, the first argument is supposed to be the interest rate, but if it has been assigned to the cell that contains the loan amount, the PMT function will produce the wrong result.

Figure 11-4: Click the PlayIt! button for tips on how to check the accuracy of your worksheets.

Oops! An "A" would be nice, but this student's spreadsheet is inaccurate. The percentage should be 89% and the grade should be "B." Can you spot the errors?

■FAQ How do I create graphs?

Most spreadsheet software includes features that create graphs, sometimes called "charts" in spreadsheet terminology. A graph is based on the data in a worksheet. When you alter the data in your worksheet, the graph will automatically reflect the change. Typically, you'll want to graph the data contained in one or more ranges. A **range** is a series of cells. For example, the range B3:B6 includes cells B3, B4, B5, and B6. The range for a graph is also referred to as a "data set" or "data series." To create a graph comparing apple and grape production, one range of data would be apple production and the other would be grape production.

Your spreadsheet software allows you create many types of graphs, such as bar, line, pie, column, scatter, area, doughnut, and high-low-close graphs. You can even add graphics to bar and column charts. For example, instead of a plain bar depicting fruit yield, you can stack up a series of apples on one set of bars and a series of grapes on the other set.

Creating a graph requires a few easy steps:
- Plan your chart by deciding which worksheet data you want to chart and the type of chart you want to use.
- Activate the Chart wizard for step-by-step instructions on creating the chart.
- Use the Chart and formatting menu options to change the appearance of the chart labels, data markers, and dimensions.

Play It!

Figure 11-5: Excel's Chart wizard escorts you through the process of creating a graph from the data in a worksheet. Click PlayIt! to see how it works.

■Hardware
Computer projection devices

Presentation software, which is one of the components of a typical office suite, helps you create a series of graphics called **slides** to use as a backdrop for a speech, lecture, or sales presentation. It provides all the tools you need to combine text, diagrams, worksheets, graphs, animations, and sound effects into a series of electronic slides. You can display these slides on a PC monitor for a one-on-one presentation. For group presentations, a **computer projection device** can project your slides on a wall screen in a conference room or theater.

Computer projection devices are commonly used in schools, libraries, and businesses. You are likely to have an opportunity to use one—for example, when you pitch a new publicity campaign to your company's best client, when you give that oral report in your anthropology class, when you brief volunteers for the United Way campaign, or even when you're trying to convince the city council to put some effort into urban renewal. Two types of projection devices popular today are **LCD projectors** and **DLP projectors**.

LCD projectors shine a bright light through a small LCD panel. As pixels on the LCD panel change color, the light projected through the LCD panel changes color to create the projected image. DLP projectors shine a bright light on an array of miniature mirrors. The miniature mirrors rotate to create different colored dots on the projected image. Prices for LCD and DLP projectors range from U.S.$900 on up.

DLP projector

Figure 11-6: DLP projectors tend to produce a sharper, clearer image but typically cost more than LCD projectors.

■Hardware
continued

Some factors that affect the price of LCD and DLP projectors are the **ANSI lumen** rating, resolution, and the weight of the projector. Projection devices with higher ANSI lumen ratings produce a brighter picture and can be more easily viewed without turning down the lights. DLP and LCD projection devices typically range from 800 to 3,000 ANSI lumens. Resolution refers to the number of pixels that can be displayed on the projection device. As is the case with most computer screens, higher resolution projection devices typically cost more than lower resolution projection devices. Most current LCD and DLP projection devices support either SVGA (800x600 pixels) or XGA (1024x768 pixels) resolution. Smaller and lighter projection devices typically cost more than larger, heavier devices with similar specifications. Portable projection devices—those designed to be carried from presentation to presentation—typically weigh from 3 to 14 pounds. Projection devices intended for built-in use weigh from 20 to 40 pounds.

While many projection devices are used for training and group presentations, video buffs have discovered that an LCD or DLP projection device can work very well as a large screen projection device for television, video tapes, and DVD movies. Most LCD and DLP projection devices include S-video or composite video ports that allow them to be connected to cable TV boxes, DVD, or VCR players. Even a mid-range laptop computer with a DVD drive can serve as the core of a portable home theater system when connected to a set of large speakers and a projection device.

LCD and DLP projectors typically include "bells and whistles" to enhance presentations. A built-in loudspeaker is handy for playing any sound effects that you've added to your presentation slides. A remote control lets you adjust the focus and turn the projector on and off from across the room. Some projectors feature computerless operation—you copy slides from your PC to a PCMCIA memory card, which you then insert into the projector's PCMCIA slot.

Keystone control is available on several LCD and DLP projector models. **Keystoning**, the bane of professional speakers and audio-visual specialists, is the tendency of projected images to appear more like trapezoids than true rectangles. It occurs when the projector is not positioned directly in line with the middle of the screen. Because it is often practical to mount the projector on a table that's lower than the screen or on the ceiling above the screen, keystoning is a common artifact of presentations. Keystone control compensates for the position of the projector to produce a professional-looking rectangular image.

Play It!

Figure 11-7: LCD projectors are hot items for business and education. Manufacturers include Proxima, ViewSonic, Philips, Toshiba, Sony, and InFocus. Click PlayIt! to find out how to connect an LCD projector to a notebook PC.

▪Hardware
continued

Technology is great—when it works. But it doesn't always work. Occasional problems with your PC will typically affect only your personal productivity, but when you must depend on presentation equipment, technology glitches can become very public. It's awfully nerve-wracking to stand in front of a group of 100 people while someone tries to track down a replacement bulb for the LCD projector. You can avoid many of the curveballs that technology throws your way if you get serious about planning and preparing for your presentation.

▪ Determine whether presentation equipment will be available. If you plan to use your own notebook computer, make sure it is compatible with the projection device and that the correct connecting cables will be supplied. If you will use a computer other than your own, make sure the necessary software has been installed.

▪ Check out the equipment ahead of time. If possible, schedule a trial run the day before your presentation. Connect your computer and display a few slides so you are certain that everything works.

▪ Make sure that your audience will be able to see and hear your presentation. During your trial run, sit in the back of the room and make certain that the text on your slides is large enough to be easily read.

▪ Arrive early. Allow at least 30 minutes to set up your equipment and connect it to the presentation device.

▪ Know how to get technical support. If you are unfamiliar with any of the equipment, you might request the presence of a technical support person during your trial run or while you set up. Find out how you can contact a technician if you run into problems during the presentation.

▪ Be prepared for problems. Find out what to do if the projector bulb burns out. If you're using a notebook PC with batteries, keep your power cord handy. If this presentation can make or break your career, you might consider printing copies of your most important slides so that you can distribute them to your audience in case of a power failure.

Figure 11-8: You can make an effective presentation using a PC, presentation software, and an LCD or DLP projector, but it requires advance planning and preparation.

■Tutorial

How to make slides for an effective presentation

Grab It!

PowerPoint Templates

Presentation software is optimized to create slides containing text, sound effects, and graphics. You can design your slides from scratch, but you'll also find a good selection of ready-made **slide templates** that contain professionally designed background graphics and fonts in sizes that are easy to read when projected on a wall screen.

Most office suites include a collection of clip art images that provide eye-catching additions to documents, spreadsheets, and slides. For a truly multimedia presentation, you can add sound effects to your slides. You can incorporate even more visual interest by selecting active **transition effects** between slides, such as fades, wipes, and dissolves.

When you have completed the tutorial, you should be able to:

■ Select a slide template to use as the theme for your presentation.

■ Create a slide with a bulleted list.

■ Add clip art and sound effects to a slide.

■ Select a transition effect.

■ Add lecture notes for your script.

Play It!

Figure 11-9: Click the PlayIt! button to begin the tutorial and learn how to assemble slides for a presentation. Estimated time: 10–15 minutes. Tracking Disk points: 10.

Is it the medium or the message?

A Canadian professor named Marshall McLuhan coined the phrase "the medium is the message" to express the idea that media, such as films, books, and television, have an impact far greater than that of the material they communicate. Suppose that you're surfing the Web and encounter a site with light pink text. This site might as well carry no message as far as you're concerned. You might skip it because the text is too difficult to read. A clear case of the medium (that awful light pink text) becoming the message (nothing).

"The medium is the message" is not, however, the last word of advice for people who create documents, spreadsheets, and presentations. It would be a miscalculation to believe that your content doesn't matter as long as it is wrapped up in a flashy package. Today's media-savvy audience might be entertained by flash, but easily penetrate its thin veil to critically examine your ideas.

According to a recent Knowledge Networks/SRI study, children's bedrooms have become media havens with almost two-thirds (61%) containing a TV and 17% a PC. The study also shows that kids with own-room media technologies have less supervision and will more often go online while watching TV. The parents and grandparents of these children, having divided their attention between print and electronic media, might quite literally be on a different psychological wavelength. While print allows time for reflection and constructing mental images to supplement the words on a page, the rapidly changing collage of TV, video game, and Web-based images requires participants to develop quite a different set of mental skills. The new media mix can well affect the evolution of individuals and cultural groups.

What do you think?

1. Do you believe that McLuhan was correct in saying that "the medium is the message"?   ○ Yes   ○ No   ○ Not sure

2. Do you agree that, as a rule of thumb, the time you devote to preparing for a presentation should be divided as 50% research and writing, 50% designing electronic slides?   ○ Yes   ○ No   ○ Not sure

3. Do you believe that the Web can fundamentally change the personality and thought patterns of an entire generation?   ○ Yes   ○ No   ○ Not sure

Save It!

QuickCheck A

1. You can design a worksheet to be a numeric [_____] that you can use to examine "what-if" scenarios.

2. D9, A6, and Q8 are examples of cell [_____].

3. SUM, PMT, and AVERAGE are spreadsheet [_____].

4. True or false? If you create a graph showing baseball players' homeruns, you can change the number of runs for a player on the worksheet and the graph will automatically reflect the change. [_____]

5. True or false? All computer projection devices use LCD technology. [_____]

Check It!

QuickCheck B

Indicate the letter that correctly matches each description.

1. A cell containing a label [____]

2. A cell containing a number [____]

3. A cell containing a formula [____]

4. The formula for cell B11 [____]

5. A "what-if" analysis [____]

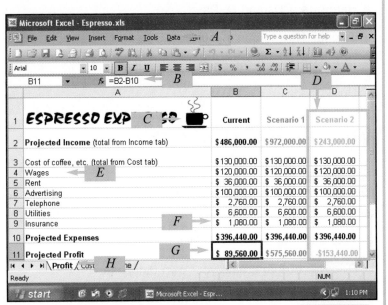

Check It!

Get It?

While using the BookOnCD, click the Get It? button to see if you can answer ten randomly selected questions from Chapter 11.

Get It?

Chapter 12

Accessing Databases

What's Inside?

In Chapter 12, you'll find out how to decide if you need database software, learn how to create your own databases, and think about some of the privacy issues associated with databases that contain information about you. The Hardware section examines CD and DVD storage—key technologies for storing and distributing large files and databases.

What's on the CD?

Chapter 12 screen tours and videos show you the inner workings of databases and DVD technology.

■FAQ What's a database?

In popular usage, the term "database" simply means a collection of data, such as a phone book, flight schedules, or a store's inventory list. You've probably encountered a collection of information, usually stored as documents. You could consider the documents stored on your computer to be a freeform database. A CD containing back issues of *Time* magazine would be another example. You could even regard the Web, with its millions of documents, as a freeform database.

A **structured database** contains information that is organized as fields, records, and files. A **field** contains a single piece of information, such as a name, birth date, or ZIP code. A **record** contains fields of information about a single "entity" in the database—a person, place, event, or thing. A group of similarly structured records form a **file**, also referred to as a "table."

When two or more related files are treated as a single unit, you have a **relational database**. For example, a video store database might include a file of movies and a file of customers. Suppose that a customer checks out the *Star Wars* movie, *Attack of the Clones*. The clerk simply enters the customer number on the Star Wars record. If the movie is never returned, the customer number acts as a link to the customer file that displays the customer's address, phone number, and credit card billing information.

Figure 12-1: In a relational database, two or more files can be linked or "joined" to display related data.

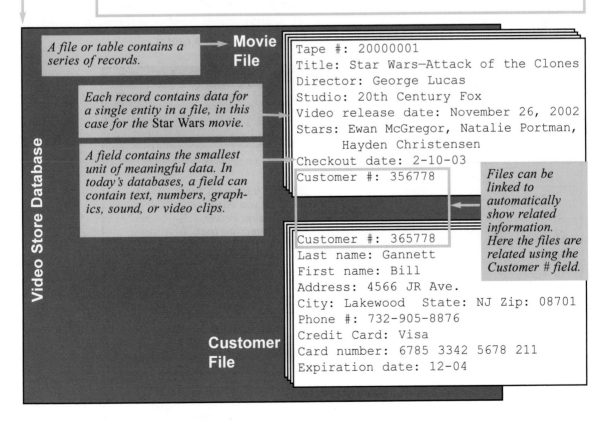

A file or table contains a series of records.

Movie File

Each record contains data for a single entity in a file, in this case for the Star Wars movie.

A field contains the smallest unit of meaningful data. In today's databases, a field can contain text, numbers, graphics, sound, or video clips.

```
Tape #: 20000001
Title: Star Wars—Attack of the Clones
Director: George Lucas
Studio: 20th Century Fox
Video release date: November 26, 2002
Stars: Ewan McGregor, Natalie Portman,
       Hayden Christensen
Checkout date: 2-10-03
Customer #: 356778
```

Files can be linked to automatically show related information. Here the files are related using the Customer # field.

Video Store Database

Customer File

```
Customer #: 365778
Last name: Gannett
First name: Bill
Address: 4566 JR Ave.
City: Lakewood  State: NJ Zip: 08701
Phone #: 732-905-8876
Credit Card: Visa
Card number: 6785 3342 5678 211
Expiration date: 12-04
```

■FAQ Do I need database software?

Grab It!

Simple File and Database Software

Database software, sometimes referred to as database management software (DBMS), provides a set of tools to enter and update information in fields, delete records, sort records, search for records that meet specified criteria, and create reports. Most people use databases with surprising frequency, but might not need database software. Why? Consider the databases that you typically access. You might access a database to register online for a class at a college or university. You might search a product database at a Web site such as Amazon.com. You might access your bank's database at an ATM to check your account balance. To access such databases, you use database software that runs on a computer at the host site—not on your own PC. Therefore, you do not need database software to interact with the databases at school, on the Web, or at your bank. Having database software is useful only to create and maintain your own databases.

If you have a use for database software, a variety of options are available. For example, Microsoft Access provides a wealth of data management capabilities, but using it to create production-quality databases requires a substantial learning commitment. Corel Paradox, Lotus Approach, and FileMaker Pro might be easier to learn and include the basic features needed to manage typical files and databases. For dealing with simple files, you might use the database modules of Microsoft Works or Claris Works. You can also use spreadsheet software for simple databases. You'll learn more about this option in a later FAQ.

Play It!

Figure 12-2: Click the PlayIt! button for a tour of database software. You'll learn how you might use the tables, search, query, form, and report functions, plus you'll find out why you might want to join two tables.

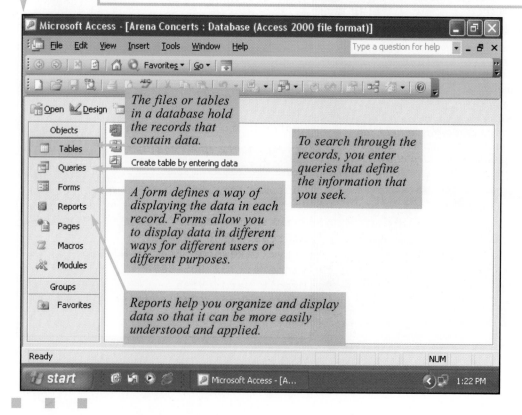

▪FAQ How would I create my own database?

Creating a database consists of two tasks: creating a file structure to hold the data and adding the data for each record. The specific procedure you'll use depends on the database software that you've selected, so you will want to refer to your software documentation for exact instructions.

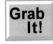

Grab
It!

Access
Database
Templates

Suppose that you want to create a household inventory in case you need it for an insurance claim. First, you will use your database software to create the **file structure**—a specification for the database fields and their characteristics. You'll need to assign a name to each field, such as Category, Item, Description, Purchase Date, Value, and Photo. Some database software might require you to specify the maximum length of each field and the type of data that it will hold—text, numbers, date, or graphic.

Once you have created the file structure, your database software will display it as a blank form that you can use to fill in the data for each household item. You will be able to reliably locate data in your database only if you enter data accurately and consistently. Keep these tips in mind when you enter data:

■ As you enter each record, compare the on-screen data to your original documents to verify its accuracy.

■ Be consistent with the entries for fields that might be used to group your data. Suppose that you plan to group your household inventory by categories such as jewelry, furniture, appliances, and electronics. You must then enter "jewelry" —not "jewels"—in the Category field for your diamond ring.

■ Use consistent capitalization. Most database software is case-sensitive. Be aware that if you enter "Microwave oven," case sensitive database software will not find anything when you later search for "microwave oven."

■ Make sure your spelling is correct. If you misspell an item, such as "portable jacuzzi," when you add it to the database, you won't be able to find it if you later search for "portable jacuzzi."

■ Use abbreviations consistently. To your database software, TV and T.V. are completely different.

■ Be careful about symbols. The telephone number (906)227-1000 is not the same as 906.227.1000.

Play
It!

Figure 12-3: Click the PlayIt! button to learn how to create a database using Microsoft Access. You'll find out how to define the database structure, specify field names, and select data types.

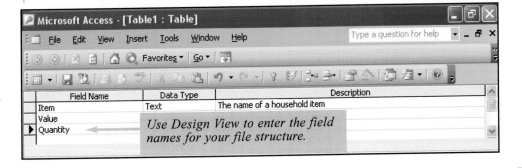

■FAQ Can I really create databases with spreadsheet software?

You can use most spreadsheet software to create and maintain files of information. You cannot, however, use it to join files together and create a relational database. Spreadsheet software typically has special data-handling features that allow you to manipulate the rows and columns of a worksheet as if they were records and fields in a database. You can sort your data, search for data that meets specific criteria, and create reports. As a rule of thumb, spreadsheet software can handle any data that you could put on a set of cards in a card file.

When managing data with spreadsheet software, the Form View displays each row of the worksheet as a "card" containing a series of fields, as shown in Figure 12-4. If you already know how to use spreadsheet software and your data lends itself to the card-file approach to data management, you'll find it easy to use the Form View for basic operations such as entering, modifying, searching, and sorting data.

A process called **filtering** or "extracting" data is a bit more complicated, but useful for creating reports that show only selected data. Suppose, for example, that you have 100 rows in a worksheet that you're using as a database. Each row contains information on doctor visits for members of your family. If you want the worksheet to display only those records for your oldest daughter, you'll need to filter the data using her name. You could then print the filtered version of the worksheet to produce a hard-copy report of her medical history.

Figure 12-4: *Click the PlayIt! button for a demonstration of how to use spreadsheet software to manage data.*

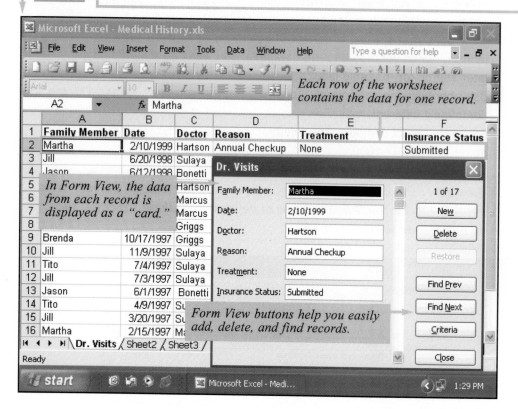

∎FAQ What about databases on the Web and CDs?

You'll find many databases on the Web and CDs that are prepopulated with all sorts of information. For example, you can look for your old roommate in a phone-book-style database that covers the entire country; find a low-cost airfare to Beijing in a database that contains flight schedules for the major airlines; look for the author of *Trout Madness* in the U.S. Library of Congress database; check the value of a 1964 Ford Mustang in a digital "Blue Book" database; find a definition of the term "CD-R" in a database of technical terms; or look up the December 1965 feature article in a database of back issues of *National Geographic* magazine.

There is a great deal of overlap between Web and CD databases. As you might expect, the Web is optimal for data that's constantly changing—air fares, for example. CDs provide a low-cost distribution method for less changeable data, which is why CD encyclopedias and medical references are so popular. CDs have an added advantage because the specific data that you access is not tracked by a cookie or Web site and therefore remains private.

On the Web, you'll also encounter databases that actively collect information. To access a Web site you might be required to register and complete a questionnaire about your income level, interests, computer ownership, and so on. The information that you supply is added to a database. You might assume that your registration information would not be made public, but businesses frequently sell their customer databases to research and marketing firms.

Figure 12-5: Click the PlayIt! button to see some samples of Web and CD databases.

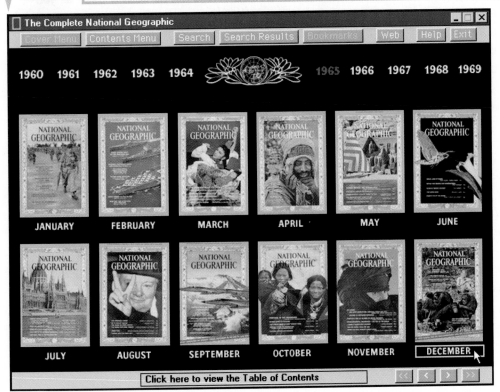

■Hardware
CDs and DVDs

Those silver disks that you nonchalantly slide into your boom box or computer are commonly called "CDs." Technically, several types of these disks exist, and each has unique characteristics and uses. The term CD or "audio CD" originally referred to only those disks that contained music or other audio data. These CDs were designed to replace LP records and cassette tapes. They comfortably held the songs from a typical music album. Why not use a similar technology to store computer data? This brilliant idea produced computer CDs with a typical storage capacity of 720 MB. Computer CDs are sometimes called "CD-ROMs" to distinguish them from audio CDs. The term **CD-ROM** is an abbreviation of "compact disc read-only memory," a reference to the fact that CD-ROM drives only read from disks preloaded with data, but cannot record or store data on them.

Standard CD-ROM drives only read data from premastered CD-ROM disks. However, variations of this technology allow you to store data as well as read it. **CD-R** (CD-recordable) technology allows you to create your own CDs using a CD-R drive and special CD-R disks. The disks you create will also work in standard CD-ROM drives. If you're shopping for a CD-R drive, you'll find one priced between U.S.$20 and U.S.$50. A blank CD-R disk typically costs less than U.S.$1.00 depending on the number included in the package.

Another variation of CD technology, **CD-RW** (CD-rewritable), allows you to write data to CD-RW disks, and later change the data that they contain. Most CD-R drives can also read and write CD-RW disks. Blank CD-RW disks are U.S.$1.00 each, just a bit more than CD-R disks. But CD-RW is not as heavily used as you might think. One reason is that most CD-RW disks must be formatted before use—a rather time-consuming process. Because the cost of CD-R disks has dropped, many users prefer to write to another CD-R, rather than use CD-RW disks, to save updated data.

Figure 12-6: CD-ROM drive speed is indicated as a multiple of the original single-speed drive. Today's 56X drives can access up to 8.4 MB of data in one second—a considerable speed improvement on the original drives, which accessed only 150 KB of data per second.

Speed Specification	Data Transfer Rate (per second)
Single-speed	150 KB
2X	300 KB
4X	600 KB
8X	1.2 MB
16X	2.4 MB
24X	3.6 MB
32X	4.8 MB
48X	7.2 MB
56X	8.4 MB

■Hardware
continued

DVD (Digital Video Disc) is a new type of storage and distribution media designed to replace VHS video tape. DVD has more than enough storage capacity for an entire feature-length film—up to 9 hours of video or 30 hours of CD-quality audio. DVDs can also store computer data. Although it is the same size as a CD-ROM disk, a DVD platter can hold far more data. Data can be stored on a DVD platter using one of four formats, as shown in Figure 12-7.

Figure 12-7: DVD storage capacity depends on whether data is stored on one or two sides of the disk, and how many layers of data each side contains.

Number of Sides	Number of Layers	Storage Capacity
1	1	4.7 GB
1	2	8.5 GB
2	1	9.4 GB
2	2	17.0 GB

DVD access rates of between 600 KB per second and 3.32 MB per second are slower than the latest generation of CD-ROM drives, but technological innovations allow them to provide similar video playback and database search speed. DVD technology does not currently provide any way to record data from your PC.

DVD players can access data from both CDs and CD-ROMs. The newest DVD players, called **DVD-2 drives**, can also access data from CD-R and CD-RW disks. Some PC manufacturers now include DVD drives as standard equipment, but software in DVD format remains somewhat limited. You might consider DVD when you purchase a new computer, but it is not necessary to replace the CD-ROM drive on your current PC with a DVD player.

Play It!

Figure 12-8: DVD technology looks and works much like CD technology. Click the PlayIt! button for a closer look at DVD.

■Hardware
continued

CDs and DVDs are examples of **optical storage technology**, which records data as a trail of tiny pits in the disk surface. The data that these pits represent can then be "read" with a beam of laser light. To manufacture a commercial CD or DVD platter, a special glass master disk stamps an imprint on reflective aluminum foil. The stamping process creates a series of microscopic pits in the foil that represent data. The foil is then bonded to the plastic disk that you insert into the player.

Optical storage media are very durable. Unlike magnetic media, such as floppy and hard disks, CD and DVD platters are not susceptible to humidity, dust, fingerprints, or magnets. If you spill Coke on a CD, simply rinse it off and your platter will be as good as new. CDs are not indestructible, however. You should be careful not to scratch the disk surface or expose the disk to high temperatures.

The data on CDs and DVDs is permanent—an advantage for archival storage when you intend to keep the data for many years. It is also a disadvantage because, with the exception of CD-RW technology, optical technology does not provide the flexibility of magnetic media for changing data once it has been stored. Magnetic media, such as hard, floppy, and Zip disks, allow you to easily and quickly modify stored data. Therefore, your PC's hard disk is the storage medium of choice for files that will be updated frequently—your documents, spreadsheets, and databases. Optical media are the choice for storing and distributing large data files that will remain relatively stable—a multimedia encyclopedia, a clip art collection, or last year's accounting data.

→| |← 1.6 microns

↕ .83 micron

→| |← .74 micron

↕ .4 micron

Figure 12-9: Optical media store data as a series of pits. The size and spacing of the pits determine the storage capacity of the disk.

The purple image is a magnification of the size and spacing of pits on the surface of a CD-ROM. The blue image illustrates the relative size and spacing of pits on a DVD-ROM.

With smaller pits and tighter spacing, a DVD-ROM stores a considerable amount more data than a CD-ROM.

A micron is one millionth of a meter.

∎Tutorial
How to make your own CDs

For professional software developers, small businesses, presenters, multimedia designers, desktop publishers, and home recording artists, CD-R and CD-RW technologies offer inexpensive, durable storage and distribution media. Using these media, however, is different from using a hard disk.

Windows XP ships with software that makes it easy to write data to CDs. If you are using an earlier version of Windows, or if you want more advanced options, you will need to use special **premastering software** to create your own CDs. Most premastering software also allows you to create an **image file** for better performance when burning CDs. In this tutorial, you'll use the Windows XP utilities to write to CD-R disks.

When you have completed the tutorial, you should:
- Be able to prepare files and write them to a CD using Windows XP.
- Understand how to use CD-RW disks.
- Understand how you would use premastering software to create a CD.

Figure 12-10: Click the PlayIt! button to begin the tutorial and learn how to create your own CDs. Estimated time: 10–15 minutes. Tracking Disk points: 10.

Gather the files that you want to include on your CD.

Use this option to write the files from the temporary location to the CD.

Who owns information about me?

There is an astounding amount of information stored about you in computer databases. Your bank has information on your financial status, credit history, and the people, organizations, and businesses to which you write checks. School records indicate something about your ability to learn and the subjects that interest you. Medical records indicate the state of your health. Credit card company records track the merchants with whom you deal and what you purchase in person, by mail, or over the Internet. Your phone company stores your phone number, your address, and a list of the phone numbers you dial. The driver's license bureau has your physical description. Your Internet cookies track many of the Web sites that you frequent. Using this data it would be possible to guess some very private things about you, such as your political views or even your sexual orientation.

When records were manually stored on index cards and in file folders, locating and distributing data was a laborious process that required hand transcriptions or photocopies of sheaves of papers. Today, this data appears in electronic format and is easy to access, copy, sell, ship, consolidate, and alter. Privacy advocates point out the potential for misusing data that has been collected and stored in computer databases. They are encouraging lawmakers to restrict the sale and distribution of information about individuals. One proposal would require your permission before information about you could be distributed.

The wisdom of such a proposal has been questioned, however, and not just by corporate interests. Information about you is not necessarily "yours." Although you might "reveal" information about yourself on an application form, other information about you is collected without your direct input. For example, suppose you default on your credit card payments. The credit card company has accumulated information on your delinquent status. Shouldn't it have the freedom to distribute this information, for example, to another credit card company? Balancing privacy with freedom of speech is a tricky issue for the Information Age.

What do you think?

1. Can you identify an actual incident when you discovered that data about you had been distributed without your approval?　　　　○ Yes　○ No　○ Not sure

2. Do you accurately fill out all the questionnaires that you encounter on the Web?　　　　○ Yes　○ No　○ Not sure

3. Do you think that you have a right to be consulted before anyone distributes information about you?　　　　○ Yes　○ No　○ Not sure

Save It!

QuickCheck A

1. A(n) [＿＿＿＿＿＿＿] database is able to link the records from two or more files and treat them as a single unit.

2. True or false? To access databases on the Web and CDs, you'll have to purchase database software. [＿＿＿＿]

3. To create your own databases, you must first design the file [＿＿＿＿＿＿＿] by specifying the names for each data field.

4. You can record and change data on [＿＿＿＿＿＿＿] disks, but you can read them only by using MultiRead CD-ROM drives.

5. CDs and DVDs are classified as [＿＿＿＿＿＿＿] storage technology because data is stored as a series of pits and read with a beam of laser light.

Check It!

QuickCheck B

Carefully examine the entries in the database. Give each record indicated by an arrow an **A** if it meets the criteria described on page 137 for accurate and consistent data. Otherwise, give it an **F**.

1. [＿＿]
2. [＿＿]
3. [＿＿]
4. [＿＿]
5. [＿＿]

Microsoft Access - [Equipment : Table]

File Edit View Insert Format Records Tools Window Help   Type a question for help

	Category	Company	Toll-Free Number	Purchase Date
1.	Computer	Dell	800-467-1255	8/30/2003
	Printer	Epson	800-377-0620	9/1/1998
2.	Softare	Microsoft	800-642-7050	9/1/1998
	Printer	Hewlett-Packard	888-439-5387	11/16/2001
	Computer	IBM	888-426-4260	3/27/1999
3.	Printer	I.B.M.	888-426-4260	8/12/1997
	Computer	IBM	888-426-4260	6/28/2003
4.	Computer	dell	888-655-8191	7/12/2003
	Software	Adobe	800-230-2320	6/20/2002
5.	Printers	Epson	800-377-0620	9/30/2004
	Computer	Compaq	800-467-1255	9/1/1998

Record: [I◄] [◄]   14   [►] [►I] [►✱] of 58

Company that created the product   NUM

start   2 Microsoft Office A...   10:53 AM

Check It!

Get It?

While using the BookOnCD, click the Get It? button to see if you can answer ten randomly selected questions from Chapter 12.

Get It?

Chapter 13
Working with Graphics

What's Inside?

You live in a world filled with strong visual images—kaleidoscopic MTV videos, photo-rich magazines, and lavishly illustrated Web sites. It is more important than ever to learn how to incorporate graphical images in the documents, presentations, and Web sites that you create. Chapter 13 will get you started.

What's on the CD?

▪FAQ What kinds of graphics can I work with on my PC?

The pictures that you can create, modify, store, download, and transmit using your PC are referred to as **graphics** or **images**. Graphics add visual interest to documents, worksheets, presentations, and Web pages.

Clip Art

If you have any "artistic genes" you'll probably enjoy creating artwork and illustrations using your PC. You don't, however, have to be an artist to spice up your projects with graphics. You can obtain ready-made images from a variety of sources. You'll find clip art collections containing thousands of professionally designed images on CDs and on the Web. You can use a scanning device to convert pictures from books and magazines into image files that you can manipulate on your PC. Even photos from your own collection can be converted into a computer-compatible format. You can also use a digital camera to take photos that don't require any conversion for use on your PC. When using images that you have not created, always make sure that you credit the source and adhere to any applicable copyright laws or licensing restrictions.

You'll typically work with two types of graphics on your PC: bitmap graphics and vector graphics. Understanding the difference between the two allows you to select the type of graphic that is best suited for a project. The rest of the FAQs in this chapter provide the basic information that you need to work with bitmap and vector graphics.

Figure 13-1: *A bitmap graphics image (upper left) has a distinctly different appearance than a vector graphics image (lower right). Click the PlayIt! button to view a gallery of bitmap and vector graphics.*

▪FAQ When should I use bitmap graphics?

Bitmap graphics, sometimes called "raster graphics," represent an image as a grid of colored dots. Because bitmap graphics produce photograph-like images, you would use them for photos, the images you add to Web pages, and pictures that you convert from paper to computer format. Bitmap graphics can be stored in a variety of file formats, including BMP, TIFF, GIF, and JPEG, and are easily converted from one format to another. To create and manipulate bitmap graphics, you would typically use **paint software**, such as Adobe Photoshop, Micrografx Picture Publisher, and Microsoft Paint.

Grab It!

Paint Software

The quality of an image depends on its resolution and color depth. The resolution of an image is expressed as the width and height of the grid that holds the dots. For example, an image with 1024 X 768 resolution is formed from a grid 1,024 dots wide and 768 dots high. High-resolution images exhibit details clearly. Each dot in an image is assigned a code number for its color. The number of bits required to store the color number is referred to as **color depth** and determines the number of colors that the image contains. A 1-bit color depth produces an image containing only two colors: black and white. An 8-bit color depth produces 256 colors. A 24-bit color depth produces 16.7 million colors, sometimes referred to as **true color**. The more colors an image contains, the more realistic it appears. However, an image with lots of colors requires lots of storage space. A true color image takes three times the amount of storage space as a 256-color image.

Play It!

Figure 13-2: Windows includes a basic bitmap graphics software program called Paint that you can access from the Accessories menu. Click the PlayIt! button to find out how to use Paint to create and modify graphics.

■FAQ How do I prepare graphics for Web pages?

Your goal is to keep Web graphics small so that they can be rapidly transmitted over the Internet and appear on screen as quickly as possible. "Small" refers to the size of the image file in bytes. Ideally, Web graphics files should be smaller than 20 KB. You can decrease file size by shrinking the physical dimensions of an image, saving it in a compressed file format, or reducing its color depth.

Shrinking the physical dimensions of an image allows you to reduce its file size. A 2" X 2" image can be stored in a file that is one-fourth the size of the same image at 4" X 4". Most graphics software provides the capability to "resize" or "scale" an image. If you're concerned that shrinking an image might eliminate important detail, consider using a thumbnail. A **thumbnail** is a miniature representation of an image that would typically link to a larger version of the image when clicked.

You can also use compression techniques to decrease the image file size. Some file formats provide built-in compression that reduces file size simply by using a more effective storage technique. For example, when stored in BMP or TIFF format, the image in Figure 13-3 requires about 950 KB of storage space. Stored in GIF format, the same image requires only 251 KB of storage space. Using JPEG format, the file size can be reduced to a mere 13 KB. When creating graphics for the Web, you should store them in GIF or JPEG format. If you want to work with graphics that have been stored in other file formats, you can use your graphics software to convert them to GIF or JPEG format.

A true color graphic requires 24 bits for each dot of color in an image, whereas a 16-color graphic requires only 4 bits. Therefore, by reducing the color depth from true color to 16-color, the image file shrinks to one-sixth of its original size. Unfortunately, reducing an image to only 16 colors can have alarming effects, as shown in the right-hand panel of Figure 13-3. A process called **dithering** can create the illusion of more colors by using dot patterns. For example, a pattern of red, yellow, and gray dots can create the illusion of skin color. As a rule of thumb, when preparing graphics for the Web, avoid true color. If the quality of a 16-color dithered graphic is acceptable, use it. Otherwise, convert the image to 256 colors.

Figure 13-3: The difference between a 256-color image (left), a dithered 16-color image (center), and a nondithered 16-color image (right) can be remarkable. Click PlayIt! to learn more about preparing graphics for the Web.

■FAQ When should I use vector graphics?

Vector graphics consist of a set of points, lines, arcs, and other geometrical shapes. Each shape is defined as a series of line segments called **vectors** and attributes, such as line width and fill color. A list of these vectors and attributes becomes essentially a set of instructions for redrawing the image. Vector graphics are ideal for diagrams, line drawings, and **computer-aided design** (CAD), the process of creating technical drawings and blueprints on a PC.

Vector graphics tend not to look like bitmap images. Two-dimensional vector graphics typically have large flat areas of color and more closely resemble line drawings than photographs. Vector graphics have three advantages. First, their files tend to be small because the vectors and attributes describing a shape can be stored very efficiently. Second, vector graphics can shrink or expand with no loss of quality. Third, the shapes in a vector graphic exist as individual objects that you can modify independently without affecting other parts of the image. You'll find many vector graphics files stored in Encapsulated PostScript (EPS) format and Windows Metafile (WMF) format. Popular CAD formats include DXF and DS4.

Grab It!

Drawing Software

Drawing software provides you with tools to create and manipulate vector graphics. Popular packages include Adobe Illustrator, CorelDRAW, and Deneba Canvas. **CAD software** includes AutoDesk AutoCAD, Cadopia IntelliCAD, and IMSI TurboCAD.

Play It!

Figure 13-4: Vector graphics are designed to work with layers of shapes. For example, each circle for the sun in this image is defined by its shape, position, color, and layer. Click PlayIt! to discover how to work with vector graphics.

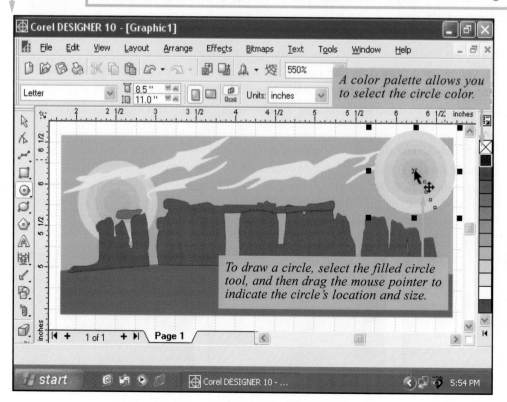

■FAQ How do I create 3-D graphics?

The **3-D graphics** you create on your PC contain one or more objects that appear three-dimensional. A **3-D object** not only looks three-dimensional, but also includes the data necessary to display and view it from any angle, viewpoint, or perspective. Composed of vectors, 3-D objects are typically created using the same drawing and CAD software as two-dimensional vector graphics.

To create a 3-D object, you first produce a line drawing called a **wireframe** by outlining every surface on the front, back, and inside of the object. Once the wireframe is complete, you can define the texture, transparency, and color for each of its surfaces. The process of applying surfaces to a wireframe, called **rendering**, is similar to draping a nylon tent covering over its frame. As part of the rendering process, you can specify a light source and your PC will automatically determine where to put highlights and shadows. This part of the rendering process is called **ray tracing** because your PC essentially traces the rays of light from the light source to the object.

Rendering is a complex activity that requires your PC to carry out extensive calculations. It can take minutes or hours, depending on the complexity of the objects, the speed of your PC, and the resolution of the completed image. Rendered 3-D graphics have a new-car-brochure look that's sometimes referred to as "super-realistic." Objects within the image are perfectly shaped and highly defined. Surfaces appear unflawed and brilliantly highlighted.

Figure 13-5: Click the PlayIt! button to learn how to construct a wireframe, render a 3-D object, and apply ray tracing.

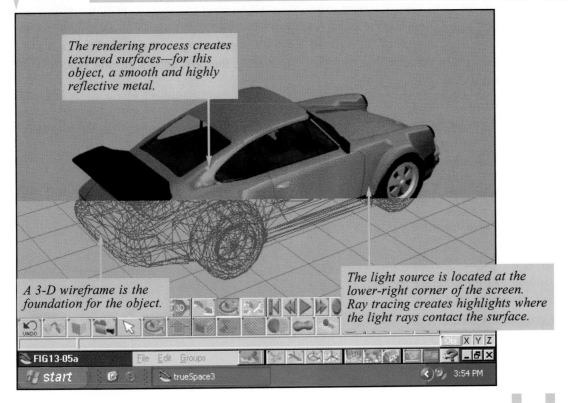

The rendering process creates textured surfaces—for this object, a smooth and highly reflective metal.

A 3-D wireframe is the foundation for the object.

The light source is located at the lower-right corner of the screen. Ray tracing creates highlights where the light rays contact the surface.

∎Hardware
Digitizing devices

Before you can work with images on your PC, they must exist in digital format. **Digitizing** is the process of converting an image into a series of 1s and 0s that your PC can store, transmit, and display. **Digitizing devices**, such as graphics tablets, scanners, and digital cameras, allow you to convert real objects, such as sketches and photos, into digital format. These fun-to-use devices can help you produce impressive results, even if you're not a professional artist.

A **graphics tablet** works like an electronic canvas. You use a pen-shaped **stylus** to "paint," and the movement of the stylus is picked up by the electronics in the pad, converted into a bitmap format, and displayed on the screen. The pad is sensitive not only to where you move, but also to the degree of pressure that you apply. When you press hard, you draw a thick, dark line. Lighter pressure produces a thinner, lighter line.

Some graphics software does not fully support the use of a graphics tablet. For example, although you can use the stylus to select tools and draw shapes in Microsoft Paint, this software does not recognize different pressures. If you are serious about using a graphics tablet, you will want to choose graphics software that specifically supports its features—select bitmap painting software rather than vector drawing software, and read the box to make sure it works with a graphics tablet or pressure-sensitive pen. Adobe Photoshop, Corel Painter, and Jasc Paint Shop Pro are good companion software packages for graphics tablets.

A graphics tablet typically connects to the serial port of your PC and requires the installation of special device driver software to establish communications with Windows. The price of a basic graphics tablet and stylus starts at U.S.$70. Prices go up from there and can exceed U.S.$500, depending on the size of the pad and the pen accessories that you select. Currently, the best sellers include Wacom's Intuos and Graphire tablets.

Figure 13-6: A graphics tablet is a fun addition to your PC for doodling, and an essential tool for serious artists. You can use the stylus to "paint" pictures. It also substitutes for a mouse to control the menus and tools of your graphics software.

■Hardware

continued

A **scanner** is a digitizing device that "reads" text, images, and bar codes. It is typically used to digitize flat objects, such as photos, newspaper clippings, and documents. These digitized images can be stored on your PC, modified, e-mailed to friends, or posted on the Web.

Among the many types of scanners, **flatbed scanners** that resemble small photocopiers are the most popular with PC owners. To use one, place the item you want to digitize face down on the scanner glass. Next, fire up your scanning software and select the resolution for the scan. Remember that higher resolutions produce sharper images, but can require a tremendous amount of storage space on your PC. For Web graphics, a scan at 300 dpi is usually sufficient. For images that you plan to print, you should use a much higher scan resolution, typically 600 or 1200 dpi. Once the actual scan begins, the digitizing process typically takes several minutes to complete. If you're satisfied with the results displayed on your PC's screen, you can save the image as a file, which you can then manipulate with any paint software.

Scanners are surprisingly inexpensive. You can purchase a serviceable basic unit for about U.S.$49. Most scanners are easy to connect—you just plug them in to a USB port.

Scanners are typically bundled with several types of software. The scanner's device driver software, which establishes communication between the scanner and Windows, must be installed when you connect the scanner. **Scanning software** allows you to preview a scan, select a resolution, and initiate the scan from your PC. **OCR (optical character recognition) software** allows you to convert a scanned image, such as a newspaper clipping, into a text file that you can edit with a word processor. The accuracy of today's OCR software is fairly high, but not perfect. Therefore, it is a good idea to use a spelling checker and proofread documents produced by OCR software.

Figure 13-7: When preparing to scan an image, use your software's preview feature to ensure that your photo or document is squarely aligned on the scanner. Specify the part of the image that you want to scan, then select a resolution that produces a sharp image, but WITH a manageable file size.

■Hardware
continued

A **digital camera** takes photos and stores them as bitmap images, instead of capturing them on film. When paired with a color ink jet printer and your PC, a digital camera puts you in control of the entire picture taking process—from snapping the picture to printing the final image or posting it on the Web. A digital camera resembles its film-based counterparts, and taking pictures is just as easy. Basically, you point and shoot.

After finishing your photo shoot, you must transfer the photos to your PC. You can plug your camera into the USB port on your computer, then use Windows Explorer to copy the photos to your hard disk drive. If your computer includes slots that can accept the type of memory card used in your camera, you can remove the card from your camera and insert it into the memory slot of your PC. The process of transferring images from your camera to the hard disk drive of your PC can take several minutes, depending on the number of photos you've taken and the size of the files. As the images are transferred, they're stored as files on your PC. You can open these image files using most paint or photo editing software.

Manufacturers of digital cameras include familiar names, such as Canon, FujiFilm, Nikon, Olympus, Eastman Kodak, and Minolta. Prices depend on the camera's resolution, which is typically measured in **megapixels** or the number of dots or pixels contained in each photo. The quality of digital photos has increased dramatically over the past few years, while prices have plummeted. With the increased capabilities of digital cameras, combined with the excellent output from color inkjet printers, even professional photographers are switching from film to digital photography.

Basic digital cameras, priced under U.S.$200, feature resolutions of between 2 and 3 megapixels. These cameras are suitable for capturing images for use on the Web and for casual printouts. Mid-range digital cameras, priced at U.S.$200 to U.S.$1,000, provide resolutions from 3 to 7 megapixels, resulting in very high quality photos.

Figure 13-8: Click the PlayIt! button to learn how to produce your own digital photos. This video takes you through the entire process. You'll find out how to take the photo, transfer it from your camera to your PC, save it, and print it.

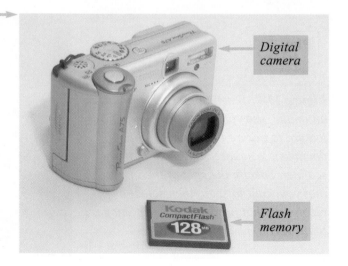

▪Tutorial
How to edit a digital photo

Grab It!

Photo Editing Software

Photo editing software is a specialized type of paint software that provides a set of tools for manipulating and retouching digital photographs. It can rescue pictures that are washed out, too dark, too bright, and out of focus. It even eliminates those poltergeist-like red eyes caused by your camera's flash mechanism.

You can use photo editing software to have some fun with your photographs. For example, you can turn current photos into old-fashioned tin-types. Or you can go for a "Pleasantville look" by hand-coloring parts of black-and-white photos. You can delete unwanted objects from a photo or create an entirely new reality by superimposing objects on backgrounds—like pasting your dog on a lunar landscape. For this tutorial, you'll use Microsoft Picture It! to learn about photo editing.

When you have completed the tutorial, you should be able to:
- Erase "red eye," adjust lighting, and sharpen a photo image.
- Add or remove objects from a photo.
- Change the size and orientation of a photo.
- Apply special effects to change the appearance of a photo.

Play It!

Figure 13-9: Can this photo be rescued? Click the PlayIt! button to begin the tutorial and learn how to use photo editing software. Estimated time: 10–15 minutes. Tracking Disk points: 10.

Shoes, UFOs, and Forrest Gump

The highly publicized O. J. Simpson murder trial was followed by an equally high-profile wrongful-death suit. Introduced into evidence were a bloody footprint from the crime scene made by a size 12 designer shoe, and a photo of Mr. Simpson wearing such a shoe. Conclusive evidence of guilt? Not according to the defense attorney, who raised doubts about the photo's authenticity.

Faked photos are not a product of the digital age. Long before the first digital cameras, tabloid newspapers in supermarket checkout lanes carried blurry photos allegedly depicting UFOs, the Loch Ness monster, and so on. In those days, most people had confidence that experts could detect photos doctored by amateurs or even by professionals—the deception discovered by a missing shadow, an obvious trace of cut and paste, or inconsistencies in coloration. In today's digital world, however, it is possible to alter the individual dots in a photo. When done carefully, these alterations can be difficult or even impossible to detect. Sure, it can be innocent fun, like when you digitally paste your roommate's head onto a picture of the Three Stooges. Unfortunately, it also introduces a note of uncertainty into the evidence we rely on to form opinions of everyday events and life-and-death situations, such as a murder trial or war crimes investigation.

Even videotapes, once virtually impossible to alter, can today be digitized and doctored. In the film *Forrest Gump*, digital editing techniques were used to paste the star, Tom Hanks, into authentic newsreels of past events—Forrest Gump meets with President Kennedy and history appears to be changed. In *Simone* (2002), Al Pacino is a desperate director who uses a computer-generated actress as his leading lady. The unknowing audience causes Simone ("Simulation One") to rise to stardom. Pacino's character quips, "Our ability to manufacture fraud now exceeds our ability to detect it." Living in a digital world, it is important to consider how you can responsibly evaluate the images that you see in newspapers, on television, and at the movies.

What do you think?

1. In your opinion, should photos and videotapes be allowed as evidence in civil and criminal trials? ○ Yes ○ No ○ Not sure

2. Do you think that it would be possible for someone to use doctored photos and video-tapes to convince people that a fake event actually took place? ○ Yes ○ No ○ Not sure

3. Do you have a set of criteria for judging the authenticity of newspaper and TV images? ○ Yes ○ No ○ Not sure

Save It!

QuickCheck A

1. An image with 8-bit [_____] can contain up to 256 colors.

2. True or false? To prepare an image for Web use, you should store it in true color BMP format. [_____]

3. [_____] graphics are stored as a set of instructions for recreating the shapes and attributes of an image.

4. To create 3-D graphics, you can use drawing software or [_____] software.

5. The part of the rendering process that creates highlights and shadows for a 3-D object is called [_____]. (Tip: The answer contains two words.)

> **Check It!**

QuickCheck B

There is only one way to correctly match the five objects pictured at right to the five descriptions below. Indicate the correct letter for each description.

1. A wireframe [_____]

2. A vector graphic [_____]

3. A bitmap graphic [_____]

4. A dithered image [_____]

5. A rendered image [_____]

> **Check It!**

Get It?

While using the BookOnCD, click the Get It? button to see if you can answer ten randomly selected questions from Chapter 13.

> **Get It?**

Chapter 14

Recording and Editing Sound

What's Inside?

Sounds, such as music and speech, are important features of your environment, so it seems natural for PCs to use sound to provide feedback, entertainment, and education. In Chapter 14, you'll learn how your PC generates sound and how to incorporate sound in your own projects.

What's on the CD?

Because sound is the topic of Chapter 14, you'll get the most benefit from these screen tours and videos if your PC is equipped with a sound card and speakers (or headphones).

■FAQ How does sound capability enhance my PC?

Your computer generates sound using a hardware device called a **sound card**, which then routes the sound to headphones or speakers. Sound cards are standard equipment on most of today's PCs. Sound adds a new dimension to your computing experience. Beeps and other sound effects can provide you with feedback as you use your PC. For example, when you click a button that isn't available, a beep might inform you that the action cannot be performed. Music lovers can connect to their favorite music store on the Web and listen to sample tracks. Sound effects can enliven once-dull business presentations. Children can listen while their PCs read stories. Computer game enthusiasts can hear a riot of sound effects as monsters attack, grenades explode, and tanks rumble past. Individuals with visual disabilities can also gain access to computers through technology that reads aloud the content of a PC screen.

Computers work with two general categories of sound: digitized sound and synthesized sound. **Digitized sound** is a recording of real music, vocals, sound effects, or speech that has been converted into electronic signals, which a computer can then store, manipulate, and transmit. **Synthesized sound** has not been recorded from a live source, but instead has been generated by a machine such as a computer. Each category of sound has its unique characteristics and applications. With a little background information on digitized and synthesized sound, you can select the one that is most suitable for your projects.

Figure 14-1: Click the PlayIt! button to take a journey through a PC sound-scape. Note: To get the most out of this tour, your computer should be equipped with a sound card and speakers (or headphones).

▪FAQ How does my PC record, store, and play digital sound?

To digitally capture sound, you need a microphone, a sound card, and sound software. After you start the software, simply point the microphone at the sound source, and click the software's record button. You can save your digital recording in sound formats such as WAVE (.wav), AUDIO (.au), RealAudio (.ra), VOICE (.voc), and MP3 (.mp3).

You probably know that a sound consists of energy waves, which your ears and brain convert into the voices, music, and assorted sound effects that you hear. A sound wave provides information about a sound. The height of a wave indicates volume, technically called sound **amplitude**. The time between wave peaks indicates the sound's **frequency**—that is, whether it is a high note or a low note.

To digitally store a sound wave, your PC periodically records a **sample** of the wave and stores code numbers for its amplitude. The sequence of samples is then stored as a sound file. The more times your PC samples the wave per second, the more accurately it can reproduce that wave. Sampling rates are measured in KHz (kilohertz), where 1 KHz is 1,000 samples per second. An 11 KHz sampling rate produces fairly realistic digitized human speech. Music, however, requires sampling rates of 22 KHz or 44 KHz for good fidelity. Each sample uses two bytes of storage space, so noncompressed digital sound files are BIG! One second of digitally recorded music requires more than 88 KB of storage space.

Figure 14-2: *At higher sampling rates, digital sound samples (shown in green) more closely follow the shape of the sound wave (shown in purple). Click the PlayIt! buttons to compare the sound quality at each sampling rate.*

Play It!

11 KHz

Play It!

22 KHz

Play It!

44 KHz

■FAQ How does speech synthesis work?

Speech synthesis is the process by which machines, such as computers, produce sound that resembles spoken words. Most speech synthesizers string together basic sound units called **phonemes**. For example, the phonemes "reh" and "gay" would produce the word "reggae."

A speech synthesis system typically includes text-to-speech software and synthesizing hardware. **Text-to-speech software** examines the text stored in a file, displayed on the screen, or entered from the keyboard, then breaks it down into a series of sounds that can be output. **Synthesizing hardware** consists of a sound card or other device that can generate speech or musical sounds.

Grab It!

Screen Readers

Unlike digitized speech, synthesized speech can theoretically produce any words or phrases—not just those that you have recorded. Though not a mainstream PC technology, synthesized speech is ideal for applications that require a computer to generate spoken responses to typed or voice input. It provides the underlying technology for voice-response systems, such as telephone directory assistance. It may be instrumental in integrating voice and e-mail, so that you can phone your voice mail system and hear not only your voice mail messages, but also your computer e-mail. Perhaps most important, a speech synthesizer's ability to read a computer screen aloud is the key that unlocks access to PCs and to the Internet for individuals with visual disabilities.

Play It!

Figure 14-3: Using speech synthesis software, your PC can generate speech using a standard sound card. Click PlayIt! to tour a Web site that demonstrates the quality of synthesized speech.

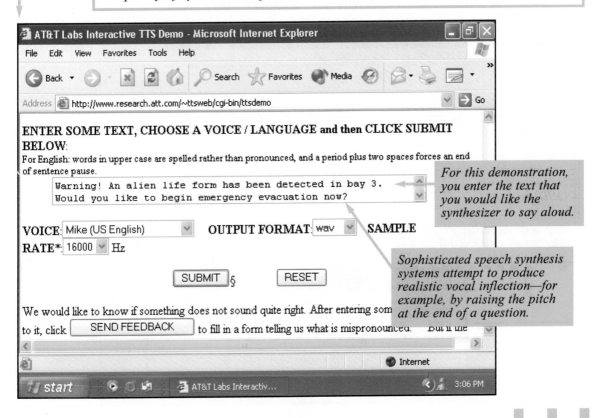

For this demonstration, you enter the text that you would like the synthesizer to say aloud.

Sophisticated speech synthesis systems attempt to produce realistic vocal inflection—for example, by raising the pitch at the end of a question.

■FAQ What should I know about MIDI?

MIDI (musical instrument digital interface) specifies a standard way to store music data for synthesizers, electronic MIDI instruments, and computers. Unlike digital sound files, which contain digitized recordings of real sounds, MIDI files contain a set of instructions, called **MIDI messages**, for synthesizing music based on the pitch, volume, and duration of each note made by each instrument. Digital sound is analogous to a tape recording, whereas MIDI music is like a player piano roll that produces notes based on the position of punched holes. MIDI is suitable for instrumental music, but not for vocals because of the complexity of synthesizing the human voice singing lyrics. Its advantage lies in its ability to store lengthy musical sequences in a small file. Three minutes of MIDI music might require only 10 KB of disk space, compared to 1,500 KB for three minutes of digitized music.

Most sound cards allow you to capture music from a MIDI instrument, as well as generate music from MIDI files. However, making MIDI music is not as simple as pointing a microphone at a musician. To create MIDI music, you must assume the role of composer. Special MIDI software helps you enter the notes for your composition on a musical staff or capture the musical themes you play on any MIDI instrument. You can then edit your composition by assigning the notes to different instruments, adding harmony, and inserting a percussion track. Basic MIDI software is often bundled with your sound card. Professional musicians typically prefer to use full-featured MIDI software, such as Cakewalk Pro Audio or Coda Finale.

Figure 14-4: *To find out what it's like to compose MIDI music, click the PlayIt! button. Note: To get the most out of this tour, your computer should be equipped with a sound card and speakers (or headphones).*

How do I add sound clips to presentations and Web pages?

Before you can use a sound clip, it must exist as a digitized sound file or as a MIDI file. You can, of course, create your own compositions by recording voices, music, and sound effects or by composing MIDI music. You can also find collections of sound files on the Web and CDs. Before using a sound file that you have not composed yourself, make sure that you have permission to use it. Most sound clip collections clearly specify your rights for using the sound clips they contain. When in doubt, request permission via e-mail or written letter.

To incorporate sound in presentations, check your presentation software documentation for a list of acceptable file formats. Unlike graphics, which are easily converted from one file format to another, it can be difficult to convert sound files. For example, MIDI files don't easily convert to WAVE files. You should capture or create sound files in a format that works with your presentation software.

For the Web, WAVE and MIDI are standard file formats. Remember that the people who receive your Web pages must have software on their PCs to play your sound files. You can typically expect them to have basic WAVE and MIDI capability. If you use other file formats, their Web browsers might need a special software module called a **plug-in** to play your sound files. They can typically obtain the necessary plug-in from the Web site hosted by the publisher that created the file format. For example, the RA plug-in can be obtained at the RealAudio site.

Figure 14-5: Click the PlayIt! button to learn how to play sound from Web pages and add sound to your own Web pages.

■Hardware
Sound devices

Most PCs today include a basic **sound system** with a sound card, speakers, and possibly a microphone. If you're not satisfied with the quality of sound produced by your PC, consider replacing one or more components of your sound system.

A sound card is a circuit board that typically plugs into an expansion slot on the motherboard (also called system board) of your PC. It provides connectors for a microphone and speakers (or headphones) so that you can record and play back sound. It also provides a joystick port that doubles as a port for MIDI instruments. Most sound cards support both digitized sound and MIDI music. Manufacturers of popular sound cards include Creative Labs, Yamaha, and Turtle Beach Systems. Prices range from U.S.$30 to U.S.$200, depending on the features.

Because a sound card generates the sound that your PC's speakers output, its performance affects the quality of the sound you hear. For playing games, using most business software, and browsing the Web, just about any basic sound card will produce adequate fidelity. However, if you're really serious about sound or you intend to record sound for professional use, a basic card might not meet your needs. You can shop around and find comparative reviews of sound cards in computer magazines or on the Web.

To produce digitized sound, your sound card simply reproduces the digital samples stored in the sound file. The quality of digitized sound that a sound card can generate is affected by several factors. Most basic, perhaps, is its **frequency response**—the range of frequencies or notes that it can reproduce. A frequency response range of 20 to 48,000 Hz is common and includes most of the sounds audible to the human ear.

To produce MIDI music, your sound card receives messages from a MIDI file, listing notes and the type of musical instrument that plays each note. To translate these MIDI messages into music, sound cards use one of two techniques: FM synthesis or wavetable synthesis. **FM synthesis** creates sound waves, essentially from scratch, that imitate as closely as possible the sound of different musical instruments. According to a recent article on the popular MIDI Farm Web site, "FM is Dead!" Indeed, most sound card manufacturers seem to have abandoned FM synthesis in favor of a newer, more realistic-sounding technology.

Wavetable synthesis generates music by patching together a set of sounds that were prerecorded as individual notes from actual instruments. This set of sounds is sometimes referred to as a **patch set**. The larger the patch set, the more realistic the sound. Most experts agree that wavetable synthesis produces better-quality sound than FM synthesis. If you want the most realistic-sounding MIDI music, look for a sound card that features wavetable synthesis with many "voices" in its wavetable. For example, a 256-voice wavetable produces better-quality MIDI sound than a sound card with a 64-voice wavetable.

∎Hardware
continued

A sound card outputs sound to speakers or headphones. The speaker-headphone port is built into the edge of the sound card that peeks out of an opening at the back of your PC's system unit. Usually, this port is labeled "line out" or "speakers." If the ports on your sound card are not labeled, refer to the documentation to find out which one to use. Note also that your PC's CD-ROM drive might contain a headphone port designed for listening to audio CDs. On most PCs, however, the CD headphone port will not produce sounds from computer CDs. To hear the sound from CD encyclopedias, for example, you must typically use the speaker-headphone port at the back of the PC system unit.

You're probably familiar with the Bose ads in which a guy listening to speakers is literally being blown away by the sound. Reality seems to be approaching this audio nirvana as speaker and sound card manufacturers introduce new technologies such as surround sound, 3-D sound, and environmental sound. You can check your favorite computer magazine or audio Web site for information on the newest speaker technology.

Although speakers can't improve the quality of sound that your sound card generates, cheap speakers can degrade it. As a rule of thumb, you should purchase a speaker system to match the quality of your sound card. If you're using a basic U.S.$40 sound card, basic U.S.$20 speakers should suffice. With a U.S.$100 mid-range sound card, use speakers that cost about the same. If you have a high-end U.S.$200 sound card, you're probably serious about your sound system and you should look for speakers in the same price range.

Most speaker systems include two speaker units for stereo sound. Many mid-range and high-end systems also include a third unit called a subwoofer that produces enhanced bass sound. Speaker manufacturers include familiar names in the audio business: Altec Lansing, Bose, Philips, and Roland.

Figure 14-6: A sound card is the basic building block of your PC's sound system. It plugs into the system unit of your PC and contains a "mic" port, a "line out" port for speakers or headphones, and a joystick port that doubles as a MIDI port.

■Hardware
continued

A sound card receives input from a microphone or MIDI instrument. If your PC came bundled with a sound system, an inexpensive microphone was probably part of the package. If you're not picky about sound quality, you'll find the bundled microphone suitable for "radio-quality" voice recording and sound effects destined for Web pages or presentations. For multimedia or professional audio projects—and even for computer karaoke—you'll want to shop for a better-quality "mic." You can connect most standard vocal and instrumental microphones to a computer sound card—you don't need to shop for a special "computer microphone." You must also generally purchase a cable that connects the microphone to the sound card or USB port on your PC.

You can also add a MIDI instrument to your PC sound system. A **MIDI instrument** is an electronic device that synthesizes music, usually based on sophisticated wavetables. Before PC sound cards offered high-quality wavetables, the only way to produce decent MIDI sound was to funnel MIDI messages out to a MIDI instrument. Today, musicians continue to use MIDI instruments to supplement a PC sound card and to input notes during the process of composing MIDI music. The most popular MIDI instrument is a piano-like keyboard, called a **MIDI keyboard**. Nowadays, a MIDI keyboard is a standard piece of gear for recording studios, and for the personal computer systems of rock, jazz, and even classical musicians.

MIDI keyboard prices vary from a few hundred dollars to a few thousand dollars. Even if you want only a basic keyboard, most MIDI experts suggest that you shop for one with "full-size" keys (the same size as those on a piano), a four octave range, and velocity-sensitive keys that emulate the feeling of real piano keys. MIDI keyboard manufacturers include Korg, Roland, and Yamaha. A visit to their Web sites can provide lots of information about features and pricing.

Figure 14-7: Just think of "piano lessons" on a MIDI keyboard! You can save your best practice session as a MIDI file and play it back for your piano teacher or while you're playing computer games. Parents, don't forget to watch your children when they claim to be practicing!

■Tutorial
How to work with digitized sound

Windows includes a program module called Sound Recorder that lets you record, save, edit, and play digitized sound. It is very basic software for manipulating sound files, but it nicely illustrates how to work with digitized sound on your PC.

To access the Sound Recorder, click the Start button, point to All Programs, point to Accessories, then point to Entertainment.

The user interface is very simple. A series of VCR-like buttons at the bottom of the Sound Recorder window start and stop the playback, fast-forward and rewind a sound segment, and start the record mode. The sound wave that you're recording or playing is displayed in a small window.

When you have completed the tutorial, you should be able to:
■ Open a WAVE file and play it.
■ Make a digital voice recording at a selected sampling rate.
■ Edit a sound file.

Figure 14-8: Click the PlayIt! button to begin the tutorial and learn how to record, save, play, and edit digital sound files. Estimated time: 15–20 minutes. Tracking Disk points: 10.

▪Issue
RIAA vs. MP3

MP3
Software

Technology rocked the music world with the release of a music compression file format called **MP3**. MP3 stores digitized music files on computer disks in such a way that the sound quality is excellent, but the file size remains relatively small—small enough to easily download from the Web. Famous performing artists and rock-star wannabes can use MP3 files to post sample sound tracks from their albums on Web sites. It is inexpensive marketing. Fans can download a song or two and, if they like the music, they will (theoretically) purchase the entire CD.

MP3 created demand for software products, called **CD rippers**, that allow you to grab music tracks from an audio CD and store them in MP3 format. You just place an audio CD in your PC's CD-ROM drive, fire up the CD ripper software, and select the tracks you would like to store. The CD ripper stores the selected tracks in MP3 format on a hard or floppy disk. You can then play the tracks on your PC. If you have a CD-R drive, you can even create your own CD containing a collection of your favorite songs. Pop this CD in a DiscMan and listen to your tunes anywhere.

What if you don't have a CD-R drive, and you want to listen to your favorite MP3 files when you're away from your PC? Diamond Multimedia Systems created a solution—a portable, palm-size device called Rio that plays MP3 files. You could transfer your MP3 music from your PC to the Rio. Unhook the cable and voila!—your MP3 music is portable. The Record Industry Association of America (RIAA) saw MP3 and the Rio as a threat to their business and filed suit to stop Diamond Multimedia from releasing the Rio. The courts eventually ruled that Diamond could release the Rio, but the recording industry is still actively trying to find a way to limit distribution of copyrighted songs via MP3 players.

MP3 was designed for use with music from CDs that you have purchased or from files that you have downloaded from authorized Web sites. However, as the Record Industry Association of America (RIAA) points out, MP3 does not prevent illegal duplication, sales, or distribution of copyrighted music, which can lead to rampant copyright infringement.

What do you think?

1. When you purchase a music CD, do you believe that you should have the right to con-vert it into any format (such as cassette tape or MP3) for your own use? ⭘Yes ⭘ No ⭘ Not sure

2. Do you believe that Rio and MP3 would be more attractive to music pirates than cassette tape? ⭘ Yes ⭘ No ⭘ Not sure

3. Do you think that it should be illegal to sell an MP3 device, such as Rio? ⭘ Yes ⭘ No ⭘ Not sure

Save
It!

QuickCheck A

1. For the clearest, most realistic digital recording, you should use a sampling rate of [   ] KHz.

2. Digital sound is analogous to a tape recording, whereas [   ] music is more like a player piano roll.

3. [   ] synthesis generates music by patching together sounds from a set of prerecorded notes from actual instruments.

4. Windows Sound Recorder software plays, records, and stores digital sound in the popular [   ] file format.

5. True or false? MP3 is a compressed digital sound format. [   ]

Check It!

QuickCheck B

Click the Sound buttons to listen to each sound, then match it with the correct description below:

1. Synthesized voice [   ]

2. Digitized voice at 11 KHz sampling rate [   ]

3. Digitized voice at 44 KHz sampling rate [   ]

4. Digitized music [   ]

5. MIDI music [   ]

Sound A

Sound B

Sound C

Sound D

Sound E

To use this QuickCheck, your PC must be equipped with a sound card and speakers (or headphones).

Check It!

Get It?

While using the BookOnCD, click the Get It? button to see if you can answer ten randomly selected questions from Chapter 14.

Get It?

Chapter 15

Creating Desktop Video and Animation

What's Inside?

Today, people are so accustomed to watching moving images on TV that static computer screens somehow seem unsatisfying. Chapter 15 provides information on desktop video and animation that can spark up Web pages, presentations, and even business software.

What's on the CD?

Wear your director's beret and ascot for Chapter 15. When you've completed the screen tours and videos, you'll be shouting, "Lights! Camera! Action!"

■FAQ How do I equip my PC to play video?

The hardware and software necessary to play a video depend on the video source. As you know from Chapter 12, you can watch videos from DVD disks on your computer's screen if your PC is equipped with a DVD drive. Watching broadcast TV, cable TV, or video tape on your PC requires a hardware device called a **TV tuner card** that converts signals designed for a TV into signals useable by your PC's display device. Most TV tuner cards plug into the motherboard (or system board) of a PC. Accompanying software allows you to change channels and display the TV signal in a resizable area of your PC's screen.

Desktop videos—those accessed from a CD, your PC's hard disk, or a Web page—require no specialized hardware, but do need a software **player** that's designed to work with the file format in which the video is stored. Players for most video file formats are available at no cost on the Web. Popular desktop video file formats include **MPEG** (.mpg), **Video for Windows** (.avi), and **QuickTime** (.mov). Desktop videos that you access from the Web often require lengthy transfer times; depending on the video technology at the Web site, you might have to wait for the entire video to download before you can watch it. To eliminate this wait, many Web sites now use **streaming video** technology that plays the video while it downloads. You don't have to wait for streaming video, but the playback might be somewhat choppy without a fast Internet connection. Streaming video requires a plug-in that tells your Web browser how to transfer and display the video data.

Figure 15-1: Microsoft Windows includes Media Player software for MPEG and Video for Windows. Click the PlayIt! button to find out how to use its start, stop, and seek controls to view desktop videos.

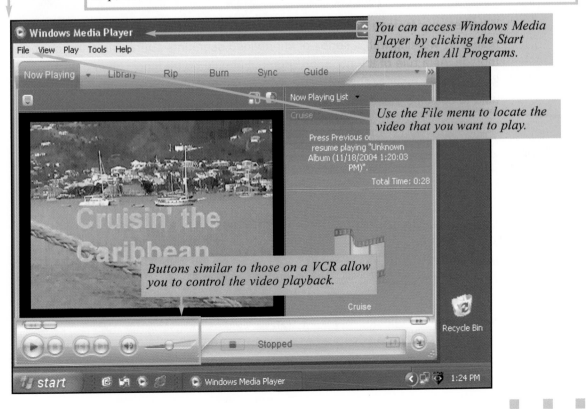

You can access Windows Media Player by clicking the Start button, then All Programs.

Use the File menu to locate the video that you want to play.

Buttons similar to those on a VCR allow you to control the video playback.

■FAQ Can I create my own desktop video?

You can create your own desktop video, which you then distribute on CDs, video tape, or the Web. Desktop video production is not as difficult as you might think. With very little effort, you can create all kinds of videos for personal and professional use, such as a video scrapbook of your children or grandchildren, a digital wedding album, a desktop sales video, or a video holiday greeting. The equipment needed and the procedures for creating desktop video depend on whether your original footage comes from a nondigital source or a digital source.

Suppose that your video footage originates from a nondigital source, such as a VHS camcorder or a VCR tape. As explained in the previous FAQ, a TV tuner card allows you to watch video tape on your computer screen. However, to "capture" video from a nondigital source in preparation for editing, you'll need a different device. A **video capture device** digitizes video footage by taking periodic "snapshots" from the video, converting each snapshot into a bitmap graphic, and then storing the series of bitmap graphics in a computer file. The documentation for your PC's video card should explain whether it includes video capture capabilities. If it does not, you must purchase a separate video capture device, available either as a card that plugs into your PC's motherboard, or as a small unit that plugs into your PC's USB or FireWire port. You control the digitizing process by using **video capture software** supplied with your video capture device. Video capture software allows you to select the display size, frame rate, length, and file format for your digitized segments.

Footage from a digital source, such as a digital video camera or digital video tape, already exists in digital format. You can buy a high-speed **1394 communications link**, popularly known as "FireWire," to transfer this digital video data directly from the video source to your PC.

Whether your footage originates in nondigital or digital format, you'll get the best results by working with a series of short video segments containing only your best footage. As a rule of thumb, each segment should be no longer than one minute to keep file size manageable and to provide good flexibility for editing. You'll later be able to combine these segments and create longer videos.

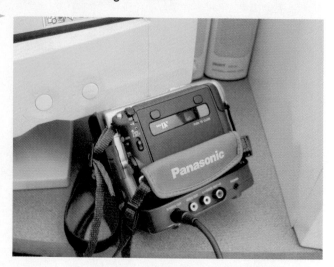

Play It!

Figure 15-2: Click the PlayIt! button to take a tour of desktop video production. Learn how to shoot footage, connect your digital camera to a video capture card, and select the footage that you want to digitize.

■FAQ How do I edit a digital video?

The process of capturing and digitizing video segments produces several large files, each containing about a minute of action. **Video editing software** helps you cut out unwanted frames, add special effects to any segment, assemble segments into the sequence of your choice, overlay a soundtrack, and designate transitions from one segment to the next. Popular video editing software includes Adobe Premiere, Ulead Systems VideoStudio, and Pinnacle Studio.

Your completed video will consist of audio tracks containing voices and music, plus video tracks containing video segments and transitions. To begin the editing process, open your video editing software and import the files that contain any video and audio clips you'll need for the final video. Once imported, you'll be able to drag these clips onto a timeline that represents the video stream. Your video editing software also allows you to insert predefined transition effects that control the way one clip blends into another—for example, by fading, flipping, overlaying, or simply cutting to the next scene. To complete your video, you can add titles and other special effects.

Video editing software also allows you to preview your entire video production, complete with sound and transitions. When you're satisfied with your work, you can select a video file format, choose a compression format, then save the video. The next FAQ explains how compression affects the quality of your finished video.

Figure 15-3: Click the PlayIt! button to learn the basic steps of video editing: importing video and sound clips, arranging the clips in sequence, selecting transition effects, and previewing the final masterpiece.

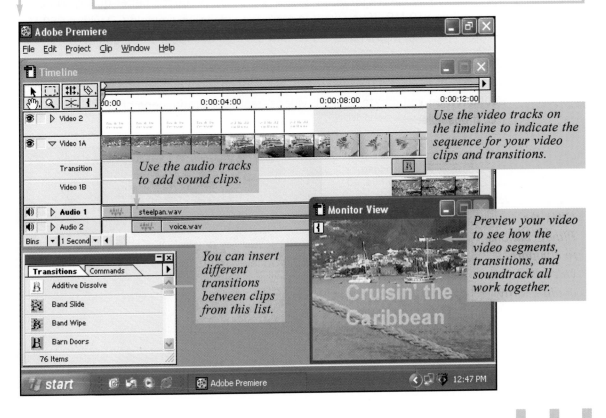

■FAQ How does compression affect desktop video quality?

Each frame of a digitized video is essentially a full-screen, true color graphic. When stored in an uncompressed format, a single frame would require about 900 KB of storage space. The series of 30 such frames necessary for one second of high-quality video would consume nearly 27 MB of storage space. Therefore, to display this one second of video, your PC would have to read and process 27 MB of data in one second—not practical with today's technology. You can whittle this enormous amount of video data down to a more manageable size by using one or more of the following methods:

■ Shrinking the video to one-quarter or one-eighth of the size of your PC screen.
■ Reducing the number of frames displayed per second.
■ Selecting a **compression technique**, such as MPEG, Indeo, Cinepak, or Video 1, that reduces the amount of data in each frame or stores only the data that has changed from one frame to the next.

With today's PC technology, desktop video production necessitates a tradeoff between quality and file size. Video can be compressed into a small file that downloads from the Web in a reasonable amount of time and occupies a manageable amount of storage space. Unfortunately, a highly compressed video typically looks blurry and has "scratchy" sound. On the other hand, using a different compression technique to create better-quality video often produces a larger file.

When you produce desktop videos, you must balance quality factors against file size as you select a compression technique. For example, you might discover that Indeo compression at 15 frames per second stores a collection of videos in 620 MB. Cinepak compression at the same frame rate produces better-quality video, but requires 850 MB. If you want to store the videos on a single CD with a 650 MB storage limit, you might have to live with the less desirable video quality.

Unfortunately, some older, slower computers cannot keep up with the processing demands of even compressed video, resulting in jerky motion and unsynchronized sound. When you create desktop videos, test your productions on an "average" PC, if possible.

Figure 15-4:
Click the
PlayIt! buttons
to compare
video and
audio quality
produced by
different
compression
settings.

Indeo video
Frame rate: 15
Compression: 0
File size: 1,072 KB

Indeo video
Frame rate: 5
Compression: 0
File size: 466 KB

Indeo video
Frame rate: 15
Compression: 50
File size: 503 KB

Video 1
Frame rate: 15
Compression: 0
File size: 6,959 KB

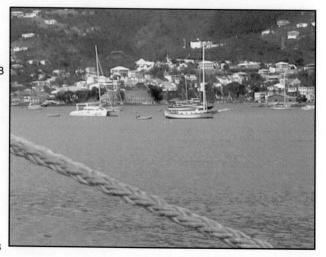

▪FAQ How do I create and play an animation?

In elementary school, you probably played with a "flip book" containing drawings of a cartoon character. When you quickly fanned through the pages, the cartoon character appeared to move. Computer animation works on the same principle as a flip book. You create a series of images, each showing a "freeze frame" from a scene in motion. You then compile these scenes into an animation, which you save as a single file in an animation file format such as FLC, known as "Flick." To play the animation, you use the appropriate player software for the animation file format.

Although you can create the individual frames for an animation using almost any bitmap, 3-D, or vector graphics software, you must use animation software to compile the frames into an animated sequence. Consequently, most animators prefer to use an animation software package for the entire process. Adobe After Effects, NewTek LightWave 3D, and Poser by Curious Labs are popular options.

Grab It!

GIF Animation Software

Web page designers tend to use a unique set of animation tools and formats. The most popular format for Web page animation, called **animated GIF**, is a series of graphics stored in GIF format, then compiled with GIF animator software. The resulting files require relatively few bytes of storage space, so they can be transmitted quickly over the Internet. Each frame for the animation arrives on your computer screen separated by the few seconds required for transmission. Once all frames have arrived, the animation cycles smoothly from one frame to the next.

Play It!

Figure 15-5: Click the PlayIt! button to find out how to create animated GIFs for Web pages.

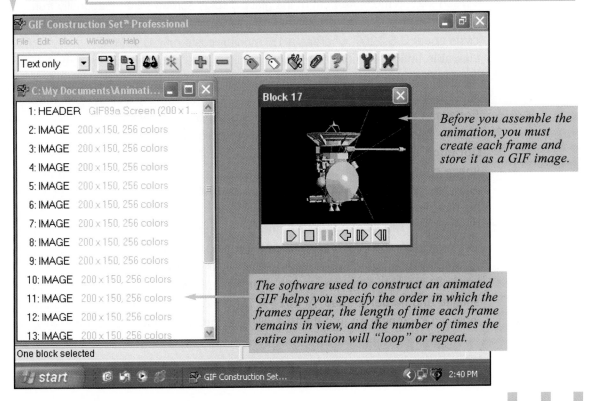

Before you assemble the animation, you must create each frame and store it as a GIF image.

The software used to construct an animated GIF helps you specify the order in which the frames appear, the length of time each frame remains in view, and the number of times the entire animation will "loop" or repeat.

■Hardware

PC display devices

A **PC display device**, such as a monitor or LCD display, provides feedback about what's going on as you use your PC. It displays what you've typed. It displays icons to click and menu options to select. It displays windows, dialog boxes, prompts, error messages, graphics, and text. Everything that appears on your PC screen is produced by dots of light called **pixels** (short for "picture elements"). Even vector graphics, which are stored as commands for drawing lines and shapes, must be "rasterized"—that is, converted into dots—before being displayed as points of light on the screen.

The clarity of the image that your PC displays depends on the quality of the source image and the capabilities of the display equipment. Good equipment can't improve a fuzzy bitmap graphic, but a cheap display system can make a high-quality image appear fuzzy and make text difficult to read. Because you will likely spend a good deal of time gazing at your PC screen, it is useful to understand the factors that affect display quality. If you are not satisfied with the quality of your PC display, you can often improve it by purchasing better-quality components.

The least expensive display device for a desktop PC is a **CRT monitor**, sometimes called simply a "monitor." CRT (cathode ray tube) technology, which is based on rays of electrons that are beamed into a big vacuum tube, is dependable and relatively inexpensive. If you're shopping for a new monitor, experts advise you to buy the one with the biggest viewable area that you can afford. Factors that affect monitor quality and price include the following:

- **Screen size**. A measurement of the glass display screen taken diagonally from corner to corner. Standard sizes are 15", 17", 19", and 21". A 19" monitor typically costs about U.S.$250, whereas a 15" monitor costs only U.S.$100.
- **Viewable image size** (vis). On some monitors, the picture does not stretch to the edges of the glass screen, creating a black border. The viewable image size is a diagonal measurement of the screen area that actually displays the image. For example, a 15" monitor might have only a 13.8" vis. When comparing display devices, use the vis measurement instead of the screen size.
- **Dot pitch**. The distance between the dots of colored light that display the image on screen. The smaller the dot pitch, the crisper the image. A .26 dot pitch means that the dots are 26/100ths of a millimeter apart. Most of today's monitors have a .28 to .24 dot pitch.
- **Resolution**. The size of the pixel grid. The minimum resolution is 640 X 480. The next step up is to 800 X 600, and the next step is 1024 X 768. Higher resolutions open up more screen area for your desktop, enabling you to view larger documents or graphics. At higher resolutions, however, text becomes smaller and harder to read. At 1024 X 768 resolution, you'll probably want at least a 17" monitor so that the text will be large enough to read comfortably.

■Hardware
continued

Most of today's notebook computers use an **LCD panel**, which produces an image by manipulating light as it passes through a layer of liquid crystal cells and color filters. These panels are compact, lightweight, and have low power consumption requirements. Recent innovations in LCD technology have improved LCD displays so that they produce a clear, bright image that rivals the display quality of many CRT monitors.

LCD technology is now available for your desktop PC. An **LCD monitor** or "flat panel display" incorporates an LCD panel in a free-standing case that you can use instead of a CRT monitor. A 15" LCD monitor costs about U.S.$250, a 17" LCD costs about U.S.$350, and a 19" LCD costs about U.S.$600. However, the viewable area of an LCD means that a 17" LCD displays an image about as large as a 19" CRT, so the price difference can be as little as U.S.$100. For an extra U.S.$100 or so, some LCD monitors include the ability to function as LCD TVs. They come complete with connections on the back for cable TV and VCR or DVD players.

LCD monitors do have lower power requirements than CRT monitors. Although this factor is important on a notebook computer that runs on batteries, your desktop PC generally remains anchored to the wall outlet where power is plentiful. Environmentalists, once worried about the amount of power consumed by millions of computer monitors, have been pleased to see new energy-saving features that automatically power down a monitor when it is not in use.

Some health officials have been concerned with the amount of electromagnetic radiation, particularly X-rays, emitted by CRT monitors. It has been suggested that LCD monitors might pose less of a health risk because they do not emit X-rays. Research on the link between CRT radiation and health has been inconclusive, so buyers must weigh the potential risks of each display technology.

An LCD monitor doesn't take up much desk space and is very light compared to a CRT. Many users prefer the "look" of an LCD display. You just have to decide if the difference is worth the extra price.

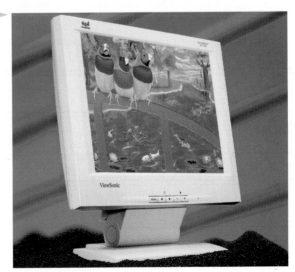

Figure 15-6: The image on an LCD display stretches to the edges of the glass, unlike the image on most CRT monitors. When comparing LCD displays and CRT monitors, remember that the specifications for viewable image size provide a more accurate comparison than specifications for screen size.

■Hardware
continued

A monitor connects to a socket in the back of your PC called a **video port**, which is part of the display circuitry housed on a circuit board called a graphics card. A **graphics card** converts data from your PC's processor into electronic signals for a display device. It comes as standard equipment with almost every new PC. In ads and product descriptions, you might see graphics cards also referred to as video cards, graphics adapters, or display adapters. The term "video card" might mislead you to expect that it has some special features for desktop video or animation; it does not. A video card is just another name for a graphics card, which handles the display of text, all types of graphics, videos, and animation. A "video capture device," described on page 172, has a similar name, but a different purpose—to digitize data from a camcorder or VCR.

A basic graphics card will suffice for most word processing, Web, and spreadsheet applications. For 2-D graphics, 3-D graphics, video editing, desktop publishing, and computer games, you might want a graphics card with extra memory or graphics acceleration.

Most graphics cards contain memory chips where an image can be constructed before being sent to the display device. These memory chips remove a substantial burden from your PC's main processor and help improve the overall performance of your PC. Because each pixel in an image requires storage space, the amount of memory on your graphics card limits the resolution and color depth available on your PC. A true color 640 X 480 image requires about 1 MB of memory, but a 1024 X 768 image requires more than 2 MB. Your graphics card must supply enough memory for the resolution and color depth that you typically work with.

As a further performance enhancement, some graphics cards also have specially designed accelerator circuitry that speeds up specific 2-D and 3-D graphics operations. These **graphics accelerator cards** are particularly prized by graphics designers and computer game players. You can add a state-of-the-art graphics accelerator card to your PC for between U.S.$80 and U.S.$400.

Figure 15-7: The amount of memory on your graphics card determines the highest resolution and color depth available on your PC. Use this chart as a guide to the amount of memory that's optimal for your computing activities.

Graphics Card Memory	Application
Shared video memory	Word processing, spreadsheets, Web browsing, and other nongraphical applications
8 to 16 MB	Basic 2-D graphics
16 to 128 MB	3-D graphics, video editing, desktop publishing, and computer games

■Tutorial
How to change display settings

You can adjust your PC's display settings to control its color depth, resolution, and power management options. If your display sometimes switches to odd colors, you are seeing an example of **palette flash** caused by the color depth setting. To avoid palette flash, you can switch to a higher color depth.

The resolution setting affects the size of objects that you see on the screen, as well as the number of objects that fit in a window. At lower resolutions, such as 640 X 480, text appears larger, but you might see only a small part of a document in the word processing window.

Your preferred display settings might depend on the software you are using. For example, you might prefer a high resolution when you're working with graphics, but a lower resolution for word processing. Once you know how to adjust display settings, you can experiment to find your preferred settings. When you have completed the tutorial, you should be able to:

- Change the display resolution for your PC screen.
- Change the color depth displayed on your PC screen.
- Adjust energy saving settings for your display device.

Figure 15-8: Click the PlayIt! button to begin the tutorial and learn how to adjust your PC's display settings. Estimated time: 15-20 minutes. Tracking Disk points: 10.

■Issue
Dead celebrities live again

Frank Sinatra in concert five years after his death? How? Through technological wizardry, of course. At the Radio City Music Hall in the fall of 2003, this feat was accomplished through the use of advanced audio/video techniques combined with elaborate staging and live musical accompaniment. For 12–14 shows, three-dimensional images were projected on 13-meter-high screens to make it appear like "My Way" Frank was moving and singing his own hits. He was backed by a 10-piece orchestra, a choir, and the RADIO CITY ROCKETTES. At the same time, Sinatra also helped to pitch Mercedes Benz, one of the show's sponsors. Leaning against a new Mercedes, a young Frank appeared in a New York magazine ad.

The use of dead celebrities represents the latest, most ambitious example of a growing trend in show business and marketing. These late movie stars and singers sell everything from beer to vacuum cleaners to concert tickets at $95 a pop. Everyone from John Wayne to Fred Astaire to Lucille Ball has appeared on some recent TV commercial. Other countries like Japan are also on this "dead celebs" bandwagon.

In the United States, some states have enacted postmortem "right of publicity" laws that prohibit unlicensed exploitation of deceased celebrities. The application of these laws to digital technology has not yet been fully explored in the courts, however. Outstanding issues include whether a multimedia developer has a right to create a digital image of a deceased celebrity, even if there is no intent to use the image for commercial gain. Further, would the laws that prohibit using the image of a deceased celebrity also prohibit the use of a digital character that was created from the image of a celebrity look-alike? The issue becomes even more cloudy when you consider that a digital character could combine the traits of several celebrities. In the music industry, it is a violation of copyright law to create a song using tunes "borrowed" from other artists' compositions. Would similar restrictions prevent a developer from creating a digital actor who is a composite of Humphrey Bogart, Clark Gable, and River Phoenix?

What do you think?

1. Have you seen deceased celebrities featured
in any new TV ads or films?   ◯ Yes ◯ No ◯ Not sure

2. Do you think that multimedia developers
should have the right to create a digital
character by digitizing a celebrity look-alike?   ◯ Yes ◯ No ◯ Not sure

3. Should laws prohibit the creation of digital
characters based on the composite traits of
several deceased celebrities?   ◯ Yes ◯ No ◯ Not sure

**Save
It!**

QuickCheck A

1. Popular desktop video file formats include Video for Windows, [＿＿＿＿＿＿], and QuickTime.

2. If you view a(n) [＿＿＿＿＿＿] video from the Web without a fast Internet connection, the playback will be rather choppy.

3. The video [＿＿＿＿＿＿] technique that you select for a desktop video will affect its quality and file size.

4. The most popular format for Web page animation is called animated [＿＿＿＿＿＿].

5. True or false? If you have a 15" monitor set at 1024 X 768 resolution, the text will appear rather small. [＿＿＿＿]

Check It!

QuickCheck B

For each task described below, indicate the letter of the appropriate tool.

1. Transfer video footage from a digital video camera to your PC [＿＿＿]

2. Digitize a video from a camcorder or VCR [＿＿＿]

3. Connect a monitor to your PC [＿＿＿]

4. Watch TV or video tapes on your computer screen [＿＿＿]

5. Play desktop video [＿＿＿]

   a. Video capture device

   b. TV tuner card

   c. Graphics card

   d. Windows Media Player

   e. FireWire

Check It!

Get It?

While using the BookOnCD, click the Get It? button to see if you can answer ten randomly selected questions from Chapter 15.

Get It?

Chapter 16

Looking "Under the Hood"

What's Inside?

Suppose that your new desktop PC arrives with a warning, "The microprocessor and graphics card might have been loosened during shipping. Make sure all chips and boards are properly seated before turning on the PC." If you're familiar with the components inside of your PC's system unit, you can deal with messages like this one, perform some basic troubleshooting, and even perform your own upgrades. Chapter 16 gets into the nuts and bolts—more specifically, the chips and circuits—of computers.

What's on the CD?

It's impossible to actually see what's happening inside the chips on your PC's motherboard, so Chapter 16 contains animated tours to help you visualize the way computers work.

■FAQ How does a computer work?

A computer works by manipulating data in various ways. **Data** refers to the symbols that describe people, events, things, and ideas. Basically, a computer works with data in four ways: (1) accepting input data, (2) processing data, (3) producing output data, and (4) storing data. **Input** is the data that goes into a computer. A computer gets input from many sources, including the keyboard, modem, and disk drives. What happens to this input? The computer puts it in RAM (random access memory). Recall from Chapter 1 that RAM is a temporary holding area for data. You might think of it as a halfway house for computer data—a place for it to "hang out" until it is processed, stored, or displayed.

How does a computer know what to do with this data that's hanging out in RAM? In addition to data, RAM holds instructions that tell the computer what to do. A computer's processing circuitry "reads" these instructions, then processes the data accordingly. **Processing data** means manipulating it in some way. For example, a computer might process numeric data by performing a calculation. It might process the data in a list by sorting it, or it might process the dots in an image by changing their color. After processing ends, the resulting data is returned to RAM.

Sometimes an instruction indicates that the computer should transfer data from RAM to a device, such as a printer, modem, or display screen. The data sent to these devices is called **output**. Other instructions might direct the computer to transfer data from RAM to a storage device, such as a hard disk drive. This process of **storing data** moves it from the temporary RAM "halfway house" to a more permanent "home."

Figure 16-1: *When you think about how a computer works, remember that input data arrives in RAM, then instructions tell the computer how to process, store, or output this data.*

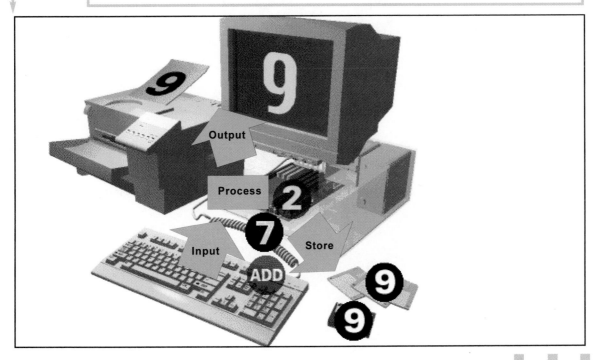

▪FAQ What does RAM and processing circuitry look like?

RAM and processing circuitry are contained in "chips" inside your PC's system unit. **Chip** is a nickname for an integrated circuit (sometimes called a microchip or IC). An **integrated circuit** is a thin slice of silicon that has been etched with microscopic circuitry. Different chips are designed to perform different tasks. For example, a **microprocessor chip** carries out most of the processing work that takes place in your PC. **RAM chips** temporarily hold data. One or more **ROM chips** (read-only memory chips) hold the instructions that your PC uses to boot up. Other chips perform support activities to keep the data moving quickly and smoothly from input devices, to output devices, and to storage devices.

A chip is housed in a small, black, rectangular **chip carrier**. Thin wire "feet," which extend from the carrier, can be soldered directly to a circuit board or plugged into a chip socket on a circuit board. A **circuit board** contains electrical pathways that allow data to travel between chips. In a typical PC, a fairly large circuit board, called the system board, **motherboard** or "main board," houses the microprocessor chip, ROM chips, and a variety of support chips. A series of RAM chips are connected to a small circuit board called a **memory module**. Memory modules plug into special slots on the motherboard, allowing data to flow between RAM chips and the microprocessor chip. Other small circuit boards, such as a graphics card, sound card, or modem, also plug into the motherboard, allowing data to travel between RAM and input and output devices.

Figure 16-2: Click the PlayIt! button to learn more about the chips on your PC's motherboard and to see how to reseat loose components.

▪FAQ How does data get into chips?

Your intuition probably tells you that miniature letters, pictures, and other kinds of data don't somehow squirt through the electronic circuitry inside your PC. Instead, your PC works with data that has been converted into a code and then into electronic signals, which can easily travel through circuits on chips and circuit boards. This treatment of computer data is similar to the way Morse code converts the letters of a message into a series of dots and dashes that can be represented by the flashing of a signal light. Keep in mind, however, that "code" in this context simply means converting data from one form to another and has nothing to do with secret codes, security codes, or encryption.

Computers do not use Morse code, but instead use special computer codes that are based on ones (1s) and zeros (0s). For example, an uppercase "A" might be coded as 01000001. Each 1 or 0 is referred to as a **bit** (short for binary digit). Eight bits form a **byte**, the unit of measurement for data storage.

Once data has been coded, it is a relatively easy task to convert the 1s and 0s into a form that can be stored or transmitted electronically. When data is stored in memory, a 1 is represented by the presence of an electrical charge in a miniature electronic circuit; a 0 is represented by the absence of a charge. On a disk, 1s and 0s are represented by metallic particles with different magnetic polarities. On a CD, 1s and 0s are represented by nonreflective pits and reflective surfaces called "lands." When data is transmitted to print or display devices, the 1s and 0s might be represented by different voltages.

As data is gathered, processed, stored, and transmitted, it is constantly converted from one type of signal to another. Special **controller chips** that convert data are found on the motherboard, graphics card, sound card, and modem of your PC. For example, a controller chip on the motherboard converts each key that you press on the keyboard into the electronic code that corresponds to the letter of the key.

Figure 16-3: In your PC, data has been coded and converted into electronic signals so that it can travel from chip to chip.

The smallest unit of information in a computer is a bit. A bit can be 0 or 1. The electronic circuits in your PC represent a 1 bit as a pulse of electricity.

0 1 1 1 1 0 0 1 **=y**

A series of eight bits is called a byte and typi-cally represents one character.

■FAQ Does a computer use the same code for all types of data?

Computers use different codes for different types of data. The codes used for text differ from those used for graphics. The coding method for graphics differs from that used for sound.

Computers represent text data (such as letters, numerals, and symbols) by using ASCII, extended ASCII, ANSI, Unicode, or EBCDIC codes. Numbers for calculations are often coded using the binary number system. Computers code bitmap image data by using a binary color code for each dot in the image. Data for recorded sound is coded by using a binary number to represent the height of each wave sample.

Although many methods for coding computer data exist, all of the computer codes that your PC uses share certain characteristics:

■ *Digital.* A digit is a single character in a numbering system. To say a code is digital means that it converts data into a finite set of numbers, rather than an infinite set of analog values.

■ *Binary.* The binary number system uses only two digits: 0 and 1. Binary coding allows computers to represent all kinds of complex graphical, sound, text, and numeric data using two simple signals, such as "off" and "on."

■ *Fixed length.* The length of a computer code is measured by the number of 1s and 0s required to represent each data item. Codes that are fixed length use the same number of bits to represent each data item. For example, if the code represents the letter "A" using a string of eight bits, it represents a "B" and every other letter of the alphabet using the same number of bits.

Figure 16-4: By looking at this table of ASCII codes, you can see that the underlying code is digital, binary, and fixed length. Just for fun, try writing your name in ASCII code.

0	00110000	C	01000011	V	01010110	i	01101001
1	00110001	D	01000100	W	01010111	j	01101010
2	00110010	E	01000101	X	01011000	k	01101011
3	00110011	F	01000110	Y	01011001	l	01101100
4	00110100	G	01000111	Z	01011010	m	01101101
5	00110101	H	01001000	[	01011011	n	01101110
6	00110110	I	01001001	\	01011100	o	01101111
7	00110111	J	01001010	]	01011101	p	01110000
8	00111000	K	01001011	^	01011110	q	01110001
9	00111001	L	01001100	_	01011111	r	01110010
:	00111010	M	01001101	`	01100000	s	01110011
;	00111011	N	01001110	a	01100001	t	01110100
<	00111100	O	01001111	b	01100010	u	01110101
=	00111101	P	01010000	c	01100011	v	01110110
>	00111110	Q	01010001	d	01100100	w	01110111
?	00111111	R	01010010	e	01100101	x	01111000
@	01000000	S	01010011	f	01100110	y	01111001
A	01000001	T	01010100	g	01100111	z	01111010
B	01000010	U	01010101	h	01101000		

■FAQ How does software tie into chips, codes, and circuits?

Think back to the concept that instructions in RAM tell the microprocessor how to manipulate data (page 183). These instructions come from operating system software and application software. Software is simply a collection of one or more computer programs or "program modules" containing a list of instructions designed to help you and your PC accomplish a task. These instructions are written using a computer **programming language**, such as Visual Basic, Java, or C++.

Today's programming languages allow programmers to use English-like words and syntax to write the instructions for a program module. However, these English-like instructions must be converted into **machine language** before they can be executed within a microprocessor chip. Machine language instructions are coded in 1s and 0s in a form that can be directly executed by a microprocessor.

The process of converting a programmer's English-like instructions into machine language instructions is called **compiling**. Compiling creates the executable EXE files, which are stored on disk as software applications. When you want to use a software application program, your PC copies the EXE file instructions from disk into memory. Once in memory, these instructions direct the activities that take place in memory and the microprocessor.

Figure 16-5: A programmer writes a computer program using English-like instructions, which must then be compiled into machine language for computer execution.

■Hardware
Microprocessors

A microprocessor and a microcomputer are not identical. A microprocessor is a single integrated circuit. A microcomputer is a type of computer that uses a microprocessor as its main processing unit. Your PC is a microcomputer that contains a microprocessor. The type of microprocessor that's inside a computer indicates its age, dictates the types of programs it can run, and affects how fast it can perform computing tasks.

Figure 16-6: An Intel Pentium 4 slot 775 processor.

Chipmakers have produced many microprocessor models. The microprocessors in microcomputers can be classified into two categories: x86 and PowerPC. x86 processors (also referred to as IBM-compatible or Intel processors) are typically found in PCs that run Windows, whereas PowerPC processors are found in Apple Macintosh computers. Although PowerPC and x86 processors both process data, they differ in terms of their instruction sets. You read on page 187 that software is compiled into a set of instructions that the processor can execute. If software is compiled into instructions that are included in the x86 instruction set, the resulting machine language instructions can be executed directly by an x86 processor. A PowerPC processor cannot execute x86 instructions without using special conversion hardware or software.

The PowerPC is a **RISC** (reduced instruction set computer) chip designed with a streamlined instruction set to simplify its circuitry and increase processing speed.

Figure 16-7: An AMD Athlon processor.

An x86 processor is a **CISC** (complex instruction set computer) chip designed to process complex and specialized instructions. In theory, a RISC chip should be more efficient than a CISC chip. In practice, however, RISC performance is not necessarily superior, though this issue is a source of controversy.

Manufacturers of x86 microprocessors include Intel and AMD. Intel is the original x86 chipmaker and still the largest. Its current lineup of microprocessors includes the Pentium 4, Pentium M, and lower-cost Celeron models. AMD's chip offerings include the Athlon, Athlon XP, Athlon 64, and Opteron. Both Intel and AMD currently offer chips with speeds over 3 GHz.

Hardware
continued

Computer ads typically hype a processor's clock speed, which is one of several factors that contribute to overall system performance. **Clock speed** is measured in **megahertz** (MHz) or **gigahertz** (GHz). One MHz is 1 million cycles per second. One GHz is 1 billion cycles per second. Larger MHz or GHz numbers indicate faster clock speeds. For example, a 3 GHz clock speed is faster than a 2.4 GHz clock speed.

Clock speed is analogous to how fast you pedal when you ride a bike. Usually, the faster you pedal, the faster you move. During each clock cycle, the processor executes instructions. The faster the clock speed, the more instructions your microprocessor can carry out in each second. If a 2.4 GHz processor executes one instruction for each clock cycle, it performs 2.4 billion instructions per second! As a rule of thumb, PCs with faster processors are more expensive than their slower cousins.

Clock speed is not the only factor that affects processor performance. For example, two Intel microprocessors, the Celeron/2.4 and the Pentium 4/2.4, were both rated at 2.4 GHz. However, the Celeron/2.4 delivered only three-fourths the performance of the Pentium 4/2.4. What could account for this difference? Think again about the bike analogy. Your speed depends not just on how fast you pedal, but also on other factors related to the design of your bike, such as gearing and tire size. For example, if your bike allows you to gear down, you can pedal more slowly, but still maintain your speed. Likewise, several factors related to the design of a microprocessor can affect the speed at which it processes instructions:

- *Instructions per clock cycle.* Suppose that during each clock cycle, a processor could perform three instructions, instead of one. It would perform three times as much work in the same amount of time. Processors that execute multiple instructions per clock cycle are referred to as **superscalar**.
- *Cache memory.* Before processing can take place, data and instructions must exist in RAM. RAM chips are several inches away from the processor on the motherboard of your PC. Even traveling at the speed of light, data can require several clock cycles to move from RAM to the processor. **Cache memory** (pronounced "cash") is data-holding circuitry where instructions and data can be accessed faster than from RAM. Typically, cache is measured by its storage capacity in kilobytes (KB) and by the number of cache areas or levels. **Level 1 (L1) cache** is located right on the microprocessor chip. **Level 2 (L2) cache** is on a separate chip from the processor, but sometimes packaged within the same chip carrier.
- *Extended instruction sets.* All x86 processors have a core set of instructions. However, some processors have extended instruction sets that speed up certain types of processing, such as video or photo processing.

■Hardware
continued

Grab It!

Benchmark Software

If clock speed doesn't tell you the whole story about processor performance, what does? Rather than relying on clock speed ratings, you can get a better picture of processor performance from the results of benchmark tests. A **benchmark test** is a set of standard processing tasks that measure the performance of computer hardware or software. Microprocessor benchmark tests measure the speed at which a processor performs a set of tasks. Computer manufacturers and independent test labs publish the results of benchmark tests in computer magazines and on Web sites. If you're interested in finding out how your own PC stacks up, you can download benchmark testing software from the Web.

Many benchmark tests are available today, and each measures a slightly different aspect of processor performance. To make sense of the results, it is useful to have some idea of how the test relates to what your computer does in real life. For convenience, you can group benchmark tests into three categories:

■ *Multimedia benchmarks* measure processor performance when processing MPEG video, AVI video, digitized sound, and other multimedia data. The WebMark 2001, CD WinBench, Video2000, and Audio WinBench are some of the tests frequently used to measure multimedia processing performance.

■ *Integer benchmarks* measure processing efficiency for integer data, which includes the words and numbers that you manipulate when using spreadsheet, word processing, presentation, and database applications. Integer benchmark tests include SPECint2000 and SPEC CPU2000.

■ *Floating point benchmarks* measure processor performance for numbers stored in a special "floating point" format that facilitates calculations. Good floating point performance is required for 3-D graphics, computer-aided design, and many of today's computer games. Floating point benchmark tests include SPECfp2000, 3DMark2001, and 3D WinBench 2000.

Although processor performance is important, it is only one factor that affects overall PC performance. Your PC is only as fast as its slowest component. Just as you can pedal fast on an icy road but not make much headway, a processor can "spin its wheels" while it waits for data to arrive from a slow disk drive.

Figure 16-8: Using a processor-level productivity benchmark, such as SYSmark 2001, you can measure system performance on popular applications in the Microsoft Windows operating environment.

∎Tutorial

How to find the technical specifications for your PC

Which processor is in your PC? How fast is it? How much RAM is installed on your PC's motherboard? What is the capacity of your PC's hard disk drive? The type, capacity, and speed of various components in your PC are called **system specifications**. These specifications are important when you purchase software, upgrade components in your PC, or seek technical support.

Grab It!

System
Analyzer
Software

You can, of course, find your system specifications by referring to the documentation that was provided with your computer. Sometimes, however, this information is not entirely accurate. You can discover the specifications for your PC using system analyzer software supplied with Windows and with your application software. In addition, you can download shareware to help you with this task. In this tutorial, you'll learn several handy ways to find your PC's system specifications.

When you have completed the tutorial, you should be able to:

■ Use the Control Panel to discover basic system configuration information.
■ Access Microsoft System Information.
■ Find system specifications using shareware.

Play It!

Figure 16-9: Click the PlayIt! button to begin the tutorial and find out how to find the technical specifications for your PC. Estimated time: 15–20 minutes. Tracking Disk points: 10.

Who invented the first electronic digital computer?

In a 1973 lawsuit, a computer manufacturing company called Sperry Rand claimed to hold a patent on the technology for electronic digital computers. If the courts upheld this claim, then no company would have been able to manufacture computers without obtaining a license from and paying royalties to Sperry Rand.

Historically, the first inventor to produce a binary digital computer was probably Conrad Zuse, an engineer in Germany who in 1938 completed work on a computer called the Z-1. World War II made collaboration on technology projects difficult, so Zuse's work was not known until after the war. More significantly, Zuse did not file for a U.S. patent. About the same time that Zuse was building the Z-1, John Mauchly and J. Presper Eckert began work in Pennsylvania on a computer called the ENIAC, which became operational in 1946. Mauchly and Eckert obtained a patent for digital computer technology and then formed a computer company. Their company and patent were eventually acquired by Sperry Rand.

At the time of the 1973 lawsuit, Sperry Rand appeared to have a clear claim on digital computer technology. However, a seemingly insignificant meeting dating back to 1941 between Mauchly and a mathematician named John Atanasoff had far-reaching consequences on the Sperry Rand patent claim. In this meeting and in subsequent correspondence, Atanasoff shared his ideas on computer design with Mauchly. Atanasoff had been constructing a computer of his own, but had never filed for a patent. Mauchly and Eckert subsequently incorporated several of Atanasoff's ideas to build the ENIAC computer.

When these events became known during the 1973 patent dispute, the judge ruled that "Eckert and Mauchly did not themselves first invent the automatic electronic digital computer, but instead derived that subject matter from one Dr. John Vincent Atanasoff." The Sperry Rand patent was declared invalid.

What do you think?

1. Does it appear to you that the judge made the right decision, despite the fact that Atanasoff never filed for a patent?   ○Yes   ○ No   ○ Not sure

2. Do you think that Zuse, instead of Atanasoff, should be declared the inventor of the first electronic digital computer?   ○ Yes   ○ No   ○ Not sure

3. Do you think that the computer industry would be different today if Sperry Rand had won its patent case?   ○ Yes   ○ No   ○ Not sure

Save It!

QuickCheck A

1. A computer accepts input data, produces output data, stores data, and [ ] data.

2. An integrated [ ] is housed inside a chip carrier.

3. True or false? Computer codes are binary because it is a relatively easy task to convert coded 1s and 0s into electronic signals. [ ]

4. The process of converting a programmer's English-like instructions into machine language instructions is called [ ].

5. True or false? The Pentium 4 processor is a RISC chip. [ ]

Check It!

QuickCheck B

Match the letter of the correct motherboard component with each of the following descriptions:

1. A memory module [ ]

2. Microprocessor [ ]

3. ROM [ ]

4. Expansion slot [ ]

5. Battery [ ]

Check It!

Get It?

While using the BookOnCD, click the Get It? button to see if you can answer ten randomly selected questions from Chapter 16.

Get It?

Chapter 17

Upgrading and Expanding Your PC

What's Inside?

When you purchased your PC, it was a top-of-the-line machine. A year later, it might seem a little past its prime. In Chapter 17, you'll find out how to give your "old" PC a makeover by upgrading its components or expanding its capabilities.

What's on the CD?

Don't be shy about using a screwdriver on your PC. The videos in Chapter 17 show you how to install new chips, cards, and devices. Just remember that the person who disassembles a PC is also the person responsible for restoring it to working order!

■FAQ   Can I upgrade the processor in my PC?

Expanding your PC usually means adding components that increase functionality. **Upgrading** typically means replacing a component, such as a microprocessor, with one that is newer and that provides enhanced performance. You typically can upgrade your PC's microprocessor with a faster model. However, before you rush out and purchase the latest, greatest processor, you should find out whether it will fit in your PC's motherboard (or system board). You should also consider whether the upgrade will be cost-effective.

Your PC's motherboard provides only one type of connector for a microprocessor. The microprocessor that you select for an upgrade must match that connector. AMD Athlon 32-bit processors use a **Socket A** connector, while AMD Athlon 64-bit processors use a Socket 754 or 940 connector. Older Intel Pentium 4 processors use a **Socket 423** connector, while newer Pentium 4 processors use a **Socket 478** connector or a **Socket 775** connector. Intel Pentium III and Celeron processors use a **Socket 370** connector. Older processors such as the Intel Pentium II and Pentium III use other connectors such as a **Slot 2** or **Socket 603** connector. It's a good idea to check with your PC manufacturer's technical support staff or Web site to find out which processors your PC's motherboard will accept.

Practically speaking, microprocessor upgrades are not always such a good deal. Purchasing a microprocessor upgrade for the next level of speed can be relatively inexpensive—from U.S.$75 to U.S.$400—but it won't dramatically boost the speed at which your PC appears to operate. Upgrading several levels of speed to a state-of-the-art microprocessor will usually produce a noticeable speed increase, but is a much more expensive proposition—costing about U.S.$1,000.

Installing a state-of-the-art microprocessor in an older PC rarely produces performance equivalent to that of a new computer because processor speed is only one factor that affects computer performance. Other components, such as slow RAM or a slow data path to the slots holding the sound and graphics cards, might create data bottlenecks and impede overall performance. Rather than upgrade your microprocessor, you might be happier with the benefits provided by adding RAM, installing a second hard drive, or upgrading to an accelerated graphics card.

Figure 17-1: A state-of-the-art microprocessor is expensive, so you should install it carefully. Click the PlayIt! button for some tips on how to successfully upgrade a microprocessor that requires a Socket connector.

■FAQ   Will adding RAM improve my PC's performance?

Adding RAM to your PC can increase processing efficiency by providing more fast-access storage space for programs and data. Whenever your PC is on, RAM holds parts of the operating system, the software program modules you're currently using, and as much data as possible for the files you have open. With more RAM, larger sections of the programs and data you work with can be held in memory circuits, instead of remaining on disk. The processor works more quickly if it can access program instructions and data without waiting for them to arrive from disk storage. Today's PCs typically have 256 or 512 MB of RAM. Adding RAM is fairly inexpensive, with a 256 MB memory module costing about U.S.$60.

Grab It!

Finding the right memory

Before you add RAM, find out the current RAM capacity of your PC by using system analyzer software, such as Microsoft System Information (page 191). Next, refer to the documentation for your PC to find the maximum RAM capacity. You can add memory only up to this limit. The documentation should also provide the specifications for the RAM that you'll purchase. RAM specifications include speed, capacity, package, and type: For additional assistance, you might try the Web site of major memory manufacturers such as Crucial and Kingston, which typically contain step-by-step guides to help you find the right memory for your computer.

- *Speed*. Memory access time is measured in nanoseconds (ns). A **nanosecond** is one billionth of a second. Lower access speed means faster data availability. For example, 60 ns RAM is faster than 70 ns RAM.
- *Capacity*. Measured in megabytes (MB), capacity refers to the amount of data that each memory module can hold. Memory modules are typically available in increments of 128, 256, 512, or 1,024 MB.
- *Package*. RAM chips are packaged onto memory modules such as **SIMMs** (single in-line memory modules), **DIMMs** (dual in-line memory modules), and **RIMMs** (Rambus in-line memory modules).
- *Type*. The memory modules in today's PCs typically contain **DRAM** (dynamic RAM) chips, which require a constant supply of power to refresh the data that they hold. DRAM comes in several types, including SDRAM (synchronous DRAM), DDR SDRAM (double data rate SDRAM), RDRAM (Rambus DRAM), EDO (extended data output), and FPM (fast page mode).

Play It!

Figure 17-2: Adding RAM is one of the least expensive and most effective ways to increase the performance of your PC. Your PC's motherboard might contain SIMM, RIMM, or DIMM slots. It might even contain a combination of SIMM and DIMM slots. Click the PlayIt! button to find out how to install SIMMs and DIMMs.

■FAQ What if I run out of hard disk space?

If you run out of space on your hard disk drive, your first step should be to try to free up some space. In many cases, you'll find that you have plenty of disk space available once you clean out the unused and unneeded files.

Start by emptying the Recycle Bin. This will get rid of saved copies of files that you thought you had deleted. You can also free up space by deleting the temporary files from Internet Explorer.

If that doesn't free up enough space, you might want to check if your computer contains a large number of digital photos, music files, or videos. If it does, you might want to delete the files that you do not need, or consider moving them to a writable CD or DVD so you can remove them from your hard disk drive and free up that space.

To recover still more space, you might consider uninstalling unused software programs. Some programs, particularly games, can take up a tremendous amount of disk space, which you can recover by uninstalling the program using the Control Panel's Add-Remove Programs feature.

Figure 17-3: Click the PlayIt! button to find out how to free up space on your hard disk drive.

■FAQ   What if I run out of hard disk space? (continued)

If you are not able to free up enough space by removing old files and programs, you should then consider adding another hard disk drive to your computer.

The easiest way to add a hard disk drive is to purchase and plug in an external USB or FireWire hard disk drive. You can attach these drives to any desktop or notebook computer that has USB or FireWire ports, without even opening your computer system unit. External FireWire and USB hard disk drives typically cost about U.S.$120 for a 160 GB drive.

If you prefer, you typically can install a second hard disk drive inside most desktop computers. Most desktop computers ship with only one hard disk drive, but include a drive bay and connector for two drives, making it fairly easily to add a second drive. The new hard disk drive must be compatible with the hard disk controller and hard drive already installed in your computer, so you'll need to check your computer specifications to determine what kind of drive and controller you already have. Many computers use some "flavor" of **EIDE** hard disk drive (enhanced integrated drive electronics) such as "Fast IDE," "Ultra ATA," or "Ultra DMA". Other computers use a **SCSI** (small computer system interface) controller and hard disk drive. Newer computers might use a **Serial ATA** controller and hard disk drive. The basic idea is that the new hard disk drive needs to be compatible with the existing hard disk drive and controller. Serial ATA and Ultra ATA hard disk drives cost about the same, approximately U.S.$100 for a 120 GB drive.

Before you purchase a second internal hard drive, check inside your PC's case for an available drive bay. A **drive bay** is simply a shelf or compartment to which you attach the drive mechanism. Screws hold the drive in place. Most system unit cases provide a number of 3.5" and 5.25" drive bays. Some bays are accessible from outside the case to accommodate removable media such as floppy and Zip disks; bays for hard drives are not accessible from outside the case. If you don't have an available internal drive bay, you should purchase an external hard disk drive.

Figure 17-4: The easiest and most cost-effective way to increase your PC's hard disk storage capacity is to add another hard drive using an existing EIDE or SATA connection. You can also add an external USB drive. Click PlayIt! to find out how to locate these connections and complete the hard drive installation.

■FAQ How do I add or upgrade other devices?

You've learned how to upgrade the processor, add memory, and add a second hard disk drive your computer. It's even easier to connect most other devices to your computer.

Most desktop and notebook computers include USB and FireWire **ports**, to which you can connect a wide range of external devices such as a mouse, printer, digital camera, external hard disk drive, or scanner. Most current devices connect to either the USB or FireWire port, but some computers also include other ports such as the older parallel, serial, joystick/MIDI, or PS/2 ports. Installation of a USB or FireWire device is simple—you just plug the device into the port. Your computer automatically recognizes the new device and, if necessary, guides you through installation of a driver.

Desktop computers also include expansion slots located on the motherboard. An **expansion slot** (or just "slot") is designed to hold a circuit board called an expansion card. An **expansion card**, such as a modem, network card, or a graphics card, contains circuitry and often a cable connector of some sort. To upgrade a graphics card, for example, you typically remove the old card from its slot and replace it with a new one. PC motherboards typically include several types of slots:

■ **AGP** (accelerated graphics port) or the newer **PCI-E** (PCI Express). Primarily used for graphics cards, an AGP or PIC-E slot provides a high-speed data pathway that's particularly handy for 3-D graphics.

■ **PCI** (peripheral component interconnect). PCI slots offer fast transfer speeds and a 64-bit data path. You would typically use a PCI slot for a graphics card if your PC's motherboard does not include an AGP or PCI-E slot. You might also use PCI slots for a hard disk controller, sound card, SCSI card, video capture card, modem, or network card.

■ **ISA** (industry standard architecture). ISA slots are an older technology and no longer included on most motherboards.

Figure 17-5: Expansion slots were originally designed to make it possible to easily expand and upgrade a computer. Note that an expansion card can gradually work its way out of its slot if not secured in some way. Click the PlayIt! button to find out how to correctly remove, insert, and secure expansion cards.

▪Hardware
Expansion devices, ports, cards, and slots

The input, output, and storage devices that you connect to your computer are sometimes referred to as **peripheral devices**. Your PC provides a variety of ways to connect these devices. Internal devices tend to use one set of connections, and external devices tend to use others.

An **internal device**, such as an internal hard drive or modem, is housed inside your PC's system unit and taps into its power supply, if necessary. An **external device**, such as a scanner or printer, is housed in its own case, sits outside of your PC's system unit, and often comes with its own power supply. Some devices, such as printers, scanners, keyboards, monitors, and mice, are available only in external models. However, modems and most storage devices are available in both external and internal models.

Some PC owners prefer internal devices, which are usually less expensive than their external counterparts, require less space on your desk, and don't contribute to cable clutter. With the advent of high-speed ports such as USB and FireWire, external devices have grown in popularity. Today, most peripheral devices are attached to external USB or FireWire ports and most users never need to open the system unit to expand their computer.

Figure 17-6: Whether you prefer an internal or external device, don't purchase it until you're certain that your PC provides a connection for the device. Today's PCs typically provide the connectors shown in the photo.

■Hardware
continued

External devices connect to one of the ports on your PC. As you know, a port is a connection point into which you plug a cable. Your PC comes with a diverse array of ports, most of which appear at the back of the system unit. Some ports, such as the keyboard and video ports, are designed for specific devices. Other ports, such as the USB and FireWire (IEEE 1394) ports, can be used as connection points for a variety of input, output, and storage devices. Before you purchase an external device, check the box to find out what type of port it has and make sure that your PC has a corresponding unused port. You should also check if your computer has USB 1.0 or the faster USB 2.0 ports, because some devices must be connected to a USB 2.0 port. If you run out of USB 2.0 ports, you can purchase a **USB hub** that connects to a USB port on your computer and provides four or five additional USB devices.

External devices connect to ports, but what about internal devices? Your PC's motherboard provides a special set of EIDE connectors for internal storage devices, such as disk, tape, and CD-ROM drives. Adding other internal devices would usually require an expansion card. For example, a Network Interface Card is housed on a PCI expansion card. Before you purchase an internal device, make sure that your PC is equipped with an unused connector or slot of the appropriate type.

After you've selected a peripheral device, adding it to your PC is usually a straightforward process. First, you connect the device to your PC. The Windows **plug and play** software should then automatically recognize the new device and walk you through the process of installing the software device drivers. If you run into trouble during the installation process, you might need to call the manufacturer for technical support.

Some devices are **hot pluggable**, which means that you can plug them in and unplug them while your computer is turned on. However, to avoid loss of data, you should always use the Safely Remove Hardware icon to prepare USB or FireWire storage devices for removal. Usually, you can hot plug PCMCIA, USB, and FireWire devices, but never attempt to hot plug a device that requires you to open your PC's system unit case. When in doubt, check the manufacturer's documentation.

continued

> *Figure 17-7:* Use this handy chart to find out what kind of devices you might attach to your computer. Notice that a number of the devices near the bottom of the table have been largely replaced by devices using USB or newer technologies.

Port, Slot, or Connector	Maximum Speed	Types of Devices	Hot Pluggable
USB 2.0 (universal serial bus)	480 M bits/second	Scanner, monitor, digital camera, joystick, speakers, modem, keyboard, mouse	Y
IEEE 1394, "FireWire"	400 M bits/second	Video camera, DVD player	Y
AGP (accelerated graphics port)	1 GB/second	Graphics card	N
PCI-E (PCI Express)	4 GB/second	Graphics card	
Serial ATA	150 MB/second	Hard disk drives	N
PCI (peripheral component interconnect)	1 GB/second	Internal tape drive, internal hard drive, internal CD-ROM drive, network card, video capture card	N
EIDE (enhanced IDE), "Fast IDE," "Fast ATA," "Ultra ATA"	100 MB/second (Ultra ATA)	Internal tape drive, internal hard drive, internal CD-ROM drive	N
SCSI (small computer system interface)	320 MB/second (Ultra320 SCSI)	Scanner, hard drive, external Zip drive, external tape drive, external CD-ROM drive, largely replaced by USB	N
PCMCIA (Personal Computer Memory Card International Association)	132 M bits/second	Modem, network card on notebook computer, largely replaced by USB	Y
ISA (industry standard architecture)	16 MB/second	Same as PCI, replaced by PCI	N
PS/2	1,200 bits/second	Mouse, keyboard on older computers, largely replaced by USB	N
Serial	115 K bits/second	Mouse, modem on older computers, largely replaced by USB	N
Parallel and Enhanced Parallel, "EPP," "IEEE 1284"	1,200 K bits/second to 32,000 K bits/second	Printer on older computers, largely replaced by USB	N

How to get technical support

When plug and play works and a hardware installation goes smoothly, upgrading your PC is the proverbial "piece of cake." Unfortunately, you might encounter problems while attempting to install a new peripheral device. Where can you turn for technical support?

Most hardware manufacturers offer technical support via telephone, fax, or the Web. To get the help you need, however, you'll need to have a clear idea of the problem and be able to explain it intelligently. "It doesn't work" is hardly an explanation that will lead to an effective solution. In this tutorial, you will learn how to deal with technical support resources to solve hardware installation problems.

When you have completed the tutorial, you should be able to:
- Determine whether the source of a problem is hardware or software.
- Gather the information that you need to explain the problem.
- Determine the best way to access technical support.
- Find the solution to the problem.

Figure 17-8: When you've tried to solve a problem, but the solution eludes you, it's time to seek technical support. Click the PlayIt! button to begin the technical support tutorial. Estimated time: 15–20 minutes. Tracking Disk points: 10.

Upgrade, reuse, recycle, or landfill?

From 1997 to 2007, an estimated 500 million computers in the United States will be deemed obsolete and discarded. More than 20 million computers are thrown into landfills annually in the United States alone. So far, it is estimated that U.S. landfills contain more than 220 million tons of computer and electronic parts. Computers contain toxic materials such as lead, phosphorus, and mercury, which can contaminate groundwater if not disposed of properly. Many computers end up in landfills because their owners were unaware of the potential environmental hazards. Unfortunately, even well-meaning PC owners may find that landfill is the only option for their old computer.

In an effort to safely dispose of toxic waste, federal legislation imposed a U.S.$10 fee on PCs, monitors, and laptops starting midyear of 2002. The fees go towards grants for developing recycling centers. Massachusetts and California are the first to ban the disposal of old computer monitors in landfills, and other states are considering similar laws. Large businesses are already barred from sending their old computers to landfills. The result is a growing market for electronics recyclers.

If you want to discard an old PC and your local recycler does not have a program for electronic waste, consider doing an Internet search and sift through the growing number of recycling organizations. Sprint Corp. and Time Warner pay *PCDisposal.com* U.S.$35 a unit (a monitor and a computer box count as two units) to take old equipment off their hands. In many cases, the PC can be reused and PCDisposal resells it, primarily to markets overseas such as China and the Philippines. Some environmental activists believe that computer companies should be required to promote public awareness about computer reuse and recycling, and provide free recycling for all computers they manufacture. Some computer companies—including Hewlett-Packard, IBM, and Gateway—will take back used computers for a fee, although this service is not well-publicized.

What do you think?

1. If you did not have a computer, would you accept any free computer as long as it ran some basic software? ○ Yes ○ No ○ Not sure

2. Do you think that your current school or business would accept a donation of 100 five-year-old computers? ○ Yes ○ No ○ Not sure

3. Do you believe that computer companies should take more responsibility for recycling the products they make? ○ Yes ○ No ○ Not sure

Save It!

QuickCheck A

1. True or false? Upgrading your PC's microprocessor is the most cost-effective way to increase overall performance. ☐

2. Whenever your PC is on, RAM holds parts of the ☐, software program modules, and data for open files.

3. If you need to add a second hard disk drive, it is easiest to replace it with external FireWire or ☐ hard disk drive.

4. AGP, PCI-E, and PCI refer to ☐ into which you can insert expansion cards.

5. External devices usually connect to a(n) ☐ on the back of your PC.

Check It!

QuickCheck B

Indicate the letter of the component that correctly matches each of the following descriptions:

1. DIMM slot ☐

2. PCI slot ☐

3. PCI-E slot ☐

4. USB Port ☐

5. SATA hard drive connector ☐

Check It!

Get It?

While using the BookOnCD, click the Get It? button to see if you can answer ten randomly selected questions from Chapter 17.

Chapter 18

Buying a PC

What's Inside?

Whether you're purchasing your first computer or buying a replacement, Chapter 18 provides a generous collection of practical tips to help you select a dependable computer from a reliable merchant at a reasonable price. You'll learn a simple, but effective shopping strategy that's tailored to today's computer marketplace.

What's on the CD?

Getting a "good deal" on a computer system requires a little bit of research and comparative shopping. Don't be afraid to ask questions as you shop. The video in Chapter 18 provides tips on how to order a computer by phone. In the tutorial for this chapter, you'll also learn how to navigate the Web to expertly compare prices and place orders.

■FAQ So many options—where do I begin?

The thought of buying a computer might make you a bit apprehensive. A computer costs a lot of money, and you want to make sure that you get a "good deal." However, finding that good deal seems to require a certain level of technical know-how. What if you make a mistake because you don't understand the specifications in a computer ad? Could you be ripped off by a salesperson who convinces you to buy something that you don't really need?

A "good deal" on a computer means that you pay a reasonable price to a reliable merchant for a dependable computer. You don't need to find the absolute lowest price. Spending days to track down a savings of $20 wastes time that you could more profitably spend at your new computer. Follow these steps to replicate the successful shopping strategy of experienced computer buyers:

■ Choose a platform.
■ Decide whether you want a notebook or desktop computer.
■ Browse through computer magazines, computer catalogs, and Web sites to get an idea of current prices and features.
■ Make your final selection by comparing prices, features, availability of technical support, and warranty coverage.
■ Buy it!

Your first step is to choose a platform. A **computer platform** is simply a category or "family" of computers. Two platforms currently compete for consumer dollars: the PC platform and the Mac platform. The PC platform includes any computers that run Microsoft Windows and contain an x86 microprocessor, such as the Intel Pentium 4. More than 95% of computer buyers select the PC platform, the most popular option. The Mac platform includes all of the Macintosh computer models manufactured by Apple Computer. Much of the extensive selection of hardware and software that's designed for the PC platform is not compatible with the Mac platform. As a result, most experts recommend that you choose the PC platform unless Macintosh computers are the standard in your school or workplace.

After selecting a platform, you should decide whether you would like a desktop or notebook computer. Obviously, if you need to carry around a computer, you should select a notebook. But would it be reasonable to purchase a notebook PC even if it was destined to spend most of its life on your desk? The answer to this question is different than it was a few years ago, when notebook PCs had barely readable screens, limited storage capacity, and no CD-ROM drive.

The features of today's notebook PCs essentially match those of a desktop PC. In addition, a notebook PC is housed in a compact case that you can easily tote around—for example, when you move back home at the end of a semester or if you need to temporarily convert your home office into a guest bedroom. You pay a premium for this mobility, however. A notebook PC can be more than twice as expensive as a desktop PC with equivalent specifications. If you're on a tight budget and don't really require computing mobility, then go for a desktop PC.

Where can I find prices and specifications?

Assuming that you've decided on the PC platform and whether you want a notebook or a desktop computer, your next step is browsing to get an idea of current prices and specifications. Contrary to what you might expect, in this shopping phase, you're not yet looking for the computer you want to purchase. Instead, you are trying to get a handle on the current market by identifying PC specifications in three price ranges: under U.S.$1,000, U.S.$1,000–$2,000, and over U.S.$2,000. Finding these specifications can be quite an interesting project.

As you look at computer ads, pay particular attention to the (1) microprocessor manufacturer and model, (2) microprocessor speed, (3) RAM capacity, (4) hard disk capacity, (5) monitor size, and (6) price. After looking at several ads, a pattern will emerge; specifications in each price range tend to be similar. You can create your own price-range table like the one in Figure 18-1 and fill it in with the results of your research. You should be aware, however, that such a table will remain valid for only a few months, because computer prices and features are constantly changing.

You'll find that the specifications are similar in each price range, regardless of the merchant. Once you recognize these specifications, you can be assured of getting a reasonable deal. Be wary of any computer that doesn't meet the specifications for the price range—it is probably overpriced.

To find information on current prices and specifications, you can look at the ads in computer magazines and in computer catalogs. Each monthly issue of computer magazines such as *Computer Shopper*, *PC Magazine*, and *PC World* contains ads and reviews of computers and peripheral devices. You or a friend might also receive computer catalogs from Dell, MicroWarehouse, or PC Connection. You can also check pricing at Web stores, such as Dell (*www.dell.com*), Computer Discount Warehouse (*www.cdw.com*) and PC Connection (*www.pcconnection.com*).

Figure 18-1: As you browse through computer magazines, catalogs, and Web sites, consider creating a table like the one below and filling it in with current information on the average specifications for each price range.

Specification	Under $1,000	$1,000–$2,000	Above $2,000
Processor manufacturer/model	AMD Duron, AMD Athlon, AMD Athlon XP, Intel Celeron, Intel Pentium III/4	AMD Athlon, AMD Athlon XP, AMD Athlon 64, Intel Pentium 4	AMD Athlon XP, AMD Athlon 64, Intel Pentium 4
Processor speed	2.0–3.0 GHz	2.8–3.6 GHz	3.4–3.8 GHz
RAM capacity	128–512 MB	512 MB–2 GB	1–4 GB
Hard disk capacity	20–80 GB	60–250 GB	160–400 GB
Monitor size	15"–17" CRT	17"–19" CRT, 15"–17" LCD	19"–22" CRT, 17"–20" LCD
Video Card and Memory	Shared video memory	ATI or NVIDIA with 64–128 MB	ATI Radeon or NVIDIA with 128–256 MB

■FAQ How much computing power do I need?

After you have completed your price-range research, it is time to decide how much computer power you need and can afford. Starting at the top, a PC priced higher than U.S.$2,000 is the computer equivalent of a luxury automobile. A computer in this price range contains state-of-the-art components: the latest, greatest Intel microprocessor, the newest, fastest graphics card, and the coolest sound system. You can also expect a generous amount of RAM and a copious amount of disk storage space. A top-of-the-line PC runs the newest versions of the operating system and application software with ease, and typically works with older versions as well. Because such a computer contains state-of-the-art components, you're not likely to replace it as quickly as a less expensive computer.

Computers that retail for between U.S.$1,000 and U.S.$2,000 might be considered the "four-door sedans" of the computer marketplace, because the majority of buyers select a PC in this price range. These popular PCs lack the flashy specifications of their state-of-the-art cousins, but provide ample computing power to run current versions of the operating system and application software.

In the computer industry, the equivalent of a compact car is a sub-U.S.$1,000 PC. Some budget PCs cost as little as U.S.$500. The technology in these computers is usually a few years old and you can expect reduced processor speed, memory capacity, and drive capacity. Nevertheless, these budget PCs are equivalent to state-of-the-art PCs with which people were perfectly happy just a few years ago. Barring any drastic change in the operating system or application software, you can expect current software to perform adequately on a sub-U.S.$1,000 PC. You might, however, need to replace a budget PC sooner than a more expensive PC.

If you're on a budget, you'd consider buying a used car. Should you also consider a used computer? The answer is yes if the specifications for the used computer at least match those you've listed for sub-U.S.$1,000 PCs in your price-range table. You should be able to negotiate a price that is approximately half of what you would pay for a new computer with similar specifications. You are not likely to get a warranty with a used PC, so make sure that it works before you buy it.

Figure 18-2: Once you decide on a price range, you can use this checklist to compare specific brands and models.

Manufacturer:
Model:
Price:
Processor model:
Processor speed:
Cache:
RAM capacity:
Hard drive capacity:
CD/DVD drive type:
Network card:
Modem:
Sound card type:
Speaker description:
Graphics card type:
Graphics card RAM:
Monitor type (LCD, CRT):
Monitor size:
Type of pointing device:
USB port included?
IEEE 1394 port included?
Operating system:
Bundled software (list):
Warranty coverage:
Technical support quality:

■FAQ Where can I find the best deal?

You can purchase a PC from a computer superstore, mass-market merchant, computer reseller, manufacturer, or computer catalog. By understanding the advantages and disadvantages associated with each of these shopping outlets, you can better evaluate the "deals" that they offer.

When shopping for a computer in a conventional store, you can "kick the tires" by comparing the speed and response of PCs with different microprocessors, trying out keyboards and pointing devices, and examining the image quality of different monitors. Computers are sold in a variety of stores, including huge computer superstores such as CompUSA, where you'll see a staggering array of products at great prices. The sales staff is trained to help you select a computer to meet your needs and budget, but you might have to pay for after-purchase technical support.

If you don't live close to a computer superstore, check your local office superstores, such as Staples, Office Depot, and OfficeMax, as well as mass-market stores, such as Wal-Mart, Best Buy, Circuit City, and Sears. These stores typically provide a smaller selection and have slightly higher prices than a computer superstore. The sales staff might have very little computer background, so you're on your own as far as your selection goes. These stores rarely offer after-purchase technical support, instead directing you to the computer manufacturer's toll-free support line.

Most cities and even small towns have computer stores run by **independent computer resellers** who specialize in selling computers and providing consulting services to individuals and small businesses. When you make a purchase from an independent reseller, you're likely to pay a premium price for a brand-name computer, such as Dell, IBM, Gateway, Hewlett-Packard, or Compaq. You might also have to wait for delivery if the model you've selected is not in stock. Independent resellers also assemble **generic PCs** using standard computer circuit boards, cases, and storage devices—often the same parts as those used by computer manufacturers to build brand-name computers. A generic PC may offer a cost-effective alternative to a brand-name PC.

Some computer manufacturers sell computers directly to customers. With this **manufacturer direct sales** option, you can place your order over the phone or at a Web site. Most manufacturers offer a range of models. You can purchase one of these models in the standard configuration, or you can have it customized with more RAM, a faster processor, a better graphics card, and so on. When you buy direct from a reputable manufacturer, you can expect good pricing and the flexibility of having a computer made to order. One disadvantage of buying direct is that you can't typically try the computer before you buy it. Also, local technical support might not be available. Instead, you must contact the manufacturer's technical support center by phone or access its Web site. Companies that provide direct sales include Dell, HP, Compaq, Gateway, and IBM.

Computer catalogs, such as PC Connection and Computer Discount Warehouse (CDW), offer another shopping option that allows you to place your order by phone or on a Web site. Prices are often competitive with manufacturer direct sales, and you can choose from a variety of brands and models.

▪FAQ Is it O.K. to "mail order" a PC?

"Mail order" is one of the most popular ways of buying a computer—you either phone in an order or place it at a Web site. Your new computer arrives "by mail," which usually means by a courier service such as FedEx, UPS, DHL, or Airborne Express. The main caution about mail order is to buy from a reputable dealer. When in doubt, check with the Better Business Bureau (*www.bbb.org*).

If you're ordering a computer by phone, a salesperson will answer your questions about equipment or warranties, take your order, and provide details about current pricing. Make sure that you obtain the following information related to your order: the salesperson's name, order number, expected ship date, total price (including shipping), and who to contact if you have questions or problems with the order.

When ordering on the Web, you'll typically follow prompts on the screen to select a computer, choose custom options, enter your shipping address, and provide your credit card billing information. You'll receive confirmation of your order by e-mail or regular mail. Review the order confirmation to make sure that it includes all of the items that you ordered, the correct price, and the right shipping address. Hang on to your order confirmation—it contains your order number and information on how to keep track of your order.

Whether you've placed an order by phone or on the Web, your new computer won't fit in your mailbox, so you must make arrangements for someone to be home when your shipment arrives. Otherwise, you can arrange to pick up your packages at the courier's office. Be aware that shipments are occasionally delayed or lost. If your computer does not arrive when promised, immediately contact your vendor to initiate a search for your packages.

No matter where you buy your computer, you should receive a purchase receipt. Keep it handy in case you need it as proof of purchase date for warranty claims. Most computers come with a one-year parts and labor warranty. Read the warranty carefully so that you understand what it covers and exactly which repair services it provides. Many merchants also offer extended warranties—some lasting as long as five years. Depending on the price and coverage, an extended warranty can be an excellent deal.

Figure 18-3: When you order a computer by phone, make sure that you get the information necessary to track your order. Click the PlayIt! button to eavesdrop on an experienced shopper who is ordering a computer by phone.

■Hardware
Accessories and add-ons

In some ways, ordering a computer is similar to ordering a hamburger at a fast-food restaurant. You can purchase a standard sandwich, or you can customize it a bit by adding extra pickles or holding the onions. A computer ad or catalog description typically lists the important specifications for standard PC systems. In many cases, these standard systems can be customized with accessories or other add-ons—for a price, of course.

Notebook PC accessories include extra batteries, an A/C adapter for using an electrical wall outlet, a D/C adapter for in-car use, an external battery charger, and a docking station. Because many of these accessories are designed specifically for a particular notebook PC model, you should purchase any accessories you are likely to need at the same time that you buy your notebook PC. After a year or two, as models change, these accessories might no longer be available.

You can often customize your notebook PC with add-ons, such as extra RAM or a larger hard disk. If you include these add-ons when you make your purchase, they will be installed and tested by a trained technician. Usually, the price of an add-on includes installation charges.

Figure 18-4: Many notebook ads include pricing for add-ons and accessories, as well as specifications and pricing for the standard system. If your budget allows, buy all accessories and add-ons at the time of your initial purchase.

For serious work—and serious play!
These powerful notebooks arrive multimedia-ready. You can further enhance your system with additional memory, extra batteries, floppy drive, or a port replicator.

Inspiron X2000 Series Notebook Computers

Model	Processor	HDD	RAM/MAX	Display	CD-ROM	Price
2100	Celeron-M 1.7GHz	40GB	256/1024	14" XGA TFT	DVD/CD-RW	$881
2200	Pentium 4-M 1.8GHz	60GB	512/1024	15" WXGA TFT	DVD/CD-RW	$971
2650	Pentium 4-M 2.8GHz	80GB	768/1024	17" WXGA TFT	DVD-RW/CD-RW	$1259

■ Powerful processor & Brilliant Display
■ Mobile ATI Mobility RADEON™ 9700 Graphics
■ Removable 24X CD-RW & 8X DVD-ROM Combo Drive
■ Integrated 3x USB 2.0 & 1x Firewire Ports
■ Bluetooth & 802.11g/Wi-Fi Wireless (Optional)
■ Integrated 10/100 Ethernet LAN & V.92/56K Modem Drive
■ 1x Type II PCMCIA Slot
■ Built-in Sound Card, Speakers, and Mic
■ Built-in Touchpad Pointing Device with Scrolling Slider
■ Hi-Performance Smart Lithium-Ion Battery
■ Microsoft Windows XP Home Edition, Works Suite 2005
■ 1-Year Limited Warranty

Accessories!

Item	Description	Price
OP2435	External USB Floppy Disk Drive	$43
OP3217	72-Watt AC Adapter	$55
OP1473	Leather Carrying Case	$99
OP1573	Lithium-Ion Battery	$139
OP1117	3-Year Extended Warranty	$179
OP2137	256 MB DDR SDRAM	$189
OP2142	Port Replicator	$199

∎Hardware
continued

Unlike notebook PC ads, the ads for desktop computers tend not to offer options for accessories. They do, however, provide options for add-ons, such as a faster processor, additional memory, a larger hard disk, a Zip disk drive, or a larger monitor. The price of a desktop PC can change dramatically, depending on the options that you select. Before you settle on a system with lots of custom add-ons, check other models in the product line to make sure that an equivalent "standard system" is not offered at a lower price.

Most merchants offer add-ons at very reasonable prices—especially considering that the price includes installation. A trained technician will install any extra equipment that you select, load the required software drivers, and verify that everything works. Even computer experts take advantage of these installation services because they know from experience that some hardware devices are "tricky" to install. For example, some DVD drives don't work with certain sound cards. Your computer merchant should know which devices pose compatibility problems and can save you the headache of trying to install an incompatible device.

Figure 18-5: A desktop computer ad might look daunting, but just think of it as the menu from your favorite burger joint. Select a standard system first, then decide which add-ons you might like.

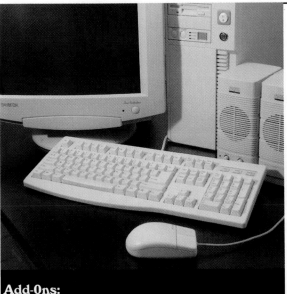

Add-Ons:

Intel® Pentium 4 Processor 3.0 GHz $55
Intel® Pentium 4 Processor 3.6 GHz $229
HP 32-bit Color Flatbed USB Scanner $79
Lexmark Z43 Color Printer $99
Samsung 22" LCD Flat Panel Monitor $249

Ask for pricing on our digital photo and small business add-on packages!

ABS™ Bravado 2500
$1,189

- Intel Pentium 4 Processor 2.8 GHz
- 1 GB DDR SDRAM Memory
- 160 GB Ultra ATA-100 Hard Drive
- 24X DVD-RW Drive & 52X DVD/CD-RW Drive
- 1.44 MB Floppy Disk Drive
- 256 MB NVIDIA® GeForce™ 6800 Ultra Graphics Video Controller
- 19" NEC MultiSync Flat Screen CRT 1600x1200 Color Monitor
- Creative Labs SoundBlaster™ Live! 5.1 Sound Card & Mic
- Klipsch Promedia Ultra 5.1 Speaker System
- 6 USB 2.0 Ports & 1 FireWire Port
- PCI 10/100 Network Interface Card
- 56K V.92 PCI Data Fax Modem
- Logitech Keyboard & Optical Mouse
- Microsoft® Windows® XP Home Edition
- 3 Year Limited Parts Warranty/Lifetime Labor Warranty/Optional 24-Hour Tech Support Available.

Call 1.800.555.1212

Price, specifications, and terms are subject to change without notice. Warranty terms and conditions available on request. Onsite service may be provided by contracted third-party provider. Technician will be dispatched if necessary following phone support.

■Hardware
continued

The merchant that sells you a computer would like to supply you with as much additional gear as you can afford. Obviously, the merchant's primary motivation is maximizing profit, but another reason exists as well—the merchant wants you to be happy with your purchase. Merchants have discovered that customers are happiest with their PCs when they can use them for fun, interesting, educational, and productive projects. Eliminating the hassle of installing hardware add-on devices and software is truly a useful service to customers.

A new trend in add-on marketing is task-related packages. For example, a digital photo package might include a digital camera for taking pictures, photo-editing software for touching up your photos, a color printer for making photo prints, and a CD-RW drive for archiving digital photo files. A deluxe game package might include a super-fast graphics card, a force-feedback joystick, and a selection of popular game software. These add-on packages can be great deals if they include equipment and software for the kinds of computer projects you want to undertake.

What about software? The software that's supplied with your PC is called **bundled software**. PCs typically come with the current version of Microsoft Windows preinstalled. Many merchants also offer a bundle of basic productivity software, including word processing, spreadsheet, money management, desktop publishing, game, and encyclopedia software. Computers with bundled software are inevitably priced a bit higher than those without comparable packages, but the additional cost is far less than what you would pay to purchase each application separately. Unless you already own software that you're planning to legally remove from an old computer, you'll save money if you buy a PC that includes bundled software. Look carefully, however, at the software titles that are included in the bundle to make sure they coincide with the software packages that you would like to use.

Figure 18-6: As a prospective computer buyer, you should be aware that the prices in some desktop computer ads do not include a monitor. The picture in the ad might show a monitor, but the fine print says "monitor not included." If the specifications do not list a monitor, assume that one is not included.

BEST.COM

$749*

This is the computer you've been waiting for!

- AMD Athlon 64 2.2 GHz
- 512 MB DDR-SDRAM
- 160 GB Hard Drive
- 24X CD-RW Drive, 12x DVD-ROM Combo Drive
- 1.44 MB Floppy Drive
- PCI 10/100 Network Interface Card

- V.90 ITU 56K Modem
- Integrated Intel Extreme Graphics
- Integrated Intel AC97 Sound
- JBL Platinum Speakers
- Keyboard & Mouse
- Microsoft Windows® XP Home Edition
- 3 years parts and labor warranty

Call 24 hours a day 7 days a week 800-555-1212 or visit best.com on the Web   *monitor not included

■Tutorial
How to buy a computer online

You can use the Web to access online versions of computer manufacturers' sales outlets, computer superstores, and mass-market merchants. At these Web sites, you can shop at your leisure and without pressure from a salesperson. You can browse through the descriptions and review the prices for standard PC packages. At some sites, you can create customized computer systems, without committing to a purchase until you submit your credit card billing information.

The Web provides another shopping option. At "price quote" sites, you can enter the brand and model of the PC you'd like to purchase. After a brief search, you'll see a list comparing prices at different online stores. Just be aware that some price quote sites search only those merchants that have paid to participate.

When you have completed the tutorial, you should be able to:
■ Purchase a standard computer package from a manufacturer's Web site.
■ Select custom options for a standard computer package.
■ Purchase a computer from an online store.
■ Use a price quote Web site to compare prices for a computer system.

Figure 18-7: Click the PlayIt! button to begin the tutorial and learn how to shop for a PC online. You'll check manufacturers' sites and visit a price quote site. Estimated time: 15–20 minutes. Tracking Disk points: 10.

■Issue
Ethics and computer users

When discussing ethical issues, we often do so from the perspective of the victim. We imagine how it might feel if someone else—an employer, the government, cyberpunks, and so on—pilfered our original artwork from a Web site or read our e-mail. It is quite possible, however, that at some time in your career, you will encounter situations in which you could become the perpetrator—the copyright violator, the snoop, or the thief.

Every day, computer professionals must cope with ethical dilemmas in which the right course of action is not entirely clear, or in which the right course of action is clear, but the consequences—such as getting fired—are not easy to face. Suppose, for example, that you are hired to manage a local area network in a prestigious New York advertising agency. On your first day of work, your employer hands you a box containing the latest upgrade for Microsoft Office and asks you to install it on all computers in the organization. When you ask if the agency owns a site license, your boss responds, "No, do you have a problem with that?" Would you risk your job by insisting that the agency order enough copies for all the computers before you install it? Or would you go ahead and install the software, assuming that your boss would take responsibility for this violation of the software license agreement?

A code of ethics can help computer professionals thread their way through a sometimes tangled web of ethical decisions. Published by many professional organizations—such as the Association for Computing Machinery and the Computer Ethics Institute—each code varies in detail but supplies a similar set of overall guiding principles for professional conduct. A code of ethics can provide guidelines, but it might not offer ready answers to every dilemma that arises in the course of your career. When confronted with a difficult ethical decision, you should consider ethical guidelines, but also consider the policies of your workplace and relevant laws. You might also seek legal advice, consult the human resources advocate at your job, or ask advice from your union representative. Ultimately, the decision about the right course of action is yours, and you must be willing to take responsibility for the consequences of your decision.

What do you think?

1. Would you follow your boss's orders to install unlicensed software?   ○ Yes   ○ No   ○ Not sure

2. If you went ahead and installed the software, but it was later discovered by the software publisher, do you think you should be held responsible?   ○ Yes   ○ No   ○ Not sure

3. Have you read a code of ethics published by some professional organization?   ○ Yes   ○ No   ○ Not sure

Save It!

QuickCheck A

1. One of the first steps in selecting a computer is to choose between the PC and Mac [_____].

2. True or false? To prepare yourself to evaluate the "deals" offered by computer merchants, you can create a table of current specifications in three price ranges. [_____]

3. True or false? Experts advise you to avoid purchasing a used computer, no matter how good a deal it appears to be. [_____]

4. A(n) [_____] PC, uses standard computer circuit boards, cases, and storage devices, but does not carry a brand name.

5. For warranty service, you'll need a copy of your [_____] as proof of purchase date.

Check It!

QuickCheck B

Fill in the blanks to complete this computer ad:

Check It!

- [_____]Pentium 4 Processor 2.8 GHz
- 1024 [_____] SDRAM
- 160 GB Ultra-ATA [_____]
- 16X DVD-ROM Drive & 1.44 MB Floppy Drive
- 40X CD-ReWritable Drive
- 256 MB ATI Radeon 8500 [_____] Card
- 0.26mm Dot [_____] 17" Monitor (16.0" vis)
- SoundBlaster Audigy Platinum Sound Card & Mic
- Creative Labs Inspire 5700 5.1 Subwoofer/Speakers
- 3Com 10/100 Network Card & U.S. Robotics V.92 56K Modem
- Microsoft Internet Keyboard & IntelliMouse
- Microsoft® Windows® XP Home Edition
- Three-Year Parts and Labor Warranty

New!

Val-U-Point Model P43200

Call Today!

Get It?

While using the BookOnCD, click the Get It? button to see if you can answer ten randomly selected questions from Chapter 18.

Get It?

.Index